HEIDEGGER

THE SEMINARS OF JACQUES DERRIDA

Edited by Geoffrey Bennington and Peggy Kamuf

Heidegger: The Question of Being and History

Jacques Derrida

Edited by Thomas Dutoit
With the assistance of Marguerite Derrida

Translated by Geoffrey Bennington

The University of Chicago Press ‡ CHICAGO AND LONDON

The University of Chicago Press, Chicago 60637
The University of Chicago Press, Ltd., London

Published 2016
Paperback edition published 2019
Printed and bound by CPI Group (UK) Ltd, Croydon, CR0 4YY

Originally published as *Heidegger: la question de l'Être et l'Histoire*.

28 27 26 25 24 23 22 21 20 19 1 2 3 4 5

ISBN-13: 978-0-226-35511-5 (cloth)
ISBN-13: 978-0-226-67892-4 (paper)
ISBN-13: 978-0-226-35525-2 (e-book)
DOI: https://doi.org/10.7208/chicago/9780226355252.001.0001

Library of Congress Cataloging-in-Publication Data

Derrida, Jacques, author.
[Heidegger. English]
Heidegger : the question of being and history / Jacques Derrida ; edited by Thomas Dutoit ; with the assistance of Marguerite Derrida ; translated by Geoffrey Bennington.
pages cm. — (Seminars of Jacques Derrida)
Translation of: Heidegger: la question de l'être et l'histoire.
Includes index.
ISBN 978-0-226-35511-5 (cloth : alk. paper) — ISBN 978-0-226-35525-2 (e-book) 1. Heidegger, Martin, 1889–1976. 2. Heidegger, Martin 1889–1976. Sein und Zeit. I. Dutoit, Thomas, editor. II. Derrida, Marguerite. III. Bennington, Geoffrey, translator. IV. Title. V. Series: Derrida, Jacques. Works. Selections. English. 2009.
B3279.H49D48413 2016
111—dc23
2015035914

♾ This paper meets the requirements of ANSI/NISO Z39.48-1992 (Permanence of Paper).

CONTENTS

GENERAL INTRODUCTION

As of the publication date of the volume for this course, *Heidegger: The Question of Being and History* (October 2013 for the French edition), the edition of Jacques Derrida's seminars at the EHESS (École des hautes études en sciences sociales) comprises three titles, corresponding to three years of teaching.[1] As we wrote in the general introduction to those volumes, the aim of the publication of Derrida's courses and seminars is to give readers access to his teaching as a sort of working laboratory in which his oeuvre was developed. Here we present the new series opened by this volume: Derrida's teaching prior to the EHESS, at the Sorbonne from 1960 to 1964, and at the ENS (Ecole normale supérieure–Ulm)[2] from 1964 to 1984. Contrary to the series

1. Jacques Derrida, *Séminaire La bête et le souverain: Volume I (2001–2002)*, ed. M. Lisse, M.-L. Mallet, and G. Michaud (Paris: Galilée, 2008); *Séminaire La bête et le souverain: Volume II (2002–2003)*, ed. M. Lisse, M.-L. Mallet, and G. Michaud (Paris: Galilée, 2010); *Séminaire La peine de mort: Volume I (1999–2000)*, ed. G. Bennington, M. Crépon, and Th. Dutoit (Paris: Galilée, 2012). The publication of the EHESS seminars has taken place in reverse chronological order. [Jacques Derrida, *The Beast and the Sovereign: Volume I*, trans. Geoffrey Bennington (Chicago: University of Chicago Press, 2009); *The Beast and the Sovereign: Volume II*, trans. Geoffrey Bennington (Chicago: University of Chicago Press, 2011); *The Death Penalty: Volume I*, trans. Peggy Kamuf (Chicago: University of Chicago Press, 2013).]

2. Regarding the terms *course* and *seminar*: For quite some time, it had become customary for Derrida, his students and his auditors, to refer to his "seminar," a practice that persists today, as concerns other authors of a similar vein of teaching. In the French university system, however, this term is not as ordinary as it could elsewhere be — particularly in Germany, where the religious valence of the word had found its way into the university milieu since the nineteenth century. This practice was adopted earlier and more widely in the Anglo-Saxon world than in France, where the term *course* has remained alive in the university (even at the Collège de France). At the time when Derrida was beginning to work at the Sorbonne as a teaching assistant, the term *seminar* was used to refer only to meetings headed by a professor and devoted to presentations and exchanges

of EHESS seminars, these courses or seminars have lengths and formats that differ, sometimes greatly, from year to year, and their material presentation—handwritten until 1967, then typed until the move to computer in 1987—presents particular difficulties (decipherment and transcription, etc.) for those publishing them. For these reasons, the order of appearance of this part of Derrida's teaching will not necessarily follow a chronological order.

At the Sorbonne (1960–64), as the only assistant in General Philosophy and Logic, Derrida was, as he wrote later, "free to organize [his] teaching and seminars as [he] wished, depending only in a very abstract way on all the professors whose assistant [he] was: Suzanne Bachelard, Canguilhem, Poirier, Polin, Ricoeur and Wahl."[3] So he alone decided on subjects and syllabi; his courses were so successful that he was obliged to double or even triple the number of sections. The archive contains written-out courses, but also courses that take the form of detailed plans and lectures or model essays. The courses vary between four and seventeen sessions, not always of the same length from one year to the next. One lecture or model essay can fit

between selected participants (so in the 1960s, for example, Paul Ricoeur's seminar was attended by teaching assistants, such as Derrida and Levinas, as well as masters' and doctoral students). This practice without clear institutional definition remained quite distinct from teaching per se. When he taught, Derrida offered *courses*. Or, more idiomatically, he *gave* courses—the latter verb implying an *ex cathedra* dispensation in itself different from the freer and more egalitarian nature of a seminar.

As Derrida began to work at the *École normale supérieure* (a mixed-character establishment aiming at both university-professional education and free research), he had to deal both with the *agrégation* curriculum—which dictated the authors and themes to be treated—and with the freedom to share his own work. At this point, it seems as though the terms *course* and *seminar* began to be confused with one another. Later, at the *École des hautes études en sciences sociales,* Derrida had nothing more to do with the university curricula.

It follows that, up until 1984, it is both useful and pertinent to differentiate between these two levels of teaching (the word *teaching* itself meaning different things at one level or the other). Even if there is no consistency in using strictly one term over another on the part of Derrida and his auditors, it still seems fitting to designate as *courses* what gets taught under the umbrella of a university and a professor (be it as part of a curriculum—such as the *agrégation*, for example — or as a selection of certain themes, authors, or periods). The term *seminar* would thus be left to indicate other kinds of teaching, it being naturally understood that this distinction is only applicable to the French teaching system.

3. Jacques Derrida, "La parole—Donner, nommer, appeller" in *Paul Ricoeur: Cahier de L'Herne* (Paris: L'Herne, 2004), 21. See the pages devoted to this subject in Benoît Peeters, *Derrida* (Paris: Flammarion, 2010), 145–47. [Translator's note: Benoît Peeters, *Derrida: A Biography*, trans. Andrew Brown (Cambridge: Polity Press, 2013), 65–67.]

TABLE 1. Courses given at the Sorbonne, 1960–64

Year	Course title	Number of sessions
1960–61	"'Evil is in the world like a slave who draws the water'—Claudel"	8
	"To Think Is to Say No"	4
	"Substance"	9
	"Reason"	10
	"The Sensory"	15
1961–62	"What Is Appearance?"	8
	"The Meaning of the Transcendental"	17
1962–63	"Husserl's Fifth *Cartesian Meditation*"	5
	"Method and Metaphysics"	11
	"Phenomenology, Teleology, Theology: Husserl's God"	4
	"Can One Say Yes to Finitude?"	6
1963–64	"Irony, Doubt, Question"	15
	"Phenomenology and Empiricism"	6
	"History and Truth"	6

into one or several sessions. As at the ENS between 1964 and 1969, some courses were given in more than one year. A list of courses given at the Sorbonne appears in table 1:[4]

In 1964–65, at the ENS, before an audience of between twenty and forty people—ENS students, university students, and auditors—Derrida began a new stage in his teaching career, after the four years spent as an assistant at the Sorbonne. At the ENS, a first period, up to 1969, contains some courses aimed not at the ENS audience, but at American students in Paris, coming from the graduate schools of Johns Hopkins University and Cornell University. During this first period—for which part of the archive has lacunae[5]—

4. This list and the following list from the ENS were put together on the basis of data collected up till now. Both thus call for future revisions and improvements. We have included therein only courses or seminars that are either completely written out or, as is the case in 1960–61, outlined in notes while nonetheless retaining all the features of a course (excluding notes for only one or two sessions).

5. As the ENS does not possess anything like a real archive, we were unable to gather any further information from it. Nevertheless, invaluable insights were gained with the assistance of four different eyewitnesses from this period, to whom we would like to

TABLE 2. Courses given at the ENS, 1964–69

Year	Course title	Number of sessions	Institutional context
1964–65	"Heidegger: The Question of Being and History"	9	ENS
	"The Theory of Signification in the *Logical Investigations* and *Ideen I*"	12	ENS (*agrégation*)
1965–66	"The *Dialogues on Natural Religion* and the Concept of Religion in the 18th Century"	6	ENS (*agrégation*)
	"Nature, Culture, Writing; or, the Violence of the Letter: from C. Lévi-Strauss to J-J. Rousseau; Writing and Civilization"	13	ENS
1966–67	"The Foundations of Critique"	5 (?)	JHU, CU (Paris)
1967–68	"Course on Hegel"	?	ENS
1968–69	"Literature and Truth: The Concept of *Mimesis*"	9	JHU
	"Writing and Theater: Mallarmé/Artaud"	9	JHU

Note: Tables 2 and 3 use the following abbreviations: CU = Cornell University; San Sebastián = Universidad Zoroaga, Spain; UT = University of Toronto; UM = University of Minnesota; UCB = University of California–Berkeley; UG = Université de Genève; UC = University of Chicago; NYU = New York University (Paris); FUB = Freie Universität Berlin; UZ = Universität Zürich; OU = Oxford University; JHU = Johns Hopkins University (Baltimore); YU = Yale University.

Derrida taught one course corresponding to the *agrégation* curriculum, and one course independent of that curriculum.

In the second period, from 1969–70 to 1983–84, the title of the course refers to the topic specified in the *agrégation* curriculum for that year, although Derrida was completely free in how he chose to develop it.[6] During these same years, Derrida taught for several weeks at Yale, usually before the beginning

extent our warmest gratitude: Étienne Balibar, François Galichet (ENS student, 1963–68), Alain Gigandet (ENS student, 1968–1972), and Bernard Pautrat (ENS professor since 1968). In 1966–67, Derrida also gave a seminar on art, as part of the *agrégation* curriculum; in 1967–68, a Hegel course was definitely given, even though no archive of it remains; in 1968–69, Derrida also gave a seminar on Hegel and one on French epistemology.

6. We would like to thank our colleague Philippe Sabot for providing us—regarding the period in Derrida's French career that concerns us here—with a list of the curriculum concepts from 1970 onward; the essay subjects since 1949 and the History of Phi-

TABLE 3. Courses given at the ENS, 1969–84

Year	Course title and institutional context	Number of sessions	*Agrégation* topic
1969–70	"Theory of Philosophical Discourse: Metaphor in the Text of Philosophy" [ENS]	10	"Language"
1970–71	"Theory of Philosophical Discourse" [ENS]	5	
	"Lautréamont" [JHU (Paris)]	8	
	"Psychoanalysis in the Text" [ENS, JHU]	11	"Matter"
1971–72	"Hegel's Family" [ENS, JHU, OU]	14	"Right and Politics"
	"Philosophy and Rhetoric in the 18th Century: Condillac and Rousseau" [ENS, JHU, UZ]	8	
1972–73	"Religion and Philosophy" [ENS, UZ, JHU]	8	"Religion and Philosophy"
1973–74	"Art (Kant)" [ENS, FUB, NYU, JHU (Paris)]	8	"Art"
1974–75	GREPH ("The Concept of Ideology in the French Ideologues") [ENS, JHU, YU]	10	"Society"
	"Life Death" [ENS, YU, UG, UCB]	14	"Life and Death"
1975–76	"The Thing (Heidegger/Ponge)" [ENS, YU]	3	
	"Theory and Practice" [ENS, YU]	9	"Theory and Practice"
	GREPH ("Seminar on Gramsci")	1	
1976–77	"Benjamin" [YU Paris, ENS]	3	
	"The Thing (Heidegger/Blanchot)" [ENS, YU]	6	
	"Blanchot—*Thomas the Obscure*" [YU Paris, ENS]	8	
1977–78	"The Thing (Heidegger and Heidegger's Other)" [ENS, YU, UCB, ENS]	4	"The Idea of Order"
	"To Give—Time" [ENS, YU, UC]	15	
1978–79	"The Right to Literature" [ENS, YU, UCB, UT]	6	"Time"
1979–80	"Hegel's Aesthetics" [= "Representation"]	?	"Art and Nature"
	"The Concept of Comparative Literature and the Theoretical Problems of Translation" [ENS, YU, TU, UCB, UM]	6	

TABLE 3. *(continued)*

Year	Course title and institutional context	Number of sessions	*Agrégation* topic
1980–81	"Respect" [ENS, YU]	12	"Morality"
	"Representation" [ENS, YU]	8	
1981–82	"The Language and Discourse of Method" [ENS, YU, San Sebastián]	13	"Method"
1982–83	"University Reason" [ENS, YU, CU]	13	"The Rational and the Irrational"
1983–84	"The Right to Philosophy"	4	"Right"

of the ENS academic year. He would repeat at Yale the previous year's ENS teaching, but would sometimes present a new research seminar conceived especially for the Yale audience. For example, in 1979–80, he presented "The Concept of Comparative Literature and the Theoretical Problems of Translation."[7] What also changes is the number of other institutions at which Derrida presents his teaching.[8] Further seminars at the ENS take place in the framework of the GREPH (Groupe de recherche sur l'enseignement philosophique).[9]

The period during which Derrida taught at the ENS-Ulm coincides with

losophy exams from 1949 to 1969; the subjects for textual commentary, and the authors included in each year's curriculum (from 1970 onwards).

7. The first two sessions of this seminar, as well as the beginning of the third, were published in English translation in the special, double-volume issue of the American journal *Discourse* under the title "Who or What Is Compared? The Concept of Comparative Literature and the Theoretical Problems of Translation"; see *Discourse, "Who" or "What?" — Jacques Derrida,"* ed. Dragan Kudjundzic, trans. E. Prenowitz, *Discourse* 30, nos. 1–2 (2008): 22–53.

8. It is also worth mentioning that during the 1970s, 1980s, and 1990s (up until the new millennium), Derrida was in the habit of responding to numerous international invitations by delivering, usually during a one-to-five-week time frame, samples of his regular seminar teaching. As for the years concerning us here, Derrida taught at the following universities: Johns Hopkins—Baltimore (1968, 1971, 1974); Alger (1971); Oxford (1971–72); Zürich (1972); Berlin (Freie Universität, 1973–74); Yale, winter or spring, uninterruptedly (1975–1986); California (Berkeley, 1978); Geneva (1978); Minnesota (Minneapolis, 1979); and Toronto (1979, 1984).

9. For more information on the GREPH, see the first session of the 1974–1975 seminar, published under the title "Où commence et comment finit un corps enseignant," in *Du droit à la philosophie* (Paris: Galilée, 1990), 111–53 ["Where a Teaching Body Begins

major publications, especially in 1967, which saw the appearance of *De la grammatologie*, *La voix et le phénomène*, and *L'écriture et la différence*. Even though the teaching and writing form two different fields, several analyses will be found in the courses taught during this period that will inform or prepare works such as *Glas, La Vérité en peinture*, or *La Carte postale*. When it is possible to establish a link between a course, or part of a course, and subsequent publications, we systematically point this out.

Geoffrey Bennington
Marc Crépon
Marguerite Derrida
Thomas Dutoit
Peggy Kamuf
Michel Lisse
Marie-Louise Mallet
Ginette Michaud
Jean-Luc Nancy

---

and How It Ends," in *Who's Afraid of Philosophy?* trans. Jan Plug (Stanford, CA: Stanford University Press, 2002), 67–98.]

EDITOR'S NOTE

Jacques Derrida's course, "Heidegger: The Question of Being and History" was held in nine separate sessions every other Monday at the ENS-Ulm, from 16 November 1964 to 29 March 1965, with some Saturday discussion sessions. 1964–65 was the first year that Derrida occupied the post of "caïman"—*agrégé-répétiteur*—in philosophy, alongside a single colleague in philosophy, Louis Althusser.[1] It must be emphasized that at that time, in that post, and in this particular place within higher education, Derrida could choose his subject freely. "Heidegger: The Question of Being and History" is thus a course that emerges from his own research and teaching work, and not a course on that year's *agrégation* topic, for which he otherwise prepared his students.[2]

The original of the manuscript is in the Jacques Derrida papers in the Critical Theory Archive, in the Special Collections of the University of California–Irvine. The manuscript comprises around four hundred pages of text (both sides of two hundred sheets). A photocopy is held at the Institut Mémoires de l'édition contemporaine (IMEC) at the Abbaye d'Ardenne near Caen. The transcription of the manuscript was done on the basis of a black-and-white photocopy I made for Jacques Derrida in the 1990s and the electronic file scanned from that photocopy in 2007. This transcription owes much to

1. [Translator's note:] The term *caïman* is an example of the distinctive slang specific to the *Ecole normale supérieure*. It refers to an *agrégé-répétiteur*: a professor specifically charged with preparing or "rehearsing" students for the *agrégation* examination.

2. We would like to thank Michel Tort and Françoise Dastur for their insights into the teaching milieu at the ENS-Ulm and Sorbonne during the period concerning us here. See above, "General Introduction," ix–xii.

the patience and clear-sightedness of Marguerite Derrida's deciphering. We also benefited from Marc Goldschmidt's checking of our initial transcription during the academic year 2009–10, and from the help of Jean-Luc Nancy. I thank all three warmly.

As the original manuscript—mainly written in blue ink, sometimes black, with additions in red or in pencil—has not yet been digitized by the Special Collections of the University of California, only twenty or so pages [of which sixteen are reproduced in this volume] were obtained at our request in color scans.[3] The reproductions we provide, even in reduced format, give a good idea of the manuscript as a whole—the visual aspect of the page, some of the graphic effects—and show some pages on which some illegible or uncertain words remain.

Note that the composition of the manuscript does not enter into our edition, any more than its colors: for, apart from the written-out pages of the course, the manuscript sometimes contains—following a system he commonly used before he started typing (in 1968–69)—note cards used to insert additions or transcribe quotations. This edition reconstitutes on the basis of these composite materials the continuous and complete course as Derrida delivered it.

The manuscript appears to have been written rapidly, with a pen that sometimes scarcely touches the paper. For the illegible or uncertain words that remain in spite of all our efforts, we have adopted the following procedure: [illegible word], in brackets, is placed where the word in question belongs. If there are several illegible words, we specify the number: for example, [three illegible words]. To the extent that this is possible, we also specify whether the illegible word is added between the lines. For words whose transcription is doubtful, the indication [uncertain word] appears in brackets immediately after the word concerned. The number of uncertain words is specified when there is more than one. It happens (rarely) in the manuscript that subject-verb agreement is or seems to be incorrect, or that a sentence is incomplete. When necessary, a note specifying "thus in the

3. We would like to thank University of California–Irvine librarian Stephen E. MacLeod (Special Collections and Archives) for providing us with these pages—requested owing to the specific reading challenges they posed—the deciphering of which was thereby significantly assisted. There is no doubt that the deciphering process of other Derrida manuscript courses will be, as it was here, dramatically abridged by their availability in complete, color-scanned digital versions—thereby also diminishing, as it would have here, the number of illegible or uncertain words.

manuscript" is added, and sometimes a missing word is added to the text, always in angle brackets (<>). Quite often, Derrida does not put the final *s* on plural nouns, and writes no more than *l* for masculine, feminine, and plural definite articles: in such cases we put the correct form. Additionally, he regularly uses abbreviations for common words and philosophical vocabulary. In this transcription we have kept the signs he uses for "equals" and "different from," namely, = and ≠. But when he resorts to unusual shortenings (he often reduces words to one letter or a vague sign), we have tried to decipher and transcribe them. Thus, for example, we transcribe the sign ⇔ as "comment," and we transcribe the abbreviation *H.* used for Heidegger, Husserl, and Hegel each time by the complete proper name, just as we spell out abbreviated titles of books. Derrida makes sparing use of commas, which gives rise to a syntax that suspends and sometimes challenges reading, without ever being unclear. We did not judge it necessary to modify this stylistic effect, except in cases where confusion was possible.

The transcription of the quotations given by Derrida in the manuscript follows normal rules. The quotations are transcribed as he wrote them, but we point out when he modifies a quotation or a quoted translation. Many of these quotations are his own translations, in which it sometimes happens that he does not exactly transcribe the German punctuation: for example, he underlines what is in quotation marks in the German, omits the German italics, omits quotation marks around a word, or displaces the beginning or end of quotation marks from one word to the next. Sometimes, Derrida does not copy out the quotation (as he explains, in such cases we are dealing with translations read rapidly and not examined closely), but marks it in his copy of the book quoted: we have framed such quotations with asterisks (*).

When Derrida announces a quotation he is about to read out, he often gives the German title, but the page number is often that of the French translation (where it exists). For example: "Einführung, p. 80," where page 80 in fact refers to the French translation. We have kept his way of announcing quotations and give necessary details in a footnote. Contrary to the manuscript, in which bibliographical references are kept to a minimum (title, page number, or paragraph number), and in which there are no notes, complete references are here given systematically in footnotes, which are therefore without exception editor's notes.[4]

4. [Translator's note:] I have modified some editor's notes in light of corrections to the transcription, and added translator's notes in brackets where necessary. After the

In "Heidegger: The Question of Being and History," Derrida does not present a commentary on *Sein und Zeit*, but performs on Heidegger's book an almost surgical reading-operation, guided by the very title of the course.[5] While identifying skillfully and accurately various articulations in Heidegger, Derrida simultaneously sets himself the task of constructing clearly Heidegger's difficult project, largely on the basis of parts of *Being and Time* that were not then translated into French. Even the translated parts had been published only in April 1964 (Derrida's course begins in November 1964). In other words, in the academic year 1964–65 we are still at the very beginning of the study of Heidegger's work in French higher education.[6] By almost always translating for himself, Derrida gives a reading, *his* reading, of Heidegger.

This course also heralds the analyses of Heidegger's work that Derrida would go on to propose, not only in the years immediately following (in *Of Grammatology*, of course, published as a book in 1967, or in "Ousia and Grammè," written and published first in 1968 and then again in 1972), but also others that come much later—for example, *Of Spirit: Heidegger and the Question* (1987). His 1983 article "*Geschlecht* I, Sexual Difference, Ontological Difference" returns to §72 of *Sein und Zeit*,[7] so important in this 1964–65 course, and *Aporias* (1992; published as a book in 1996) is another sustained exchange with Heidegger, whose central theme of inauthenticity is clearly broached here. On the other hand, we can observe in this course how Derrida's thinking is settling into place and elaborating its major operative "concepts." Let us emphasize rapidly that "writing," "text," and "graft," are elab-

first complete reference in a note, subsequent citations may appear in shortened form parenthetically in the text.

5. The course is throughout faithful to each title word—except perhaps for the word *question*. In the last sentence of the course, Derrida comments on the fact that the single title word not tackled by the course was precisely the word *question* (to which he comes back in his 1987 book *Of Spirit: Heidegger and the Question*) [trans. Geoffrey Bennington and Rachel Bowlby (Chicago: University of Chicago Press, 1989)].

6. The publication of this course will enable us moreover to fill in the gaps of—if not to correct—the overall picture we hitherto have as concerns the history of Heidegger's reception in France. See, for example, Dominique Janicaud's *Heidegger en France: Entretiens* (Paris: Albin Michel, 2001) and Marlène Zarader's *Lire "Être et temps" de Heidegger* (Paris: Vrin, 2012).

7. Reprinted in *Psyché: Inventions of the Other*, ed. Peggy Kamuf and Elizabeth Rottenberg, 2 vols. (Stanford, CA: Stanford University Press, 2008), 2:7–26.

orated at length here. The very term *deconstruction*, explicitly proposed as a translation of *Destruktion*, is several times put aside here in favor of other translations such as "solicitation" and "shaking up," which will, with a few exceptions, not be retained to describe Derrida's thinking. It is only much later that Derrida will lay claim to the word *deconstruction* and devote many developments to it.

This publication takes its place not only in the publication project of Jacques Derrida's seminars, but also in the wake of other publications of writings from the beginnings of his career as a student and a teacher.[8] Finally, we might also be making good on a wish of Derrida's. It appears that he had conceived of a book that would take up this course again, as he explained to Dominique Janicaud: "When I began as a caïman at the École, my first course, that has never been published, was on 'History in Heidegger;' this was in 1965–66. What's more, at that time I planned to write a book on Heidegger, which was announced by the Éditions de Minuit. I never wrote it. The title announced was *The Question of History*. You can find the ad for it in the journal *Critique*. Axelos was going to publish it. I never wrote it, but the course is entirely written out."[9]

Thomas Dutoit

8. The publication—initially supported by Françoise Dastur and Didier Franck, and brought to fruition by Elisabeth Weber—of Jacques Derrida's 1953–54 master's thesis entitled *The Problem of Genesis in Husserl's Philosophy* [Translator's note: published in French in 1990; English translation by Marian Hobson (Chicago: University of Chicago Press, 2003)] already attests to the high caliber of Derrida's early writings, dating back more than a decade before the present course.

9. "Jacques Derrida," in Janicaud, *Heidegger en France*, 96. Jacques Derrida's memory here (the incorrect course date aside) appears to be inexact: a search through the 1966–74 published volumes reveals that the Éditions de Minuit never announced the forthcoming publication of a book with such a title. However, a Derrida piece by the name of "Les questions de Heidegger" did appear among the articles yet to be published by the journal *Critique*—listed at the beginning of each monthly issue—from volume 272 (January 1970) to volume 295 (December 1971). However, no article with such a title was ever published under Derrida's name. There is also the announcement of the forthcoming publication of a Derrida article called "L'é-loignement de Heidegger"—which never saw the light of day either—in all the *Critique* volumes between December 1972 (vol. 307) and June 1973 (vol. 313).

TRANSLATOR'S NOTE

As Thomas Dutoit explains in more detail in his editor's note, the original French text of the course here printed is the result of the transcription of around four hundred handwritten pages. As anyone who has seen Derrida's handwriting can attest (and as is readily confirmed by a glance at the pages reproduced here), this was an immensely arduous and time-consuming task, which might well have been simply impossible without the help of Marguerite Derrida, who is able to decipher her late husband's handwriting with less difficulty than most. We owe them both an immense debt of gratitude for their very many hours of care and perseverance in managing to produce anything approaching a publishable text.

When the French edition was eventually published in October 2013, however, it rapidly became clear to me that a number of problems remained. I was able to check suspect transcriptions (passages that seemed incoherent or that simply did not "sound like Derrida") against the PDF file of the manuscript, which I had originally scanned for Tom and Marguerite in 2007, and after twice carefully rereading the published text against the manuscript, I was able to confirm that a significant number of errors had made their way into the French edition. These errors are of many kinds, ranging from misidentification of the *H* that Derrida often uses to refer to Heidegger, Husserl, or Hegel, through presentation as part of Derrida's discourse what are in fact direct quotations from Heidegger, and through omissions of legible words and misconstruals of syntax, to inaccuracies in registering Derrida's underlinings and punctuation marks, more or less adventurous conjectures as to the reading of words not flagged in the published text as "uncertain" or "illegible," and many misspellings of German words. Pending publication of a corrected edition of the French text by the Éditions Galilée, Marguerite Derrida has graciously agreed to the publication of this translation, based on the text as I have corrected it rather than on the French original. As publication of that corrected edition will make the detail of those corrections otiose, however, I did not think it advisable to signal every departure from the French that I have been led to make here.

I have used published translations of the texts Derrida discusses where these exist. I have on occasion modified these translations in light of the French translation Derrida uses or supplies himself (often with greater accuracy than the published versions), and I have not systematically pointed out discrepancies in the use of italics, spaced characters, and quotation marks within the quotations that Derrida gives. Interpolations within quotations are in almost all cases his, usually supplying German words (in parentheses), or providing glosses on the translation [in brackets]. In cases where Derrida's text is paraphrasing rather than quoting, I have supplied references to the relevant passages in the published translations. I have followed the French edition in letting stand some inconsistencies in Derrida's own practice (notably in the choice to hyphenate or not the German *Da-sein*). For many details involving tracking down incomplete references or identifying misspelled German words in the French original, and for a number of more humble but crucial editorial tasks, I am extremely grateful to Rodrigo Bueno Therezo for his vigilance, rigor, and patient hard work. Finally, I am indebted to all the participants in the 2014 Derrida Seminar Translation Project summer workshop for their uncompromising commitment to accuracy in the translation and their help in avoiding a fresh round of errors and omissions. Remaining mistakes and infelicities in the final translation are, of course, my own responsibility.

Geoffrey Bennington
NEW YORK, MARCH 2015

SESSION ONE

16 November 1964

I must first explain myself as to the title of this course, as to its very letter, which is important to me.

(1)[1] I say: *the question of Being* and not *ontology*, because the word *ontology* is going to appear more and more inadequate, as we follow Heidegger's tracks, to designate what is in question in his work when the question is that of being. Not only is Heidegger not here undertaking the foundation of an *ontology*, not even of a new ontology, nor even of an ontology in a radically new sense, not even, in fact, the *foundation* of anything at all, in any sense at all—what is at issue here is rather a *Destruction* of ontology. Section 6 of *Sein und Zeit* establishes as a primordial task the destruction (*Destruktion*) of the history of *ontology*. Here—only here—the destruction is destruction of the history of ontology. That is, of ontology as it has been thought and practiced throughout its entire history, this history being already described by Heidegger, from the beginning of *Sein und Zeit*, as a covering-over or a dissimulation of the authentic question of Being, under not ontological but ontic sedimentations.

> We understand this task as the destruction of the traditional content of
> ancient ontology which is to be carried out along the *guidelines of the ques-*
> *tion of being* [literally: taking the question of being as guiding thread : *am* 24
> *Leitfaden der Seinsfrage*]. This destruction is based upon the original experi-
> ences in which the first, and subsequently guiding, determinations of being
> were gained.[2]

1. The numbering begun here does not continue in the manuscript.

2. Martin Heidegger, *Being and Time*, trans. Joan Stambaugh, revised by Dennis Schmidt (Albany: State University of New York Press, 2010), 21–22. Translations from *Being and Time* are based on Stambaugh, with occasional modifications to reflect Derrida's own version. (In the manuscript, Derrida most often provides his own French translations from *Sein und Zeit,* which he quotes from the 10th German edition (Tübin-

As to this notion of *destruction*, a few remarks are necessary. (1)[3] Destruction does not mean annihilation, annulment, rejection into the outer darkness of philosophical meaning. It does not even mean *critique* or *contestation* or *refutation* within a theory of the knowledge of Being. The point is not to say that all the thinkers of the tradition were wrong or committed an unfortunate error that would need to be corrected. We shall see later that what might superficially be interpreted as an *error* about being or a forgetting of being has its basis in a fundamental *errancy* that is a necessary movement of the thinking of Being and of the history of being. In *destroying* the history of ontology, Heidegger never *refutes*. *Refutation* in the sense in which it can be understood in the sciences or in common parlance has no meaning for thinking. And here, already, we have broached the very content of our problem. The concept of *refutation* belongs—implicitly—to an anti-historical metaphysics of truth. If it is possible to refute, this is because the truth can
25 be established once and for all as an object, and only particular conceptions of truth, more or less valid approximations to this ahistorical truth, belong to history. Only knowledge, and not truth, would on this view be historical, and it would be so only to the extent of its distance from truth, that is in its error. But, as Hegel had already shown, there is no simple error in philosophy once truth is historical. The metaphysics of *refutation* thus floats on the surface of a truth without history, which is to say that it is *futile*. Refutation is futile in Heidegger's view. But that does not mean that on this point Heidegger simply agrees with Hegel. You know that Hegel meditated a great deal on this difficulty of refutation (*Widerlegung*) in philosophy. He was led naturally to do so by his fully historical concept of truth and of philosophy. "Philosophy," according to the *Lectures on the History of Philosophy*, "draws its origin from the history of philosophy, and conversely. Philosophy and history of philosophy are mirror images of one another. The study of the history of philosophy is the study of philosophy itself, and especially of its *logical* aspect."[4] And especially of its logical aspect.

---

gen: Max Niemeyer Verlag, 1963). He also refers to the partial French translation then available (which ends at §44 of Heidegger's book) by R. Boehm and A. de Waelhens (Paris: Galllimard, 1964).

3. The numbering begun here does not continue in the manuscript.

4. Hegel, *Lectures on the History of Philosophy*, trans. R. F. Brown and J. M. Stewart with the assistance of H. S. Harris, ed. Robert Brown (Oxford: Oxford University Press, 2009), 55. [Translator's note: I have modified the translation of this and the following Hegel citations to reflect the French translation Derrida used: Hegel, *Leçons sur l'histoire de la philosophie*, trans. J. Gibelin (Paris: Gallimard, 1954). As the aforementioned English and French translations are each based on a different German edition of Hegel's

And it is precisely because, for Hegel but not for Heidegger, philosophy is, in a profound and radical sense of the word, a *logic*, that, even while radically historicizing meaning, Hegel cannot purely and simply abandon the notion and value of "refutation." Being unable to abandon it, he extends its signification, inflates it to the point of making it signify the moment of negativity in general. And we know that this negativity is essential to historical production, to the production of history in general, to production, to productivity in general:

> The philosophies have not only contradicted one another, but also refuted one another. To what extent? What in them is open to refutation? What is the *meaning* of this reciprocal refutation? The answer is given by what has just been said. Only the fact that some principle or some concrete mode of the idea, the form of the idea, now has validity as the highest idea, and as
> the idea as such. In its own era it is, to be sure, its highest idea; but because 26
> we have grasped the activity of thinking as self-developing, what was highest steps down, no longer being the highest, although it remains a necessary element for the following stage. So the content has not been refuted; all that has been refuted is the philosophy's status as the highest, the definitive, stage. So the refutation is just the demotion of one determination to a subordinate role, to being an element. Thus the principle of a philosophy has not been lost, for it is essentially preserved in what follows, except that its status is now different. Nothing gets lost; only the relative position changes. This refutation occurs in all development, hence also in the development of a tree from the seed. The blossom is refutation of the leaves, such that they are not the highest or true existence of the tree. Finally, the blossom is refuted by the fruit. The fruit, which is the last stage, comprises the entire force of what went before. *In the case of natural things these levels occur separately* [Derrida's emphasis], because there nature exists in the form of division. In spirit too there is this succession, this refutation, yet all the previous steps remain *in unity*. The most recent philosophy, the philosophy of the current age, must therefore be the highest philosophy, containing all the earlier philosophical principles within itself. (*Lectures*, 59)

Let me pause for a moment in the middle of this quotation. You have seen that the natural example, the example of the tree, functions here only by analogy. In truth we have here only an inferior form of refutation, refutation in the form of *division*. Nature is the form of division, and what is left behind or refuted, the seed for example, has simply expired, and is not present as such

---

Die Vorlesungen über die Geschichte der Philosophie, it was necessary both to omit sentences appearing only in the English translation and conversely to add in translation sentences appearing only in the French translation from which Derrida quotes.]

in the tree, the flower is not *present* in the fruit. In spirit, on the contrary, and philosophy is the highest form of spirit thinking itself, refutation is preserved in presence—what one can call by a term that is not Hegelian, but that does not, I believe, betray Hegel's intention, *sedimentation* — and the sedimentation of forces (Hegel talks here of forces) is a phenomenon not natural but spiritual. It is spirit itself. With this passage from Hegel, and many other
27 passages (those from the phenomenology on error, for example) the sense of what in general is meant by *last philosophy* is clarified. Last philosophy as highest philosophy, superior philosophy, does not of course mean the last in date in the contrived succession of systems. In this regard, the *recent* is far from being always the *last*, and Hegelian philosophy is much more last than many philosophies that have followed it "in history," as they say. The Hegelian concept of "last philosophy" does not translate an empiricism of the *fait accompli* that leaves the last word to the one who speaks last. If one speaks to no purpose, or without understanding what has already happened, without following the philosophical conversation from its origin, one may well continue to hold forth, but one is not representing the last word or the last philosophy. The last philosophy, in the authentically Hegelian sense, is a philosophy that comprehends in itself the totality of its past and inquires after its origin or endlessly attempts to. To have the last word, one must truly speak last, and not just chatter on after the last speaker.

And it could well be that the philosophy that was the first to understand as such what is *meant* by *the last,* the being-last of the last philosophy, it could well be that such a philosophy—that of Hegel—was not only the last philosophy in its time but the absolutely *last* philosophy. This is often said, but we still have to understand what it means without giving in to the stupidities circulating around and about on the death of philosophy, on Hegel who believed that history would stop with him and the Prussian people, whereas, as people do not fail to add in this case, he was wrong since history continued after him, there have been several world wars, twenty-five systems of philosophy, and—ultimate proof that history continues—we are here, we exist and we are speaking and doing philosophy, as if all that were obvious, as if all that were important, and as if it had the slightest refutational relevance where Hegel stands when he declares the *Last*. It suffices to read him and to see in him something other than—let's say here precisely—a retard: it goes without saying that the end of history and of philosophy does not
28 mean for Hegel a factual limit after which the movement of history would be stopped, arrested, but that the horizon and the infinite opening of historicity has finally appeared *as such*, or finally been thought as such, that is, as infinite opening—the absolute infinite opening being thought as such. This

is indeed the end and the closing of something, but of anything but history. To come back to our specific theme of refutation, it is perhaps possible that the last philosophy is indeed the one that, not content to refute, tries to think the essence of refutation and the essence of the *last*. Hegel's philosophy was not the last philosophy in the same way that Aristotle's, Descartes's, or Kant's (perhaps) were in their time the last philosophies; Hegel's philosophy as last philosophy was the philosophy that thought in itself the essence of last philosophy in general, of what "last" meant in philosophy. The last is not the last so long as it does not appear as such. The *eschaton* as such is thus *said* in Hegel's philosophy of refutation, and Hegel's logic is indeed an *eschatology*. This eschatological logic of Hegel's is, as you know, an ontology. To say that ontology is here eschatology is to say that the essence of being, the appearing of being in its essence is *eschatological*. This is what Heidegger says in *Der Spruch des Anaximander* (a text from 1946 collected in *Holzwege*, where it is translated as "Anaximander's Saying." *Spruch*, in fact, is a sentence, a judgment pronounced, Decision, in the strong sense of this word). In particular, Heidegger writes this:

> As *geschicklich* [translated as destining, being as destining, dispensating Destiny] being is inherently eschatological. We do not, however, understand the word "eschatology" in the phrase "eschatology of being" as the title of a theological or philosophical discipline. We think of the eschatology of being in the sense in which the phenomenology of Spirit is to be thought, i.e., from within the history of being. *This phenomenology itself represents a phase in the*
> *eschatology of being inasmuch as* being gathers itself, in the extremity of its 29
> essence hitherto struck by the seal of metaphysics, as the absolute subjectivity of the unconditioned will to will.[5]

I make no commentary on that last sentence to which we shall return a little later.

So let me pick up again the reading of Hegel's text where I left off ([French] pp. 150–51).

> The most recent philosophy, the philosophy of the current age, must therefore be the highest philosophy, containing all the earlier philosophical principles within itself. Refutation is the negative side. Hence it is far easier than justification; to "justify" means [to] discern the affirmative element in a determination and to call attention to it. So, on the one hand the history of philosophy displays the limitation, or the negative, of the principles, but on

5. Martin Heidegger, "Anaximander's Saying," in *Off the Beaten Track*, trans. Julian Young and Kenneth Haynes (Cambridge: Cambridge University Press, 2002), 246–47; Derrida's emphasis.

> the other hand, the affirmative side too. There is nothing easier than exhibiting the negative side. Doing so gives one satisfaction, or the consciousness of one's superiority to that on which judgment is passed, which flatters one's vanity. In contrast, it is more difficult to recognize the affirmative side. By refutation one disposes of something easily, that is, has not fathomed it. The affirmative consists in fathoming the object and justifying it, which is far more difficult than refuting it. Insofar, then, as the philosophies are shown to be refuted in the history of philosophy, they are also shown to be preserved. But what has been refuted is not the principle, but the fact that it is the ultimate, the absolute and that it should have as such an absolute value; the point is to reduce a principle to the rank of a determinate moment in the whole. The principle does not disappear, but merely its form as absolute, ultimate. That is what refutation in philosophy signifies. (*Lectures*, 60)

In spite of the immense progress marked by this concept of refutation, as soon as one wishes to take seriously what a history of truth and a history of
30 philosophy can be, in spite of the proximity between this Hegelian relation to the history of philosophy and the Heideggerian relation to the history of philosophy, there remains a decisive difference over which I would like to pause for a moment, to verify for the first time but not the last that, as is indicated by Heidegger's itinerary and the increasing number of his references to Hegel, it is in the difference between Hegel and Heidegger that our problem is situated.

The *Destruction* of the history of ontology is not a *refutation* even in the Hegelian sense.

First of all because the Hegelian philosophy of refutation, that ontological extension of a refutation that is usually understood as a discursive and logical operation (refutation is properly speaking a discourse, a dispute), that extension is dictated by a logic and a philosophy of the Idea or the Concept in which Heidegger himself sees a moment in the history of ontology, the last moment, the moment of blossoming and of "summation" but which still remains a dissimulation of being beneath beings. Already in the first paragraph of *Sein und Zeit*, Hegel's logic is invoked as the last moment in a tradition of classical ontology that goes back to Plato and Aristotle, but as a last moment *belonging* to that tradition, recomprehending it, summing it up, but not taking that step beyond it—i.e., just as much back from it—that Heidegger wants to take. Speaking of the necessity of an explicit repetition of the question of being, Heidegger writes,

> This question has today been forgotten—although our time considers itself progressive in again affirming "metaphysics." All the same we believe that we are spared the exertion of rekindling a γιγαντομαχία περί τῆς οὐσίας ["a

> Battle of Giants concerning Being" (Plato, *Sophist* 245e6–246e1)]. But the question touched upon here is hardly an arbitrary one. It sustained the avid research of Plato and Aristotle but from then on ceased to be heard *as a thematic question of actual investigation*. What these two thinkers achieved has been preserved in various distorted and camouflaged forms down to Hegel's *Logic*. (*Being and Time*, 2) 31

And a little later, examining the three prejudices that up until that point had obscured the question of being, he cites first the prejudice that makes of being a concept and *the most general concept*, and he accuses Hegel *not only* of having determined being as the poorest concept, as the *indeterminate immediate* at the beginning of the *Phenomenology* and the *Logic*, and as a basis for all the later developments, but even, in doing this, of having neglected or forgotten, "given up" he says, the problem posed by Aristotle as to the unity of being as a non-generic generality, as transcending *generality*, as transcendental in the forced sense the scholastics gave to this expression to express what Aristotle understood by the analogical unity of being (*Being and Time*, 2).

And later, in paragraph 6, devoted precisely to the destruction of the history of ontology, Heidegger insists on this belonging of *Hegelianism* to the ontological tradition that he wishes, precisely, to *destroy*. The history of ontology that emerged from Greek ontology shows that (I quote) "the ontology that thus arises deteriorates into a tradition, which allows it to sink to the level of the obvious and to become mere material for reworking (as it was for Hegel)" (*Being and Time*, 21). And further on: "In the *scholastic* mold, Greek ontology makes the essential transition via the *Disputationes metaphysicae* of Suárez into the 'metaphysics' and transcendental philosophy of the modern period; it still determines the foundations and goals of Hegel's *Logic*" (*Being and Time*, 21).

Why is Hegel's enterprise, so close for that matter to Heidegger's, still enclosed in the circle of classical ontology? This is a question that will not leave us in peace throughout these reflections, but already the reply has 32
peeped through in the two passages I have just read: (1) the passage on the prejudice one could call *conceptualist*, the prejudice that makes of being a concept, or of the thought of being a concept, and (2) the passage on the eschatology of being in "Anaximander's Saying," the last sentence of which I read again:

> This phenomenology itself represents a phase [so only a phase, in other words the access to Absolute Knowledge in the *Phenomenology of Spirit,* when spirit is finally gathered into itself] in the eschatology of being inasmuch as [this is why it is only a phase] being gathers itself, in the extremity of its essence

hitherto struck by the seal of metaphysics, as the absolute subjectivity of the unconditioned will to will. (*Off the Beaten Track*, 247)

What does this mean? It implies that the gathering of being, what passes itself off as the gathering of being, is still only the gathering of an ontic determination of being, in the form of the *subjectivity* of the *will*. On the modern foundation of Cartesianism, Hegel determined the absolute as subject. Substance becomes subject as he says himself—and as voluntarist subjectivity, deciding, willing its manifestation. Subjectivity and voluntarism stamp with their seal Hegelian teleology: the Idea *wants* to manifest itself, and spirit is this will to epiphany. Being is the Idea, Being is subjectity, Being is the will to will, Being is God as totality and the determinations of Being are still epochal dissimulations (Comment: read *Holzwege* [French], p. 275: *"This illuminating, keeping to itself with the truth of its essence, we may call the ἐποχή of being. Here, however, this word which is taken from the language of the Stoics does not mean, as it does for Husserl, the methodological setting
33 aside of the act of thetic consciousness in objectification. The ἐποχή of being belongs to being itself. We think it out of the oblivion of being."*)[6] of the meaning of being itself (*Off the Beaten Track*, 254). Why is this seal the seal of *metaphysics*: why does "being gather itself in the extremity of its essence hitherto struck by the seal of metaphysics" (*Off the Beaten Track*, 247)? Because metaphysics is, for Heidegger, the name of the determination of the being in general or of the excellent eminent being par excellence, that is, God, metaphysics is onto-theology. Hegel's logic did indeed, moreover, present itself as Metaphysics. In paragraph 18 of the *Encyclopedia* (among other places) Hegel writes, "Die *Logik* fällt [. . .] mit der *Metaphysik* zusammen" (*Logic* thus coincides with *metaphysics*).[7]

One might be tempted to think that what Heidegger says here about the Phenomenology of Spirit as a *phase,* as only a phase in the eschatology of being, would no longer be valid for the *Logic* . . .[8] since the Phenomenology of Spirit represents the moment of the becoming-phenomenon of spirit, the

6. Derrida sometimes gives the German title and French pagination or the French title and German pagination. We have placed asterisks (**) around the quotations not copied out by Derrida in the manuscript, reproducing them: (1) when they are clearly signaled by the brackets Derrida typically uses in indicating a quotation to be read aloud during his courses and (2) when they fit clearly into the context of the present course.

7. G. W. F. Hegel, *Encyclopedia of the Philosophical Sciences in Basic Outline*, Part I: Science of Logic, trans. and ed. Klaus Brinkmann and Daniel O. Dahlstrom (Cambridge: Cambridge University Press, 2010), 58. [Translator's note: The paragraph in question is in fact §24.]

8. Thus in the manuscript. We often find ellipses inserted in this way into a sentence.

moment of *consciousness*—in truth, this moment of reflection or the subjective articulation of the Idea. This would explain why the dialogue that Heidegger undertakes with Hegel always privileges the Phenomenology of Spirit. In truth, this determination of Being as subjective, as Idea in itself for itself, persists (in the *Logic*). We shall return to these problems.

Thus, to the extent that Hegel persists in obscuring the question of the meaning of being under onto-theo-logy, the destruction of the history of ontology is also a destruction of Hegelianism, is even *especially* a destruction of Hegelianism as the "summation" of this whole history; and in spite of troubling resemblances, Heideggerian destruction is not Hegel's "recollecting" refutation. It is distinguished from it by a nothing, a slight trembling of meaning that we must not overlook, for the whole seriousness of the enterprise sums up in this its fragility and its value. A slight trembling, for Heidegger says *nothing* else after the Hegelian—that is, Western—ontology that he is going to destroy. He says nothing else, he does not propose another ontology, another topic, another metaphysics, and his first gesture is to claim that he is not doing so. In this sense he does confirm the Hegelian consciousness of the end of philosophy. But he confirms it by adding no other *proposition*, that is to say he surrounds it with an ontological silence in which this Hegelian consciousness will be put into question, will be *solicited* (i.e., shaken); will tremble and let be seen what it still dissimulates in that trembling, will let be heard that on the basis of which it can still be questioned from a place that is neither outside it nor in it. 34

The difference between interiorizing refutation, between refutation as Hegelian *Erinnerung* and Heideggerian destruction, is thus as close as possible to *nothing*. Like Hegelian *refutation*, Heideggerian *destruction* is neither the critique of some error, nor the simply negative exclusion of some past of philosophy. It is a destruction—that is, a deconstruction, a de-structuration, the shaking that is necessary to bring out the structures, the strata, the system of deposits. As Heidegger said in the passage from a moment ago, sedimentations of the ontological tradition—sedimentations that have, according to a certain necessity, always covered over the naked question of being—covered over a nudity that in fact never unveiled itself as such.

It is, then, while remaining attentive, with the most acute vigilance, to this slight, flimsy, almost immaterial but decisive displacement that happens between Hegelian refutation (*Widerlegung*) and Heideggerian *Destruction*, that one must hear the few lines I am going to read, in which Heidegger, playing as Hegel does with the concepts of positive and negative, forewarns against a misinterpretation of his project of destruction. You will see how this passage resembles the Hegel passage I read a moment ago. I quote §6: 35

> This demonstration of the provenance [*Nachweis der Herkunft*, search for, justification of the provenance] of the fundamental ontological concepts, as the investigation which displays [*Ausstellung*: ostention, monstration] their *Geburtsbrief* [letter of nobility, says the [French] translation, letter of birth, civil status, mark of origin] has nothing to do with a vicious relativizing of ontological standpoints. The destruction has just as little the *negative* [emphasized] sense of an *Abschüttelung* [the [French] translators say *rejection*, but it is much more concrete and eloquent: of the demolition which brings down, which brings to ruin by blows brought to bear from outside: a Cartesian operation and metaphor of a *methodical* destruction to find new foundations, to begin again *a primis fondamentis* on the unshakeable ground and security in certainty]. The destruction has just as little the *negative* sense of such a demolition of the ontological tradition. On the contrary, it should stake out, measure [*ab-stecken*: here the [French] translation makes a pig's breakfast of the text: *ab-stecken* becomes "unveiling"] the positive possibilities in that tradition, and that always means to stake out its *limits*. These are factically given *each time* [not translated] with a specific formulation of the question and the prescribed demarcation of the possible field of investigation. Destruction does not relate itself in a negative way to the past: its critique concerns "today" and the dominant way we treat the history of ontology, whether it is conceived as the history of opinions, ideas, or problems. Destruction does
> 36 not wish to bury the past in nullity; it has a *positive* [emphasized] intent. Its negative function remains tacit and indirect.
>
> The destruction of the history of ontology essentially belongs to the formulation of the question of being and is possible solely within such a formulation. Within the scope of this treatise, which has as its goal a fundamental elaboration of the question of being, the destruction can be carried out only with regard to the fundamentally decisive stages of its history. (*Being and Time*, 21–22)

Which means that the principles of a systematic and exhaustive destruction are here present and that Heidegger does not exclude this possibility.

The development I'm bringing to an end here was supposed to explain in the most preliminary way why I had entitled this course *The Question of Being and History* and not *Being and History* or *Ontology and History.* But this explanation is only beginning. For what we have invoked to support it is the Destruction of the *history of ontology* and not the destruction of ontology itself. One might imagine, at this point, that Heidegger, destroying the tradition of ontology, would have to save or found an authentic ontology and that he would thus think that there is some chance for ontology outside the tradition or beyond the tradition, that ontology has been obscured and that one can at last return it to its true light.

Well, this is not the case; the destruction of the history of ontology is a destruction of ontology itself, of the entirety of the ontological project itself. What I'm saying goes against appearances and against public rumor, and it is true that it is in the name of an *ontological* point of view and, especially in *Sein und Zeit*, using the word ontological, that Heidegger destroys the tradition and conducts his analyses. But if these destructions mean to be ontological, what he wants to constitute is anything but an *ontology*. Here we must consider Heidegger's thought in its movement; or here, rather than his thought, his terminology. There is no doubt that in *Sein und Zeit* the term *ontology* is taken positively and what Heidegger wishes to awaken is a fundamental ontology slumbering beneath special or general metaphysics, which is interested only in beings and does not ask the question of the being 37
of beings. He wants to awaken the fundamental ontology under metaphysical ontology and the ontological under the ontic. But immediately after *Sein und Zeit*, and increasingly as he advances, the word *ontology* will seem more and more dangerous to him, both because of its traditional use and the meaning that at bottom legitimates this traditional use, ontology meaning not thought or *logos of* being (double genitive on which he will insist in the "Letter on 'Humanism'") but discourse on the *on*[9]—that is, on the *being* in general, on the being *qua* being (general metaphysics).

To follow this progressive abandonment of the notion, and this destruction of the *history of ontology* as destruction of ontology itself, I will pick out three reference points in the path of Heidegger's thinking in this regard.

First reference point: The opening of *Sein und Zeit* (1927). In §3 of *Sein und Zeit,* Heidegger defines the primacy of the question of the meaning of being in relation to the regional disciplines, the particular regional ontologies, each of which concerns a particular type of being. To each science, to each particular discipline, mathematics, physics, biology, historical sciences, theology and . . . ,[10] there must correspond an ontology that determines in advance the meaning of the being, the being of the being that is its object. A particular positive science can unfold its theoretical field and determine the unity of its theoretical field only by presupposing that clarity has been achieved as to the meaning of the being or of the particular type of being that it has as its object. One must know what is the meaning of the being of the physical being, of the being as physical thing, in order to constitute a physics. Knowledge is in fact for the physicist always a foreknowledge, a

9. In the manuscript, Derrida writes the Greek word for "being" either in Greek letters (ὄν) or in Roman letters (*on*). We adopt transliterations throughout.

10. Thus in the manuscript.

non-thematic pre-comprehension, but one that is indispensable, and this pre-comprehension must be brought into the light of the explicit. Each regional science will therefore have to be the object of an ontological question as to
38 the meaning of the being it treats. A movement parallel to the one specified by Husserl himself. And the reference to Husserl is almost explicit in §3. Husserl also defined the need to fix the meaning of the objects corresponding to each regional or material ontology. The difference here, and it is decisive, is that the material regions or ontologies that Husserl is talking about delimit domains of *objects*; beings are objects determined by a transcendental consciousness, a transcendental subject. The regional ontologies constitute the domains of objectivity. The world is the totality of regions, and thus the totality of objects appearing to a nonworldly consciousness, the region of consciousness not being one region among others but the *UR-Region*, the *UR-Kategorie.* And formal ontology concerns not the structure of objectivity of a region but the structure of objectivity in general, referred to something like an object in general for a consciousness in general. Clearly, Heidegger claims to be more radical in refusing to take on all this transcendental idealism, the whole thematic of the reduction, and so forth, which predetermines the being in general as an object in general. For Heidegger, the object in general is merely a determinate type of being and the same goes for its correlate, the subject or consciousness in general. We shall return to this. With the exception of this fundamental difference, the movement he effectuates here is analogous, if not identical, to that of Husserl. Once particular ontological questions have determined the meaning of the different regions of the being, it will be necessary to pose the question of being itself, of nonregional being itself. Regional ontological differences presuppose, whether they speak of the being of *such and such* a being or such and such a domain of beings, they presuppose the meaning of being; they have an implicit knowledge of what the word *being* means when they ask what is the physical being, the biological being, the mathematical, historical, being, and so on. This implicit knowledge must become explicit.

This question of the meaning of being in general (which is not a constructed generality) is what, in *Sein und Zeit,* he calls fundamental ontology. In *Sein und Zeit,* he accepts the word *ontology* to designate this endeavor.
39 See for example the end of §3. (Comment.)

> But such inquiry—ontology taken in its broadest sense without reference to specific ontological directions and tendencies—itself still needs a guideline. It is true that ontological inquiry is more original than the ontic inquiry of the positive sciences. [Comment.] But it remains naïve and opaque if its

> investigations into the being of beings leave the meaning of being in general undiscussed (*unerörtert*). And precisely the ontological task of a genealogy of the different possible ways of being (a genealogy which is not to be construed deductively) requires a preliminary understanding (*Vorverständigung*) of "what we really mean by this expression 'being' ('*Sein*')." (*Being and Time*, 10)

And here is the articulation of fundamental ontology with the regional ontologies, and of these latter with determinate ontic sciences.

> *Die Seinsfrage* thus aims not only at an a priori condition of the possibility of the sciences, which investigate beings as this or that kind of being and which thus always already move within an understanding of being, but also at the condition of the possibility of the ontologies which precede the ontic sciences and found them. (*Being and Time*, 10)

And now notice that in this first text, Heidegger while accepting for the moment ontology and the term *ontology*, nonetheless begins to refer it to the higher authority that is the question or the thinking of the meaning of being. This movement, which will be confirmed later, is here only announced. I continue my translation:

> All ontology, no matter how rich and tightly knit [tightly interlocked: *fest verklammertes*] a system of categories it has at its disposal, remains fundamentally blind and perverts its innermost intent if it has not previously clar- 40
> ified the meaning of being sufficiently and grasped this clarification as its fundamental task. (*Being and Time*, 10)

Some eight years later—and this would be our second reference point—the same movement is repeated, but this time it presents itself as a movement beyond. Beyond ontology and the word *ontology*.

In the *Einführung in die Metaphysik*, which is a course from 1935 that Heidegger considers as a sort of complement to *Sein und Zeit*, Heidegger again poses the question of the meaning of being, and again, this time directing his protest against Nietzsche (being = illusion) rather than against Hegel—Nietzsche and Hegel being the two thinkers in the privileged proximity of whom Heidegger makes his own difference heard—he shows that the thinking of being is not the concept of being. Just as any general concept can be constructed and fixed only if it is guided by a pre-comprehension of the meaning of that of which one wishes to form the concept, here too the concept of being, for there is a concept of being, refers to a prior thinking of the meaning of being itself. And this is the moment at which, restricting the extension of the word *ontology* to its signification and its *de facto* usage in the tradition, he proposes to abandon it. I will read you this passage, [French] pages 49–50.

*Of course, one can show oneself to be very clever and superior, and once again trot out the well-known reflection: "Being" is simply the most universal concept. Its range extends to any and every thing, even to Nothing, which, as something thought and said, "is" also something. So there is, in the strict sense of the word, nothing above and beyond the range of this most universal concept "Being" in terms of which it could be further defined. One must be satisfied with this highest generality. The concept of Being is an ultimate.
41 And it also corresponds to a law of logic that says: the more comprehensive a concept is in its scope—and what could be more comprehensive than the concept "Being"?—the more indeterminate and empty is its content.

For every normally thinking human being—and we all want to be normal—such trains of thought are immediately and entirely convincing. But now the question is whether the assessment of Being as the most universal concept reaches the essence of Being, or whether it so misinterprets Being from the start that questioning becomes hopeless. The question is whether Being can count only as the most universal concept that unavoidably presents itself in all particular concepts or whether Being has a completely different essence, and thus is anything but the object of an "ontology," if one takes this word in its established meaning.

The term "ontology" was first coined in the seventeenth century. It designates the development of the traditional doctrine of beings into a philosophical discipline and a branch of the philosophical system. But the traditional doctrine is the academic analysis and ordering of what for Plato and Aristotle, and again for Kant, was a question, though to be sure a question that was no longer originary. The word "ontology" is still used this way even today. Under this title, philosophy busies itself with the composition and exposition of a branch within its system. But one can also take the word "ontology" "in its broadest sense without reference to specific ontological directions and tendencies" (cf. *Being and Time*, 1927, p. 11, top). In this case "ontology" means the effort to put Being into words, and to do so by passing through the question of how it stands with Being [not just with beings as such]. But because until now this question has found neither an accord nor even a resonance, but instead it is explicitly rejected by the various circles of academic philosophical scholarship, which pursues an "ontology" in the traditional sense, it may be good in the future to forgo the use of the terms "ontology" and "ontological." Two modes of questioning which, as is only
42 now becoming clearer, are worlds apart should not bear the same name. We *ask* the question—How does it stand with Being? What is the meaning of Being?—not in order to compose an ontology in the traditional style, much less to reckon up critically the mistakes of earlier attempts at ontology. We are concerned with something completely different.*[11]

11. Martin Heidegger, *Introduction to Metaphysics*, trans. Gregory Fried and Richard Polt (New Haven, CT: Yale University Press, 2000), 42–44.

Third stage. This time Heidegger is no longer content to give up on the *term ontology* because it is charged with an equivocation due to a certain usage that was in fact made of it in history. This time Heidegger will consider that the *concept* of ontology itself can only be inadequate, for reasons not of fact but of essence. The very word *ontology* cannot designate anything other than a discourse directed toward beings, either the totality of beings or beings in general, or the being of beings (beingness, *étantité*) but not being itself. Ontology concerns the *on* and not the *einai*. Ontology has therefore no privilege with respect to metaphysics, at least with respect to general metaphysics. Whereas at the beginning Heidegger wanted to ground metaphysics in ontology, he *now* thinks that onto-logy is metaphysical. Now—that is, eight years again after the *Einführung*, sixteen years after *Sein und Zeit*, in the lecture given during the war, in 1943, entitled "Nietzsche's Word: 'God Is Dead,'" on the basis of the Nietzsche lectures given from 1936 to 1940. This is a meditation on Nietzsche's Metaphysics. In spite of Nietzsche's demolition of classical metaphysics, there is a metaphysics in Nietzsche, and one that is not simply to one side of his aesthetics, of his theory of knowledge, and so forth.

This metaphysics, like all metaphysics, wants to determine being *qua* being; here it is a metaphysics of being as value, a metaphysics of value, and pursuing the explication of this metaphysics of value, Heidegger tries to show that being as such in its essence is *will to power* and in its existence "Eternal Return of the Same." But this dissociation between *essentia* and *existentia* has not been meditated on by the metaphysics that lives off this inheritance without posing the question of the unity of the meaning of being before the rupture of the *ens* qua *ens*, of being as being, as essence and existence. A rupture that came about after Aristotle and his [illegible word]. And Nietzsche *43*
is imprisoned in this metaphysical limitation.

> The essential relation between the "will to power" and the "eternal return of the same" must be thought in this way; however we cannot yet represent it here directly because metaphysics has neither considered nor even inquired about the origin of the distinction between *essentia* and *existentia*.[12]

Well, this metaphysics as determination of the being qua being, and blind to the originary question of being, this traditional metaphysics that Nietzsche wanted to demolish but was unable to destroy—Heidegger also calls it ontology in this text, consecrating this time not the depreciation (for there is none) but the limitation attributed to this concept: read [French] pages 173–74:

12. Heidegger, "Nietzsche's Word: 'God Is Dead,'" in *Off the Beaten Track*, 178.

> However, even for Nietzsche thinking means: to represent beings as beings. All metaphysical thinking is onto-logy [in two words joined by a hyphen] or it is nothing at all. (*Off the Beaten Track*, 158)

You see that Heidegger was not content with the project of "*destroying*" the history of ontology; he really did want to destroy ontology itself, which is one with its history. That is what I wanted to show today through these remarks which are not yet even *prolegomena* and by which I wanted to justify the first part of the title of my course: *the question of being*—and not ontology—*and history*. Next time we shall have to speak of history, that is, first of the *and*, that is, of the place of communication and the *passage* between Being and History, this passage, this *et* being the very place of our problem,
44 this *et* about which it is not yet decided whether we will write it *et* or *est* [is]. All the words of the title will not thereby have been justified: there is still the question here, and especially the *of* of the question of being. But we shall concern ourselves with that only periodically and well after the Prolegomena.

Questions.[13]

13. Thus in the manuscript.

SESSION TWO

30 November 1964

Last time I attempted in a quite preliminary way to justify in its literality the title of this course. I *first* had to make clear why this title said *the question of being* and *history* and not *ontology* and *history*. This led us to explain how and why Heidegger's thought was not and did not wish to be, whatever people say and write, an *ontology*. Whatever people write, because not only are people writing everywhere about Heidegger's ontology, but the author of one the two fattest books (which are not the best books) written on Heidegger in French, one of these authors, who is the co-translator of *Sein und Zeit*, writes an essay entitled *Paths and Impasses of Heidegger's Ontology*,[1] without realizing that Heidegger's path—which moreover Heidegger would not represent as an impasse, Heidegger not caring much, and for profound reasons, about the arrival of paths, those that do not arrive, like *Holzwege*, not being the worst paths of thought—is precisely, as we saw, the search for a way out of ontology in general. Which means that it is difficult to see how one can speak of a Heideggerian ontology and a fortiori of its impasse, and a fortiori of several impasses, for the word is in the plural in the title, an unconscious homage to a thought whose richness consists in arriving at several impasses at once (aporia of SZ).[2] The other, Chapelle, devotes 250 46
pages to what he calls Heidegger's phenomenological ontology.[3] It is true that this is a commentary of *Sein und Zeit* alone, in which, as we saw, the step beyond ontology is only announced.

To show that Heidegger's thought was not an ontology, we had to dwell on the problem of what Heidegger, in the opening pages of *Sein und Zeit*,

1. Alphonse de Waelhens, *Chemins et impasses de l'ontologie heideggerienne: À propos des "Holzwege"* (Paris: Desclée de Brouwer, 1953).

2. The transcription of this abbreviation is uncertain. It could refer to *Sein und Zeit*.

3. Albert Chapelle, S. J., *L'Ontologie phénoménologique de Heidegger: Un commentaire de "Sein und Zeit"* (Paris: Éditions universitaires, 1962).

calls the *Destruktion* of the history of ontology. *Destruktion* that meant neither annihilation nor demolition (we specified these concepts), nor critique, nor refutation of an error. Not even a refutation in the sense that Hegel gives this word. And to make this clear, we had to be attentive to the difference, which could sometimes appear to be null, between Hegelian *Widerlegung* — with the total extension that Hegel gives this notion which allows him to *logicize* the totality of the negativity in being—a difference that could appear to be null between Hegelian *Widerlegung* and Heideggerian Destruction.

Nonetheless, Hegel's definition of history as the development of "Spirit" is not *untrue (unwahr)*. Neither is it partly correct and partly false. It is as true as metaphysics, which through Hegel first brings to language its essence—thought in terms of the absolute—in the system. Absolute metaphysics, with its Marxian and Nietzschean inversions, belongs to the history of the truth of being. Whatever stems from it cannot be countered or even cast aside by refutations. It can only be taken up in such a way that its truth is more primordially sheltered in being itself and removed from the domain of mere human opinion. All refutation in the field of essential thinking is *töricht* [senseless, foolish, mad, verbose, crazy].[4]

This allowed us, in passing, to perceive another covering-over, and, scarcely perceptible but decisive, another displacement between the Hegelian concept and the Heideggerian concept of the *last*, and of the last philosophy. And why Hegel, even though he refutes it and fulfils it totally, belongs to the metaphysical ontology that Heidegger wants to destroy—that is, to deconstruct, de-structure, shake (solicit), to bring out the thinking of being that is hiding under the ontic sedimentations. We followed in three passages this destruction of the Hegelian moment: Hegel who reduces the thinking of being to the concept of being, and Hegel who always determines being as a whole as voluntarist subjectivity (on the basis of Cartesianism), as will to will, absolute idea, God and the concept, as will to manifest itself—the Hegelian ontology or the Hegelian metaphysics which, as Hegel says himself,

4. Martin Heidegger, "Letter on 'Humanism,'" trans. Frank A. Capuzzi, in *Pathmarks*, ed. William McNeill (Cambridge: Cambridge University Press, 2008), 256. The 1957 French translation that Derrida used while writing this course could not be located. A slightly modified translation by R. Munier appeared in a bilingual edition in 1964, and was re-issued in 1966. This last edition is still to be found in Derrida's library today, but it cannot, of course, have been the one he used during this course. Therefore, we shall confine ourselves to the 1957 edition when reproducing the citations referenced (as in "read pp. 63–67") but not copied out in the manuscript. There is thus a certain amount of uncertainty as to where exactly these citations begin and end—this not usually being the case when we have access to the brackets Derrida used in his own copies.

merges into logic and onto-theology. These precautions as to the scarcely perceptible but decisive difference between Hegelian ontology and Heidegger's thinking of being allowed us to hear in its true resonance the passage from paragraph 6 of *Sein und Zeit* in which Heidegger defines the *Destruktion* of the history of ontology in terms that closely resemble those that Hegel uses to define the *Widerlegung* in philosophy in the passage we read (*Lectures on the History of Philosophy*). The scarcely perceptible character of the difference is what allows us to avoid those spectacular overturnings of Hegelian metaphysics that, as we well know, *qua* overturnings remain, unbeknownst to themselves, prisoners of what they would like to transgress (Nietzsche and Marx). All of this only partially justified the fact that the course should be entitled "The Question of Being and History" and not "Ontology and *48*
History." For the *Destruktion* that Heidegger talks about at the beginning of *Sein und Zeit* is a *Destruktion* of the history of ontology and not of ontology. So I tried to show that this *Destruktion* of the history of ontology is *explicitly* the *Destruktion* of ontology itself.

I could also have cited a fourth text that confirms this movement of a passage beyond ontology that does not lead to a new ontology, to a new ontological proposal or to the new proposal of an ontology. This is a passage from the "Letter on 'Humanism'" in which, speaking of the relation between *Ethics* and *Ontology*, Heidegger affirms that, I quote: "ontology always thinks solely the being (ὄν) in its being" (*Pathmarks*, 271).

"Ontology thinks solely the being of beings or the being in its being":[5] that's a proposition that is difficult to understand and that is replete with many possible confusions. "The being of beings"—this expression can mean two things. One often hears tell that Heidegger is not interested in the being but in the being of beings. Yet here, he seems not to be satisfied with an ontology that only ever thinks the being of beings. What does this mean? The point is that one can understand and articulate the *of* in "the being of beings" in two ways. When he understands it in the sense of the metaphysical ontology that he wishes to "*überwinden*," overcome, Heidegger understands by the being of beings the being-a-being of beings, the being of beings *qua* beings, if you like the beingness of beings [*l'étantité de l'étant*] (*Seiendheit*). Traditional metaphysical ontology limits itself to what makes of the particular being or of beings in their totality, or of beings in general, a *being* (*on*). But it does not

5. [Translator's note:] Derrida adds "the being of beings" to the translation; the German text has, "Denn die Ontologie denkt immer nur das Seiende (ὄν) in seinem Sein." See Martin Heidegger, "Brief über den Humanismus," in *Wegmarken* (Frankfurt: Vittorio Klostermann, 1950), 162.

pose the question of the being of beings as a question of the being of beingness. At a pinch, one can also speak of the being of beings but being no longer has here the same meaning as in the homonymic expression of a moment ago. We are not here dealing with the being of beings as beingness of the being, but, through a further degree of questioning regression, of the being of beingness in general. This is what Heidegger also calls *the truth of being*, an expression that also presupposes a whole itinerary wrenching the notion of
49 truth away from its classical determination as the truth of a judicative statement, as adequation. We shall have to speak of this again. What was called fundamental ontology in *Sein und Zeit* and what will subsequently no longer even be called ontology wants to be a regression to a point not only prior to beings but even prior to the being of beings as *beingness*, toward the truth of being itself. In the passage from the "Letter on 'Humanism'" that I have just explicated, this is clearly stated by Heidegger, who appears to be very concerned to justify retroactively this title *Sein und Zeit,* the incompletion of which people often try to transform into an impasse and try to oppose to the later writings, either to prefer it, or to make of it an inconsequential misstep.

I quote, [French] p. 145:

> For ontology thinks solely the being (ὄν) in its being. But as long as the truth of being is not thought all ontology remains without its foundation. Therefore the thinking that in *Being and Time* tries to advance thought in a preliminary way into the truth of being (*das Denken, das mit Sein und Zeit in die Wahrheit des Seins* vorzudenken *versuchte*) [comment] characterizes itself as "fundamental ontology." It tries to reach back into the essential ground from which thought concerning the truth of being emerges. By initiating another inquiry this thinking is already removed from the "ontology" [in quotes] of metaphysics (even that of Kant). "Ontology" itself, however, whether transcendental or precritical, is subject to critique, not because it thinks the being of beings and in so doing reduces being to a concept, but because it does not think the truth of being and so fails to recognize that there is a thinking more rigorous than conceptual thinking. (*Pathmarks*, 271)

Naturally we shall have to repeat concretely and effectively this movement of the destruction of the history of ontology as destruction of ontology, a movement in which all we have done is to propose a few reference points.

So I think I have explained why *I did not* use the word *ontology* in the title
50 of this course. But I have not explained why I said "the question of being" and not "being" or "the truth of being." But that belongs to the order of justifications that cannot be preliminary. I could do it insufficiently and purely indicatively by radicalizing what I've just said about the history of ontology

and ontology: namely, that there is also a project of *destruction*—in the very precise sense of this word—of the notion of *being* itself and of the word *being* itself. I could do so indicatively but very precisely by pointing to a short text from 1955, offered to Ernst Jünger, the second version of which has as its title *Zur Seinsfrage*, "the question of being," a text in which, from [German] page 30 onward, *das Sein* is always written under a crossing-through that has the form of a cross, a cross, a *Durchkreuzung,* a *kreuzweise Durchstreichung* that leaves being present, visible, and legible behind the negative cipher that neutralizes it especially, says Heidegger, as an object in the subject-object relation or as a concept of the totality of beings.

But I prefer to let this justification mature, in its own time. The same goes for the justification of the term *question*, the word *of* in "the question of being," and the word *and* that links the question of being to history as well as the syntax that allows this expression to be read. These words being the most important and the most problematic.

The question that will guide us today, then, in a very preliminary way, will be the following, very simply stated. What does history have to do with the question of being, in the sense in which Heidegger appears to understand it?

It would be easy to show, and I will not dwell on it, that never in the history of philosophy has there been a radical affirmation of an essential link between being and history. Ontology has always been constituted through a gesture of wrenching itself away from historicity and temporality, even in Hegel, for whom history is the history of the *manifestation* of an absolute and eternal concept, of a divine subjectivity that, in its origin and in its end, seems to gather up its historicity infinitely—that is, to live it in the total presence of being with itself (i.e., in a non-historicity). History is phenomenology and not ontology or logic, at least if one considers Hegel literally 51
and limits oneself to a standard reading. After Hegel, philosophy's thematizing and taking history seriously took the form, precisely, of giving up on the problem of being. The most serious attempt to think the historicity of being, after Hegel, is the Marxist attempt which, according to Heidegger, has never been taken seriously as such. In defining *Entfremdung*, alienation, Marx attained an essential dimension of history as *Geschichte* which goes much further, says Heidegger in the "Letter on 'Humanism,'" than the banal and common concept of history. And Heidegger adds,

> But since neither Husserl nor—so far as I have seen till now—Sartre recognizes the essential importance of the historical in being, neither phenomenology nor existentialism enters that dimension within which a productive dialogue with Marxism first becomes possible. (*Pathmarks*, 259)

The dialogue is possible and can be fruitful only if, notes Heidegger,[6]

(1) one liberates oneself from naïve representations and cheap refutations;
(2) one stops seeing in materiality the simple affirmation that everything is only matter; and
(3) one understands it as the metaphysical determination of beings in general as the material (*Material* and not *Stoff*) of labor.

In doing this, however, and reaching the essence of historicity on the basis of the essence of *labor*, Marx remains a prisoner of the Hegelian metaphysical determination of labor: Hegel had already thought, in the *Phenomenology of Spirit*, the metaphysical and modern essence of labor as *sich selbst einrichtende Vorgang der unbedingten Herstellung,* as a process organizing itself in unconditioned production:

> The modern metaphysical essence of labor is anticipated in Hegel's *Phenomenology of Spirit* as *sich selbst einrichtende Vorgang der unbedingten Herstellung*, as the self-established process of unconditioned production, [unconditioned production here meaning that labor and the force of production, produc-
> 52 tivity, are not defined by derivation on the basis of other conditions, but are grasped in an absolute originality with regard to any other concept or signification from which one might try to derive them] which is the objectification of the actual (*Vergegenständigung des Wirklichen*) through the human being, experienced as subjectivity (*durch den als Subjektivität erfahrenen Menschen*). (*Pathmarks*, 259)

This last sentence means that the originary concept of labor or production, in Marx, cannot be uncoupled from an essential relation to man as subject of labor. Humanism, subjectivity and metaphysics are indissociable, as Heidegger will show later, and ultimately, on this view, Marx, in his concept of labor, however profound the penetration of historicity allowed by it, remained an inheritor of Hegelian metaphysics, in the form of the subjectivizing voluntarism we were speaking of last time, and ultimately of a humanist anthropologism. To free oneself from it and truly think labor (and therefore history) outside the horizon of Hegelian metaphysics, it would have been necessary to think the essence of technology sheltered and hidden in this notion of labor. See [French] page 101 of the "Letter on 'Humanism'":

> The essence of materialism is concealed in the essence of technology, about which much has been written but little has been thought. Technology is in

6. [Translator's note:] These introductory words and the following numbered points follow almost word for word *Pathmarks*, 259.

> its essence a destiny within the history of being (*Die Technik ist ihrem Wesen ein seinsgeschichtliches Geschick*) and of the truth of being, a truth that lies in oblivion. For technology does not go back to the τέχνη of the Greeks in name only but derives historically and essentially from τέχνη (*sie stammt wesensgeschichtlich aus der* τέχνη) as a mode of ἀληθεύειν, a mode, that is, of rendering beings manifest. As a form of truth, technology is grounded in the history of metaphysics, *which is itself a distinctive and up to now the only surveyable phase of the history of being* [Derrida's italics]. No matter which of the various positions one chooses to adopt toward the doctrines of communism and to their foundation, from the point of view of the history of being it is certain that an elemental experience of what is world-historical (*was weltgeschicht-* 53
> *lich ist*) speaks out in it. Whoever takes "communism" only as a "party" or a "Weltanschauung" is thinking too shallowly, just as those who by the term "Americanism" mean, and mean derogatorily, nothing more than a particular lifestyle. (*Pathmarks*, 259)

If the foundational concepts of technology or labor or production or alienation or objectification belong to the history of metaphysics, as Heidegger says here, and if this history of metaphysics—or of ontology—is only a *phase*—an important phase and the only one we can see in its entirety as a tradition—a phase of the history of being, then the profound historicity to which Marxism gains access is not yet the history of being itself, and it is this metaphysical closure that prevents Marxism's concept of history from going beyond the ontic sphere; it is this closure that prevents Marxism from radicalizing the historicity (that it nonetheless thinks) as history of being itself and of the truth of being itself. And this at bottom because, as for Hegel and Nietzsche, *being* is for Marx only the indeterminate object of the poorest *concept*. If the most serious attempt to radicalize the thinking of history was unable to escape from metaphysics and from the history of ontology, one must therefore think this *and* that links the question of being *and* history at a depth that has always been *closed off*—that is, presupposed but unthought. How then do matters stand between the question of being and history?

We can gain an entrance for ourselves into this problem by opening up the following question, which is only apparently extrinsic or simply methodological: In which *language* will it be possible for the question of being in its relation with history to be expounded and treated, to the degree of absolute radicality that Heidegger has chosen—that is, at the depth of the originarity that *on the one hand* the destruction will have laid bare, and, first 54
of all and *on the other hand*, on the basis of which the destruction itself was able to be undertaken<?>

Whence are we to draw the concepts, the terms, the forms of linking nec-

essary for the discourse of Destruction, for the destructive discourse? Clearly we cannot borrow them simply from the tradition that we are in the process of deconstructing; we cannot simply take them up again, that much is obvious. But *neither* can we, because destruction is not a demolition or an annihilation, erase them or abandon them in some conceptual storage room, as definitively outdated instruments. Because *Destruktion* is in its gesture like a *Wiederholung*, a repetition, it can neither use, nor simply deprive itself of the traditional logos.[7] Simply to deprive oneself of it would be "precisely" to give to traditionalism a meaning that is exactly the one that Heidegger does not want and that belongs to a moment of metaphysics—namely, the meaning of a beginning again from zero in the ahistorical style of Descartes or perhaps (things are less simple) of Husserl. Not that the Descartes of the *Discourse* or Husserl in his Cartesian vein decided to create from scratch a new language to escape from the historical heritage. In any case, if that had been practically possible, one can suppose that they would have done so and that nothing in their philosophical intention was opposed to it. And when they use received words, they indeed have the certainty—no doubt a naïve one in Heidegger's eyes—that the new intention animating them suffices to liberate them from their historical weight. Heidegger cannot and precisely does not want to accept the comfort of this ahistorical radicalism and, planning to destroy the history of ontology and ontology, he is always vigilant in making the most radical question of being and the most radical historicity communicate intrinsically and essentially. The problem of language that he faces is thus formidable and it goes without saying that it has no general solution, no principial solution, no solution of principle. There is no oper-
55 ative schema that will allow in each case the resolution of this difficulty on the basis of a rule. At every moment, uneasily but vigilantly, in the work of analysis, in the corrections and crossings out, the crossings out of crossings out, one will proceed slowly within the received *logos*, sometimes modifying it by itself, correcting itself by itself, and in this sense the destruction will always be an auto-destruction of the *logos* of ontology, and of philosophy by philosophy. I say of philosophy by philosophy because it goes without saying that the destruction of ontology is for Heidegger the destruction of philosophy itself (see the end of the "Letter on 'Humanism'"). Because of this problem of language, the destruction of philosophy will always be *surprised* in philosophy, surprised by philosophy, enveloped by philosophy at the very moment that it wants to destroy philosophy, if only because it is the philosophical *logos* that is undertaking its own destruction. Sometimes, one will

7. See Martin Heidegger, *What Is Philosophy?* trans. Jean T. Wilde and William Kluback (Lanham, MD: Rowman & Littlefield, 2003), 71–73.

forge new words, new concepts, drawing on the resources of the language, on certain resources of the language that are, ought to be *younger* than philosophy, later arrivals on the scene than philosophy.

But the creation of new concepts, and of new concepts not as new philosophical concepts, but as concepts new with respect to any possible philosophy — this creation of new concepts, even when it is possible, will be quite insufficient to solve our problem of language. For this problem is not only a problem of concepts and words. It is not only a problem of philosophical lexicology, but it is a problem of syntax which concerns the forms of linkage of concepts. For example, hermeneutics will be unable to satisfy itself with either a purely descriptive language, with a continuous and serene explication, or with a synthetic or deductive language. Description and deduction are methods the value of which is not self-evident, and which belong to the history of metaphysics.

— hyphen and rupture:[8] at certain moments of the subject-attribute relation so as to link their signification (for example Being and history).
— Substantivation of preposition (the *there* . . .). 56
— Double genitive [history] (the question of being, the thinking of being). See *Humanism,* p. 27. Read.

> Thinking is *l'engagement par l'Être pour l'Être* [engagement by being for being]. I do not know whether it is linguistically possible to say both of these ("par" and "pour") at once in this way: *penser, c'est l'engagement de l'Être*. Here the possessive form "de l' . . ." is supposed to express both subjective and objective genitive. In this regard "subject" and "object" are inappropriate terms of metaphysics, which very early on in the form of Occidental "logic" and "grammar" seized control of the interpretation of language. We today can only begin to descry what is concealed in that occurrence. The liberation of language from grammar into a more original essential framework is reserved for thought and poetic creation. (*Pathmarks*, 259–60; French as in Heidegger's original text)

This question of the language in which the *destruction* will operate is not a question that I am posing to or imposing on Heidegger. It is posed by Heidegger himself at the end of the introduction to *Sein und Zeit*, which is entitled "Exposition of the Question of the Meaning of Being." It is posed in an added remark, which is a little surprising and, if I have forced Heidegger's thinking, it is by placing this added remark in the foreground.

Well, Heidegger lays out a problem that is analogous, but not identical,

8. [Translator's note:] The next few lines, up to and including the quotation from Heidegger, are written on a separate sheet and inserted in the MS.

since this time it is a matter not of this or that concept but of the totality of the philosophical logos. I'll translate this remark and you'll see the new entry it gives us into our problem. End of §7.

> With regard to the awkwardness and "inelegance" of expression in the following analyses, we may remark that it is one thing to tell stories about beings [literally, to report narratively: *über Seiendes erzählende zu berichten*]
> 57 and another to grasp beings in their *being*. For the latter task not only are most of the words lacking but above all the "grammar." If we may allude to earlier and in their own right altogether incomparable researches on the analysis of being, then we should compare the ontological sections in Plato's *Parmenides* or the fourth chapter of the seventh book of Aristotle's *Metaphysics* with a narrative passage from Thucydides. Then we can see the stunning character of the formulations with which their philosophers challenged the Greeks. Since our powers are essentially inferior, and also since the area of being to be disclosed ontologically is far more difficult than that presented to the Greeks, the complexity of our concept-formation and the severity of our expression will increase. (*Being and Time*, 36–37)

Ontic metaphor.[9]

The language difficulty hangs, then—even before all the reasons for it I just gave—on the fact that for the first time we are going to forbid ourselves resolutely and absolutely from "telling stories." The writing that *tells stories* is easy, narration is easy and philosophy, in spite of appearances, has never deprived itself of it. The point is to break with the philosophical novel, and to break with it *radically* and not so as to give rise to some new novel. The philosophical novel, philosophical narration, is of course, but is not only, the history of philosophy as *doxography* that recounts, reports, gathers and lays out the series of philosophical systems. "Telling stories," in philosophy, is for Heidegger something much more profound and that cannot be so easily denounced as doxography. The Novelesque from which we must awaken is philosophy itself as metaphysics and as onto-theology.

What does this mean? And why, at the very moment at which historicity
58 must finally be taken absolutely seriously, must one stop telling stories? Why, at the moment when the question of history has the same dignity as—and not merely a dignity equal to that of—the question of being, must one stop telling stories? And why in a certain way had Plato and Aristotle also "told stories" and hadn't broken radically with the narration of Thucydides? Why would narrative and mythology and the stories of metaphysics [several illegible words] withdrawn being and history? Before attending to what in Hei-

9. Thus in the manuscript: two underlined words, rather than a subtitle. [Translator's note: here converted to italic.]

degger's gesture—dismissing stories at the moment he poses the question of being—before attending to what in this gesture is singular and difficult, we must first recognize in what way it is classical.

Heidegger is aware of this classicism. It turns out that each time in philosophy someone wanted to establish an ontology, or to renew ontology, they began by bidding farewell to stories. But it turns out that each time it was from historicity in general that one thus took one's leave.

Heidegger gives only one *reference* in this regard but one can give others and I shall do so in a moment.

Before examining this reference, I would like to say a few words about the status of historical reference, reference to the history of philosophy in Heidegger, from the point of view that interests us. When Heidegger says (§6) that "the destruction of the history of ontology essentially belongs to the formulation of the question of being and is possible solely within such a formulation" (*Being and Time*, 22), he means that references to the history of ontology (or of philosophy) are neither rhetorical or literary ornaments of the discourse elaborating the question of being, nor a methodological preamble, nor, in whatever sense, a preliminary or extrinsic phase of the elaboration of the question of being. This latter happens in the destruction of the history of ontology. What one cannot imagine, what is impossible or would have no sense, is a question of being, a positing of the question of being that would happen before or independently of a destruction of ontology—that 59
is, which essentially, in its essence, could do without historical reference to the past of philosophy. That means that the transgression of philosophy that happens with the question of being must find and maintain its support in philosophy. The question of being—beyond all regional ontologies and general ontology—has no sense if it does not question on the basis of beings and the beingness of beings in their entirety, therefore the entirety of its history and in the entirety of its explication in philosophy (as metaphysics or onto-theology). As being is not a being, it is nothing outside beings, it is not another being, therefore it is nothing ontically—outside its ontic determinations, therefore outside its totality and the totality of its history. Thus to ask questions about being outside historical reference to the totality of its ontic determinations and their explication in the history of metaphysics is to miss the meaning of being itself.

This is why *Sein und Zeit*, in a style which is anything but that of doxography, and at the very moment when Heidegger refuses to tell stories, begins with a reference (*Sophist*) and strings references throughout the length of its journey. Closing this parenthesis on references, I come back to the first reference I announced concerning "storytelling."

After having defined and criticized the three prejudices that obscure the

question of being—namely, <(1)> the prejudice that makes of the thinking of being an absolutely general concept; (2) the prejudice that dismisses the question of being on the pretext that being is by definition indefinable (Pascal: "We cannot undertake to define being without falling into the same absurdity: for we cannot define a word without beginning with the word *it is*, either expressed or understood. To define being, therefore, it is necessary to say *it is* and thus to employ the word defined in the definition");[10] and (3) the prejudice that dismisses the question of being on the pretext that being is a self-evident (*selbstverständlich*) concept and that, consequently, it merits no supplementary explication.[11] So, after having denounced these three prejudices, Heidegger lays out what he calls the formal structure of the question
60 of being. The formal structure of the question of being is what, in its structure, is analogous to the structure of any question in general. One must know what a question in general is to determine what the question of being must be. This structure cannot be drawn without the three poles of the *Gefragtes*, the *Befragtes* and the *Erfragtes*.[12] What does this mean?

Every question is a seeking and as such it has an object (*Gesuchten*) about which it is concerned. Every question has an object *asked about* [two illegible words] in general. "*Das Fragen hat als Fragen nach sein Gefragtes [. . .]*" (*Sein und Zeit*, 4). But every question also inquires of something (here the [French] translation is unintelligible—Heidegger does not say "address a question to" but "inquire of something" (*Anfragen bei*). "*Zum Fragen gehört ausser dem Gefragten ein Befragtes*" (*Sein und Zeit*, 5). "Besides what is asked about, what is interrogated also belongs to questioning" (here the asked about, *Gefragten*, is being, the interrogated (*Befragtes*) is beings) (*Being and Time*, 4). And then the intention that guides the question, what makes one pass from the *Befragtes* to the *Gefragtes*, from what is interrogated to what is asked about, if you like, is the *Erfragtes*, translated [by Stambaugh] as "what is to be ascertained." This fundamental and formal structure which is that of any question is further determined if one thinks that it can be a question posed just like that, in passing, in the vacuity of chatter that does not think

10. [Translator's note:] Blaise Pascal, *Pensées et Opuscules*, ed. L. Brunschvicg (Paris: 1912), 169 (this is the edition Heidegger quotes from in *Being and Time*). Blaise Pascal, *Thoughts, Letters and Minor Works*, trans. O. W. Wight (New York: Cosimo, 1910), 432.

11. [Translator's note:] This sentence is syntactically incomplete in the French text.

12. [Translator's note:] I use the neuter nominative singular primary ending of the adjectival nouns *Gefragtes*, *Befragtes*, and *Erfragtes* when Derrida uses them as part of his own discourse. When, on the other hand, it is a matter of simply giving or alluding to a specific German word in a given quote, I have reproduced the word with whatever ending it has in the original text.

about the word, or, to the contrary, an explicit and authentic question. It is on the basis of this *Fact* that what is asked about (*das Gefragte*) comes into question. The *Gefragtes*, being, is always already pre-comprehended and that is necessary for a being to appear to us and to be determined as a being. This horizon or this opening of being in which every being whatsoever appears can quite obviously not itself be a being. In our pre-comprehension of what is asked about (*Gefragtes*) we already know that being is not itself a being since it is that on the basis of which every being is what it is. We know, then, that the *Gefragtes* (being) is not the *Befragtes* (a being interrogated as to what makes it a being). Our question is launched, then, in the difference between the *Gefragtes* and the *Befragtes*, and thus already—although Heidegger has 61
not yet used these words—it is launched in the only space that is proper to it, the *difference* between being and beings (ontico-ontological).

Now, what is it to *tell stories*? To tell stories is to ignore this difference and confuse the *Gefragtes* and the *Befragtes*, it is to ignore the *Erfragtes*, it is to assimilate being and beings, that is, to determine the origin of beings qua beings on the basis of another being. It is to reply to the question "what is the being of beings?" by appealing to another being supposed to be its cause or origin. It is to close the opening and to suppress the question of the *meaning* of being. Which does not mean that every ontic explication in itself comes down to *telling stories*; when the sciences determine causalities, legalities that order the relations between beings, when theology explains the totality of beings on the basis of creation or the ordering brought about by a supreme being, they are not necessarily telling stories. They "tell stories" when they want to pass their discourse off as the reply to the question of the meaning of being or when, incidentally, they refuse this question all seriousness. When the sciences or theology or metaphysics say, "We're dealing with beings, with the beings in this region or beings in their totality or beingness without needing to pose the question of the truth of being," then these discourses are content to tell stories, and those who speak them refuse to pose the question of knowing what they are talking about and to make explicit the meaning of their language. Whether this gesture be that of metaphysics, of theology, or of science, it is, at root, the very expression of *obscurantism* itself; of an obscurantism in which science is complicit with theology and metaphysics, that humanism which, as we shall see later, is always associated with this refusal of the question of being.

Let me make clear again, for one is never prudent enough when one touches on these questions, one never sufficiently forestalls one's reflexes, even if the intentions—here Heidegger's intentions—are already clearer here: let me make clear, then, that all this does not come down to *condemn-*

ing metaphysics, theology or *science* (especially not science since that is the
62 sensitive point) under the name of obscurantism. There is obscurantism not in the ontic explanation as such, but when those who practice it refuse, refute or repress the question of the meaning of being that is prior—and not only theoretically—to their activity. And it also goes without saying that of course the question of being is in no way a *paralyzing reaction* with regard to the progress of ontic research, whatever it be. Not only does it exercise no paralyzing reaction but, of course, it is necessary to the movement of ontic research. It is all the more necessary as the question of the meaning of being *in general* in that it is already necessary as a determinate ontological question concerning this or that type of being as object of this or that science. See for example what Heidegger says about this in paragraph 3 of *Sein und Zeit*. I'll read directly from the [French] translation, pages 24 to 25.[13]

> *[Up to now the necessity of a retrieval of the question was motivated partly by its venerable origin but above all by the lack of a definite answer, even by the lack of any adequate formulation of the question. But one can demand to know what purpose this question should serve. Does it remain solely, or *is* it at all, only a matter of free-floating speculation about the most general generalities—*or is it the most basic and at the same time most concrete question?*
>
> Being is always the being of a being. [The totality of beings can, with respect to its various domains, become the field where particular domains of knowledge are exposed and delimited. These domains—for example, history, nature, space, life, human being, language, and so on—can in their turn become thematized as objects of scientific investigations. Scientific research demarcates and first establishes these domains of knowledge in a rough and ready fashion. The elaboration of the domain in its fundamental structures
> 63 is in a way already accomplished by the prescientific experience and interpretation of the region of being to which the domain of knowledge is itself confined. The resulting "fundamental concepts" comprise the guidelines for the first concrete disclosure of the domain. Whether or not the importance of the research always lies in such establishment of concepts, its true progress comes about not so much in collecting results and storing them in "handbooks" as in being forced to ask questions about the basic constitution of each domain, these questions being chiefly a reaction to increasing knowledge in each area.]
>
> The real "movement" of the sciences takes place in the revision of these basic concepts, a revision which is more or less radical and lucid with regard

13. Where the following quote begins and ends is unclear since Derrida signals two different starting points with two brackets and, with three brackets, three possible endings for this quote. We thus reproduce all the brackets in transcribing this quote from the copy Derrida used.

to itself.] A science's level of development is determined by the extent to which it is *capable* of a crisis in its basic concepts. In these immanent crises of the sciences the relation of positive questioning to the matter in question becomes unstable. Today tendencies to place research on new foundations have cropped up on all sides in the various disciplines.

The discipline which is seemingly the strictest and most securely structured, *mathematics*, has experienced a "crisis in its foundations." The controversy between formalism and intuitionism centers on obtaining and securing primary access to what should be the object of this science.]* (*Being and Time*, 8–9)

"Telling stories," then—that is, giving oneself over to a mythological discourse (I'm finally arriving at the reference I announced)—is something one tried to renounce for the first time in philosophy precisely at the moment when the problem of being announced itself as such. Heidegger does not multiply references; he merely cites this "first time" when storytelling was dismissed in the face of the problem of being. This is Plato's *Sophist* (242e). Paragraph 2:

> *The first philosophical step in understanding the problem of being consists* [in the present and not in the past as in the French translation, "Philosophy took its first step when . . .": Heidegger is not referring to Plato as in the past, but to indicate the necessity of a gesture that always threatens the question of being, yesterday, now and tomorrow] in avoiding the *muthon tina diēgeisthai* (*keine Geschichte erzählen*), that is, not determining beings as beings by tracing them back in their origins [the origins of beings *qua* beings] to another being—as 64
> if being had the character of a possible being [Seienden]. As *Gefragte* [what is asked about], being thus requires its own kind of demonstration which is essentially different from the discovery of beings. (*Being and Time*, 5)

This is Heidegger's second reference to the *Sophist* in the space of three pages. The first is the epigraph to *Sein und Zeit.* Read the Greek and the translation in the German text.

> *dēlon gar hōs humeis men tauta (ti pote boulesthe sēmainein hopotan on phtheggēsthe) gignōskete, hēmeis de pro tou men ōometha, nun d' ēporēkamen (Plato, *Sophist*, 244a).

> Denn offenbar seid ihr doch schon lange mit dem vertraut, was ihr eigentlich meint, wenn ihr den Ausdruck "seiend" gebraucht, wir jedoch glaubten es einst zwar zu verstehen, jetzt aber sind wir in Verlegenheit gekommen.*[14]

14. Martin Heidegger, *Sein und Zeit* (Tübingen: Max Niemeyer Verlag, 2006), 1. [Translator's note: Derrida does not give the French here. Stambaugh's translation of *Being and Time* gives, "For manifestly you have long been aware of what you mean when

Now precisely this passage on the aporia (244a) comes up a brief moment after the passage on the "*muthon diēgeisthai*" (242c). It is starting from the moment when one gives up, when the Stranger in the *Sophist* and his interlocutors give up on telling stories, that they enter into the aporia of being, that they broach the real difficulties.

What is going on here? Heidegger does not explain his reference; he quotes the Platonic expression, gives the idiomatic German equivalent and that is all. But I think it would be a good idea to dwell a little on the *Sophist* to understand clearly what is at stake in this problem. After the refutation of Parmenides and the parricide, the Stranger mentions those who carelessly (*eukolōs*) plan to determine how many beings (*onta*) there are and what they
65 are. And this is the beginning of a little history of philosophy:

> Every one of them seems to tell us a story (*muthon tina hekastos phainetai moi diēgeisthai*), as if we were children. One says there are three principles, that some of them are sometimes waging a sort of war with each other, and sometimes become friends and marry and have children and bring them up [here it's the history of being as told by the presocratics, or the sophists, the history of being as a family history, as a family tree]; and another says there are two, wet and dry or hot and cold, which he settles together and unites in marriage. And the Eleatic sect in our region, beginning with Xenophanes and even earlier, have their story that all things, as they are called, are really one. Then some Ionian and later some Sicilian Muses (Empedocles) reflected that it was safest to combine the two tales [. . .].[15]

The Stranger enumerates in this way all the past ontologies, those that say that Being is one or multiple, or both, that it is heat or cold, movement or rest, and so forth, of the materialists or of the sons of the earth, of the friends of the forms, and *in the midst* of the *Gigantomachia* that arises between them—a *Gigantomachia* that is also mentioned at the beginning of *Sein und Zeit*— there arises the *aporia* of being, in the form of the question of the *triton ti*. The schema of the question of being here is the following: you say that being is this or that, this and that (movement or rest, etc.). But what is the being which you say is this or that and what is the being of the *is* that allows you to say that being is this or that? What is this third term, being itself, which does not let itself be determined by a discourse but on the contrary allows all the determinations that come about in it? To stop telling stories, you must stop replying to the question "What is being?" in the form

---

you use the expression 'being.' We, however, who used to think we understood it, have now become perplexed."]

15. Plato. *Sophist*, trans. Harold Fowler, in *Theaetetus, Sophist* (London: Harvard University Press, 1977), 242c–e, p. 359.

of "There is being as movement, there is being as rest, there is being as sensory matter, there is being as *eidos*." A schema analogous to that of Theaetetus on science. [Comment.] Telling scientific stories. [Uncertain word] We 66
need, then, a minimal and austere answer to the question, "What is being?" Now, here are the two passages in which non-mythical discourse surfaces as the question of the meaning of being in the initial form of the question on the signification of the word *being*.

Read *Sophist* 243a–244b, [French] pp. 346 to 348.

*STRANGER: When one of them says in his talk that many, or one, or two are, or have become, or are becoming, and again speaks of hot mingling with cold, and in some other part of his discourse suggests separations and combinations, for heaven's sake, Theaetetus, do you ever understand what they mean by any of these things? I used to think, when I was younger, that I understood perfectly whenever anyone used this term "not-being," which now perplexes us. But you see what a slough of perplexity we are in about it now.

THEAETETUS: Yes, I see.

STRANGER: And perhaps our minds are in this same condition as regards being also; we may think that it is plain sailing and that we understand when the word is used, though we are in difficulties about not-being, whereas really we understand equally little of both.

THEAETETUS: Perhaps.

STRANGER: And we may say the same of all the subjects about which we have been speaking.

THEAETETUS: Certainly.

STRANGER: We will consider most of them later, if you please, but now the greatest and foremost chief of them must be considered.

THEAETETUS: What do you mean? Or, obviously, do you mean that we must first investigate the term "being," and see what those who use it think it signifies?

STRANGER: You have caught my meaning at once, Theaetetus. For I certainly do mean that this is the best method for us to use, by questioning them directly, as if they were present in person; so here goes: Come now, all you
who say that hot and cold or any two such principles are the universe, what 67
is this that you attribute to both of them when you say that both and each are? What are we to understand by this "being" (or "are") of yours? Is this a third principle besides those two others, and shall we suppose that the universe is three, and not two any longer, according to your doctrine? For surely when you call one only of the two "being" you do not mean that both of them equally are; for in both cases they would pretty certainly be one and not two.

THEAETETUS: True.

STRANGER: Well, then, do you wish to call both of them together being?

THEAETETUS: Perhaps.

STRANGER: But, friends, we will say, even in that way you would very clearly be saying that the two are one.

THEAETETUS: You are perfectly right.

STRANGER: Then since we are in perplexity, do you tell us plainly what you wish to designate when you say "being." For it is clear that you have known this all along, whereas we formerly thought we knew, but are now perplexed. So first give us this information, that we may not think we understand what you say, when the exact opposite is the case.—If we speak in this way and make this request of them and of all who say that the universe is more than one, shall we, my boy, be doing anything improper?*(*Sophist*, 359–63).

After this aporia the doxography picks up again, at a higher level. And then we see file past the unitarist and materialist doctrines, those of the friends of the forms, the partisans of movement and of rest, and to these naïve ontologies that are still telling stories, the same question is posed: that of the *triton ti* at 250b.

Read [French] 359.

*STRANGER: Being, then, you consider to be something else in the soul, a
68 third in addition to these two, inasmuch as you think rest and motion are embraced by it; and since you comprehend and observe that they participate in existence, you therefore said that they are. Eh?* (*Sophist*, 389)

Being is *other* than the determinations of the *onta*. Which does not mean that it is another *on*. And one must become *conscious* of this alterity which is not a difference between *onta* in order to transgress mythology when one asks what is the origin of beings in their being. This is the condition for ceasing to speak as if we were children. Adult philosophical discourse, then, presupposes that one takes seriously the question of being. And it is remarkable, let it be said in parentheses dedicated to Georges Lapassade,[16] that in all the philosophical discourses that may have presented themselves as radically new, one finds an *explicit* allusion to a childhood left behind. Why the value of philosophical discourse is spontaneously measured by the yardstick of adult maturity is a question to which it is not so easy to reply seriously. Why, fundamentally, is an *adult's* discourse better than a *child*'s discourse? And why would philosophy make common cause with maturity?

16. [Translator's note:] Georges Lapassade (1924–2008) had recently published *L'entrée dans la vie* (Paris: Éditions de Minuit, 1963), to which Derrida is presumably referring here.

If the question interests you, well then, note the following references: apart from Plato whom we have just read, apart from the well-known texts by Descartes and Comte, one can find this critique of childhood and childishness in Bergson (introduction to *La pensée et le mouvant*)[17] and in Husserl (*Formal and Transcendental Logic*, end of paragraph 95, where the fear of methodological solipsism and the refusal to understand transcendental egoity are presented as an issue for children philosophers.)[18]

When Heidegger says that the question of being should impose silence on stories and he reads Plato, this does not mean that in his eyes Plato did not, at the end of the day, also tell stories. I do not wish to go down that path here: we can discuss it later if you wish. Without, for that matter, even going via 69
Heidegger's reading of Plato—a reading according to which the *eidos* and above all the *agathon,* which were supposed to answer the question "What is being?" are not being but beings par excellence, beings that are truly beings (*ontôs onta*), at the very moment when the *agathon* is presented as *epekeina tēs ousias*—without even going via this reading, one can invoke many texts by Plato that are unequal to the breakthrough and the promise of the *Sophist*. Very remarkable in this respect is the *Timaeus*, in which, when it comes to explaining the origin of the *world*, the origin of the beings that appear to us, the origin of the ordered system (*Cosmos*) of phenomena, Timaeus, responding to Socrates who was asking for a true story (*alēthinon logon*) at last, and not a *muthon*, announces (29 c–d) that, when it is a question of the origin of beings, a philosophical discourse adequate to the question is impossible, a true and exact discourse is impossible, and one must be content to recite, to unroll like a genesis, like a becoming-real of things, something that is not becoming, but the origin of things. One must unroll the *Archē* like a genesis. One must produce a discourse, a narrative in terms of becoming, in what is already there, already born, even though one would need to speak of the origin and of the birth of the world. This, he says, is because "both I who speak and you who judge are but human creatures, so that it becomes us to accept the likely account of these matters (*ton eikota muthon*) and forbear to search beyond it."[19]

A resignation that can also be interpreted as the principle of an ironic answer to the question of being—in Heidegger's sense—the question of the

17. Henri Bergson, *The Creative Mind*, trans. Mabelle Andison (New York: Dover, 2010).

18. Edmund Husserl, *Formal and Transcendental Logic*, trans. Dorion Cairns (The Hague: Springer, 1969).

19. Plato, *Timaeus*, trans. R. G. Bury (London: Harvard University Press, 1999), 53.

origin of beings in their being. Basically, Timaeus seems to be saying that it is pointless to want to say anything about *being* that concerns it *itself*. On the subject of being which in itself is nothing, one can only tell stories—that is, ontic or worldly discourses (here, cosmological, metaphysical, without the Demiurge). *One* can only . . . (i.e., men, philosophers qua men, can only . . .) "We are only human [both I who speak and you who judge are but human
70 creatures]," he says (29c), which means that those who would like to proffer a philosophical—and not anthropological—discourse about being and the origin of beingness deceive themselves and rave even more than those who are content with plausible stories, with good myths. That is, with science: for it is science, the content of scientific knowledge, that Timaeus is unfolding in this dialogue.

It is true that this resignation to the plausible myth is not the only intention of this passage from the *Timaeus*. There is also, briefly suggested, the theme of an esotericism, an outcome that contradicts it a little. One must content oneself with the plausible myth—here ontic narratives, Heidegger would say—when one does not have the *rare* luck, possibility or merit to gain access to the origin of the world of beings in their being. "Now to discover the Maker and Father of this Universe were a task indeed; and having discovered Him, to declare Him unto all men were a thing impossible" (*Timaeus*, 51). Telling stories—in the sense we are now giving to that expression—is thus a necessity when one is addressing everybody; it is an expository necessity when the philosopher chosen by God or the philosopher with the patient eye of the Eagle, or in any case the philosopher who has broken with the natural attitude and non-philosophy, wants to transmit the question of the origin to those who do not yet have access to it. Necessity of the ontic metaphor.

This is not, by this comparison with the *Timaeus,* to transform the question of being or of the origin of beings and of their being into a question of initiation, and to transform Heidegger's thought into a *gnosis*. To the contrary, the possibility of acceding to the question of being beyond the natural attitude, naïve sciences, and even critical but regional ontologies, is the most radically universal. But it is first of all a possibility that can only be made explicit in a break with the natural language and attitude.

So, rather than play on this similarity to help you understand this break,
71 and by comparison, rather than invoking Husserl who would have us understand it within the horizon of a transcendental idealism, I would rather refer once again to Hegel. Hegel (for example §88, remark 3 of the *Encyclopedia*) tries to have us understand what he means by the unity of being and pure nothingness. This proposition that being is nothingness appears to be *contradictory* to common sense which cannot understand it, which cannot under-

stand it because it cannot think being outside all determination, outside this or that. The passage to the thinking of pure being, which is a break with determination in general, and which makes us understand that being, being no being in particular, is nothing, this passage to the thinking of being as a thinking of nothingness is the beginning of philosophical knowledge, and presupposes a break with the attitude of natural consciousness or scientific consciousness which is also a natural consciousness imprisoned in determination. Faced with the incomprehension of natural consciousness, "there is nothing further to be said than this, namely that philosophical knowledge is indeed of a different sort from the kind of knowledge one is accustomed to in ordinary life, as it also is from what reigns in other sciences" (*Encyclopedia*, 142). Hegel seems, then, to determine the difference between natural, common or scientific knowledge, and philosophical knowledge, between the thinking of determinate beings and the thinking of pure being as nothingness—Hegel seems to determine this difference as a difference that is a break, a difference that can be overcome only by a violent movement of conversion. But at the same time, in what immediately follows in the same text, Hegel shows that what natural knowledge claims it does not understand—namely, pure being—it has always already understood, that it has an "infinite number of representations" (*Encyclopedia*, 142) of the unity of pure being and pure nothingness and that, each time that thinking determines, it has already thought the being of determinate beings. It has thought it without thinking it, but in order to think what it has thought, it suffices that it reflect and make explicit what it has always already done qua determining thinking. In other words, the conversion or the break that supposedly moves us from the naïve knowledge of the determination to the philosophical knowledge 72
of pure being—this conversion is an explication. The Difference between difference as break and difference as interval of explication, the difference between difference as break and difference as explication, is according to Hegel a false difference, an indifferent difference; and the problem connected with it—we would still need to understand why—is a false problem.

You see, in any case, from the *Timaeus* to Heidegger, what can be meant by this secret of the question of being that one cannot share with those who do not have access to it, without running the risk, in traversing the language common to natural consciousness and philosophical consciousness, of "telling stories." And yet nothing is less secret than this secret. Nothing is more widely shared.

Now, however close Hegel's text and intention, as I have just invoked them, may once again be to Heidegger's intention, this should not leave us with the illusion that Heidegger, who is not saying anything *different*, is saying the same thing. An identical thing. While one must indeed go via this identity of pure being and pure nothingness in order to understand that being is not a being, is not one being or the totality of determinate beings, in order to understand the difference between being and beingness, for Heidegger being is however not merely non-beingness or rather indeterminate beings, it is not only *in*determination, indeterminacy, and if the expression *pure being* is not Heideggerian this is not by chance. Being, once again, is not for Heidegger the abstract poverty of an empty concept preceding possible experience and beings [three uncertain words]; it is concrete and the presence of the present. The question of being, says Heidegger in paragraph 3 of *Sein und Zeit*, is the most *basic* and the most *concrete* (and Heidegger underlines these words).

So much so that Hegel's proposition of the identity of pure nothingness and pure being, however necessary it may be, is still a preliminary proposition, an *ontic* and *metaphysical* proposition, which negatively pronounces being to be indeterminate beingness. That Hegel's proposition should be in Heidegger's eyes a metaphysical or ontic proposition, still blind to the truth of being, is what appears in *Was ist Metaphysik?* (1929), the guiding thread
73 of which is the question of nothingness, and anxiety as the fundamental experience of nothingness. In *Was ist Metaphysik?* Heidegger writes this (the point is to show that experience of nothingness does not have its origin in logical negation):

> This cursory historical recollection shows the nothing as the counter-concept to that which properly is, i.e., as its negation. But if the nothing somehow does become a problem, then this opposition does not merely undergo a somewhat clearer determination; rather, it awakens for the first time the proper formulation of the metaphysical question concerning the being of beings. The nothing does not remain the indeterminate opposite of beings but unveils itself as belonging to [attached to: *zugehörig zum Sein des Seienden*] the being of beings. "Pure Being and pure Nothing therefore are the same." This proposition of Hegel's[20] is correct. Being and the nothing do belong together, not because both—from the point of view of the Hegelian concept of thought—agree in their indeterminateness and immediacy, but rather because being itself is essentially finite and manifests itself only in the transcendence of a Dasein that is held out into the nothing (*in der Transzendenz des in das Nichts hinausgehaltenen Daseins offenbart)*.[21]

Not only does Hegel's proposition remain a metaphysical proposition

20. Heidegger's reference: Hegel, *Wissenchaft der Logik, Erstes Buch* (Hamburg: Felix Meiner Verlag, 1932), 78. [Hegel, *The Science of Logic*, ed. and trans. George di Giovanni (Cambridge: Cambridge University Press, 2010), 59.]

21. Heidegger, "What Is Metaphysics?" in *Pathmarks*, trans. David Farrell Krell (Cambridge: Cambridge University Press, 1998), 94–95.

dominated by a logic of negation but, even within metaphysics, Heidegger contests its scope. It is true but not in the sense that Hegel believed.

Historicizing the revelation of being within the borders of metaphysics understood in this way is thus in a certain way still to "tell stories." And Hegel would in this sense have been one of the great storytellers, one of the greatest novelists of philosophy, the greatest no doubt, and you can see how *The Phenomenology of Spirit* and the *Lectures on the History of Philosophy* could come to illustrate this remark.To liberate the question of being and 74
history, one must, then, stop telling stories, which is to say that one must take a step beyond ontic history. This step, which can look like an exit from history in general toward the ahistorical, is in truth the condition of access to a radicalization of the thinking of history as *history of being itself*. One must, then, constantly and firmly maintain the distrust of historicism in order to think history as the truth of being, in order truly to think history at the level of the truth of being. So there is in Heidegger—without of course everything coming down to this, but there is underlying in him—the classical distrust of history and historicism, a distrust that belongs to a Cartesian vein (think of Descartes's distinction in the *Regulae* between philosophical knowledge and historical knowledge: Descartes too is someone who wanted to be finished with novels and the childishness of "storytelling"), a Cartesian vein and therefore a Husserlian vein. For his part, Husserl, without beating about the bush, thought that all Hegel had done was tell stories and that metaphysics consists in telling stories (example: dialectics) [comment].

Before even entering, as we shall have to do, into the problem of the relations between Husserl and Heidegger, from the point of view that interests us, it is certain that Heidegger's gesture is here entirely *analogous*—I do not say identical—to Husserl's: reduce historicity, refuse to "tell stories," bracket the real ontic or practical genesis in order then to grasp in its profound originality the *historicity of meaning*. For it is not by chance that, in the history of thought, the only book, along with *Sein und Zeit*, that explicitly begins with the refusal to "tell stories" is, not the *Sophist*, which does not begin with this refusal, but in fact *Ideen I*. The first note in the first section of the first chapter of *Ideen I* expresses this refusal. I'll read from Paul Ricoeur's translation. The note comments on the text's use of the word *original*:

> No stories will be told here. Neither psychological-causal nor historical-
> developmental genesis need be, or should be, thought of when we speak 75
> here of originality. What other sense is meant will not become reflectively and scientifically clear until later.[22]

22. Husserl, *Ideas Pertaining to a Pure Phenomenology and a Phenomenological Philosophy*, trans. F. Kersten (The Hague: Martinus Nijhoff, 1998), 5.

And what is translated here as "No stories will be told here" is the common German expression, "We aren't going to tell stories." Husserl writes, "*Es werden hier keine Geschichten erzählt*,"[23] the very expression used by Heidegger.

We must now understand how, in the elaboration of the question of being by Heidegger, taking advantage precisely of the *keine Geschichten erzählen*, the theme of historicity is introduced.

It *will be difficult and slow*, and one can already say (very summarily) that the theme of the historicity of being itself, of the historicity of the truth of being, does not really belong to *Sein und Zeit*. The historicity that is an important theme in *Sein und Zeit*, which provides on this subject Heidegger's fullest and most systematic developments (contained in the fifth chapter <of division 2> of the published part, a chapter that has not yet been translated [into French]), the historicity in *Sein und Zeit* is the historicity of *Dasein* and not of *Sein* (i.e., of the privileged being that affords us privileged access to the truth of being). The historicity is, if you will, that of the *Befragtes* (of the being interrogated with a view to being) and not of the *Gefragtes* (of what is the asked about of the question, being itself). However important and revolutionary the analyses devoted to historicity in *Sein und Zeit* are, they are preliminary; they belong to the hermeneutic of *Dasein* which is only an introduction into the question of being. Historicity of *Dasein* and not of *Sein*.

76 But we will have patiently to follow this preliminary phase both because of its intrinsic importance and because here the preliminary is perhaps more than the preliminary and there is not, between *Dasein* and *Sein*, between the *Befragtes* and the *Gefragtes*, a simple relation of means to end, a route accessible to all, or a move from the threshold to beyond the threshold.[24]

If one wants to measure from a great distance and a great height the immensity of the itinerary that must lead to the question of the history of being itself, one must first realize that the question of the historicity of *Dasein* (or of *Existenz*), which is only a question preliminary to that of the historicity of *Sein*, itself constitutes an immense step forward. An immense step forward not only with regard to anti-historical idealisms, but even with regard to what one might consider to be the question of the historicity of transcendental subjectivity in Husserl. It is at the price of an immense effort and at the end of a long path that transcendental historicity was discovered by Husserl, and even then it affected only the historicity of meaning and affected it merely with a concern. If one bears in mind that Heideggerian *Dasein* is

23. Husserl, *Ideen zu einer reinen Phänomenologie und phänomenologischen Philosophie* (Halle: Max Niemeyer, 1913), 7.

24. At the bottom of the manuscript page, Derrida has written, "(perhaps stop here)."

a notion that takes us back before the distinctions proper to transcendental idealism (activity-passivity, consciousness, subject, object, etc.), distinctions that are laden with metaphysical presuppositions, then speaking of the historicity of *Dasein* already goes a long way, even if only in a preliminary way.

I[25]

So, opening here the first major part of this course, we ask ourselves the following question.

What is the necessity that links the *Gefragtes* to a given *Befragtes*? That
is, in other words, Why does the question of being pass through an analytic
of *Dasein*? And, closer to what interests us, Why does the question of the 77
historicity of being pass through the question of the historicity of *Dasein*? I
do not say of beings.

This is the very general question we must try to answer before describing this historicity of *Dasein*.

Having, in the passages I have already mentioned, destroyed the prejudices that were obscuring the question of being, having drawn out the formal structure of the question of being (i.e., the structure that it has in common with all other questions), Heidegger begins to open the path proper to the question of being itself.

To do so, he must obviously give himself at the outset no metaphysical presupposition of any sort, no metaphysical proposition of any sort. His question must be in this regard absolutely radical and radically inaugural, *de jure*. *But de jure* already, Heidegger gives himself, thinks he has to give himself, *two* . . . let's say vaguely and in quotation marks, using a word that is improper, two "assurances" in which the fully *historical* character of the question of being appears.

As always happens, what a question that is absolutely radical when it is historical in its radicality must give itself—that is, the two assurances that I have just announced—it gives to itself in the form of an *Already*, or rather of an *always already*.

And we would have to meditate on the grammatico-philosophical meaning and function of this expression *always already* (*toujours déjà*, an expression that is not French, that shocks French syntax, and I would even say French philosophical syntax, which would perhaps tell us a great deal about the relations between this French philosophical *logos* in its relations with history: the expression *always already* was only used in French texts in the wake of the translations of *immer schon*, the German always already).

25. The numbering that begins here is not followed in the manuscript.

The signification of "always already" is the historical translation or rather the historical foundation of the signification "*a priori*." The *always* modifies the *already* in such a way that the already does not depend on this or that contingent situation, but has a value of unconditioned universality. The always
78 wrests the historicity of the *already* from empiricity.

Here the essential *already* is unconditioned, the *always already* is thus the form in which Heidegger must, not give himself or simply encounter presuppositions, but begin in the sense of repeating the beginning of a question which in fact has never been posed but which has always already been made possible. We will see later—or next time—why the presence of an *Already* in a questioning that is claiming to be radical is not a circle, in the sense of vicious circle or faulty reasoning.

What, then, are the two assurances that, far from compromising the radicality of the question, make it possible *qua* radicality?

(1)[26] Given the formal structure of every question, the question of being must be guided by the very thing in view of which it questions. As Heidegger says, insofar as it is a *Suchen* (seeking, quest), the question needs to receive a prior direction from the *Gesuchten* (from what is sought, and not from the *object* of the seeking, as is translated in a translation that is not innocent, since it makes of Being the object of a question: it is what is sought in the seeking). For the question of being to receive prior direction from the very thing in view of which it is questioning, it is necessary, as Heidegger notes, that the *meaning of being* be *already* in a certain sense *verfügbar* ("*Der Sinn von Sein muss uns daher schon in gewisser Weise verfügbar sein*" [*Sein und Zeit*, 5]): "accessible" in the [French] translation, which thus implies that we already *know* it. In fact *verfügbar* means "available," available in a certain way, not available like an object at our disposal but welcoming, disposed to let itself be understood, to let itself be approached in some way, close to *us* (we do not yet know what we need to understand by this *us*—neither understanding nor reason nor man) in a certain familiarity.

79 Without this familiarity with the meaning of being or this pre-understanding of the *meaning* of being, the explicit question of the meaning of being could not even arise. So there is an *already* of the question of the meaning of being, a reference to an *always already*, to a past that is always already buried but still having an effect that allows the most radical, freest, most independent, most concrete question, the first and last, to arise. The weight of the *already* in the *originary* signifies *already* the absolute and originary his-

26. The "second assurance" is only initially taken up at the very end of this session (see below, p. 46), and is pursued in detail in the next session (pp. 47ff).

toricity of the question of being, signifies that the question of being is fully and originarily and through and through historical.

The pre-understanding or the familiarity of the meaning of being that guides our question as soon as it arises—this familiarity is a Fact (*Faktum*), but of course a fact that is unique of its kind. We could fix the originality and uniqueness of this *Faktum* according to two themes. But to do so, I must translate a few lines from Heidegger, on which I shall rely subsequently: [German] p. 5 of §2:

> As a seeking, questioning needs prior guidance from what it seeks. The meaning of being must therefore *already* be available [comprehensible?] to us in a certain way. We intimated that we are always already involved in an understanding of being. From this grows the explicit question of the meaning of being and the tendency toward its concept. We do not *know* [*wissen* emphasized] what "being" means (*was Sein besagt*). But *already* when we ask [and not "as soon as we ask"], "was *ist* "Sein"?" what *is* [emphasized] 'being'?" we stand in an understanding [comprehension, *Verständnis* . . .] of the "is" without being able to determine conceptually what the "is" means (*ohne dass wir begrifflich fixieren könnten, was das "ist" bedeutet*). We do not even know the horizon upon which we are supposed to grasp and pin down the meaning. (*Being and Time*, 4)

(A very important sentence: this means that we cannot even anticipate what will soon reveal itself as the transcendental *horizon* in which the meaning of being is determined in the first part of *Sein und Zeit*—namely, *time*. 80
This first part, the only one that was published, is entitled, as you know: "The Interpretation of Dasein in Terms of Temporality and the Explication of Time as the Transcendental Horizon of the Question of Being.") And apropos the transcendental horizon: "The 'transcendental' meant there does not pertain to subjective consciousness; instead, it is determined by the existential-ecstatic temporality of Being-there," and so forth (*Einführung* . . . , [French] p. 26) (*Introduction to Metaphysics*, 19–20).

I continue the translation I had begun: "*This* [and not "a" as in the [French] translation] *average and vague understanding of being (Seinsverständnis) is a fact (Faktum* [emphasized]) (*Being and Time*, 4).

And a little later: "What is sought in the question of being is not completely unfamiliar, although it is at first totally ungraspable" (*Being and Time*, 5).

I announced that the originality of this *Faktum* enveloped in the question of being could give rise to two determinations.

(1) It is always obvious that our pre-comprehension (as Heidegger says

elsewhere: *Vor-verständnis*) of the meaning of being is not a *Fact* among others, is not a contingent or empirical fact, for the good reason that the content of this fact is access to the meaning of being itself which will subsequently allow the determination in general of any fact in general. Understanding, even confusedly, the signification of the word *being*, is an absolutely irreducible *Faktum*, out of reach for any determinate science, for any science of fact, in particular for the sciences most hungry for that flesh—namely, the human sciences: for example, all the sciences of the psyche (be that science a logic or something else) whatever their style, or a philology or a linguistics, and so on—and to the extent that the very exercise of their scientific activity
81 and all the scientific determinations and all the propositions that they could produce presuppose as the ground of their validity, as the source of their value the very thing that they would like to account for:—namely, the understanding of the meaning of being, since all their explanatory propositions naively appeal to it. Naturally this does not mean—as one might a bit stupidly be tempted to think would crush Heidegger—that the Desire that moves these *sciences*, being deprived of the essential thing—namely, of accounting for the meaning of the signification *being*—would be deprived of everything. That does not mean, then, that all the activity mobilized by scientific desire would be vain or sterile. Quite the contrary—it can be very fruitful. It is fecundity itself and it is necessary and legitimate. All the psycho . . . (of the psyche), philological, linguistic, grammatical exploration throwing itself into an assault on the word *be* is an indispensable task, even if one can say *a priori* that it will ultimately run out of breath before the very meaning of being, not out of impotence or some limit of the rationality that animates it, out of some irrationality, but because the meaning of being is the very thing that allows it to speak, to form any proposition; it is therefore the origin and the possibility of its desire for science and research; and if the scientist happened to question as to this ultimate origin and the dawn of his Desire, then his question would no longer be simply scientific, without for all that becoming anti-scientific. On the contrary, the anticipation of this limit, which has nothing negative about it and must even be the most positive stimulant of science, and the neo-scientists by profession who refuse to ask themselves about the foundations of science, on the pretext that those foundations mean going back before science and that therefore they are non-scientific, on the pretext that they run the risk of a crisis of science—those ones, those neo-scientists are obviously the first to betray the demand of science. The authentic demand of science ought to allow one to distinguish between the pre-scientific as foundation of science and the pre-scientific as irrationality [three illegible words]
82 of the illiterate and fearful stuttering.

(2) The *Faktum* from which we are starting and which we are speaking about is determined by Heidegger as a phenomenon of language and it is not by chance if the pre-comprehension of the *meaning of being* is first presented as a pre-comprehension of the *signification of the word being*. The pre-comprehension of the *Sinn* is illustrated and even demonstrated by the pre-comprehension of the *Bedeutung* of the "is" in the sentence. Heidegger indeed says,

> We do not *know* what "being" [in quotes, the word "being"] means (*besagt*). But already when we ask, "was *ist* 'Sein'?" we stand in an understanding of the "is" [in quotes] without being able to determine conceptually *was das "ist" bedeutet*. (*Being and Time*, 4)

You already see the immensity of the problems and the implications to which this gesture of Heidegger's leads back, this gesture the necessity of which we must understand; the necessity of which will never cease to be understood, and that the later developments of Heidegger's thought will, precisely, merely lay out. For it is quite obvious that, giving himself *language* and the possibility of a language or a tongue in which the verb *to be* would be *de facto* or *de jure*, virtually or virtually[27] what makes language come to its true essence (cf. *Einführung* . . . , [French] p. 64: "but essence and being speak in language" [*Introduction to Metaphysics*, 57]; [French] p. 92: without the word *Being*, all words would disappear)[28]—giving himself that, Heidegger is not simply giving himself a premise, or a principle, or a facility (*Introduction to Metaphysics*, 86). He is giving himself only the possibility of a question and he ties the possibility of the question to that of language. That is a right that one might wish to contest: for my part I believe—and I'm saying this to put this formidable problem at least provisionally aside (and not to hide from these questions)—that this contestation has not yet been undertaken at the necessary level and with the necessary means, that it demands an immense 83
itinerary, one scarcely imaginable, and that it will not arise seriously tomorrow, except in the mode of a vague desire that can sometimes be very talkative and voluble, and that, for my part, I prefer to hold in reserve here. We shall be encountering this problem again. For the moment, I shall be

27. Thus in the ms.

28. [Translator's note:] Derrida is paraphrasing the German "das Wort »Sein« hätte nicht einmal jene verschwebende Bedeutung, gerade dann gäbe es überhaupt kein einziges Wort" (Heidegger, *Gesamtausgabe*, vol. 40 (Frankfurt a M.: Vittorio Klostermann, 1983), 62), translated by Fried and Polt as "presuming that the word 'Being' did not even have that evanescent meaning, then there would be not a single word at all" (*Introduction to Metaphysics*, 86).

content to refer you to the *Einfuhrung* . . . (grammar and etymology of the word *being*). All I wish to emphasize here is that starting from the *Faktum* of language, and of a language in which the word *be* is heard, precise and unavoidable, Heidegger ties the possibility of his question and therefore of his whole subsequent discourse to the possibility of *history*. For there is no language without history and no history without language. The question of being is the very question of history. It is born of history, and it takes aim at history. It is the absolution of history itself on itself as history of being.

The *Faktum* was, then, the first of the 2 "assurances" that I had announced. Assurances that are not "contracted for" but always already present when a discourse begins and even when a questioning discourse begins.

The 2nd is the one which, with the *Gefragtes*, the questioning, gives itself the *Befragtes*, as question*ing*. The being interrogated, *Befragtes*, in view of being, is *us*, namely the questioning being. And this us is determined as *Dasein*. Well, it is the necessity of this gesture that will interest us as we begin next time. Then we will be ready to study the structures of the historicity of the questioning *Dasein*, interrogated in view of the historicity of *Sein*, the ultimate questioned of the question.

Cf. *Einführung* . . . , [French] p. 80 for what follows.[29]

29. In his copy, Derrida brackets a passage—starting at the last paragraph of [French] page 79 ("can it still be [. . .]") and ending on the last paragraph of [French] page 80 ("[. . .] just what we *are*?")—only to read it later, during the following session (see below, p. 53).

SESSION THREE

17 December 1964

We shall make no progress today. We shall be marking time today, and we shall dwell almost the whole time on a problem that last time we were getting ready to leave behind us. We are going to hold ourselves in suspense between the two assurances with which I concluded last time, having explicated only one.

To save time, I don't want to go too far back in what was said last time. I shall recall only that, before concluding, I announced the two *assurances* that Heidegger had to give himself in posing or in repeating the question of Being. Two *assurances* that were not "*contracted for*" in a conventional or arbitrary way—and neither were they metaphysical propositions, since the question of Being that they assure goes beyond metaphysics; two assurances that, although they have to do with something like language, were not for all that begged questions or *logical* presuppositions since the question of being goes back before the *logical* itself, even the logical in the Hegelian sense inasmuch as it merges with metaphysics.

I tried to show that this double assurance was pronounced in the form of an *Already* and of an *always already*, an expression the syntax and philosophical signification of which we interrogated. The envelopment of these 86
two *assurances* in the completely unmotivated, ontically and metaphysically unmotivated containment of the question of being, the envelopment of these two assurances, of these two *always alreadys* in the question of being, appeared to us as the mark of the originary and thoroughgoing historicity of the question of being.

As you will remember, the first of these two assurances was the *Faktum* of a language *in general* (any language) in which the signification (*Bedeutung*) of the word *is* (to be) is always already pre-comprehended. I tried, via two series of considerations, to reach the originality and uniqueness of this *Faktum*. I will not go back over this but before broaching the second of these assurances, or rather the second form of the same assurance and of the same "always already," I should like to prolong a little what I said last time about the *Faktum*.

One might wonder by what right Heidegger (1) starts out from the fact of language <and> (2) affirms that the *signification* (*Bedeutung* ≠ *Sinn*) of the word *being* is always already pre-understood. Should not an absolutely radical question move back toward the origin of language—that is, question toward a pre-linguistic or pre-symbolic zone of the discourse of experience (i.e., toward an opening of experience in which the pre-understanding of the signification *be* would not yet have come about)? A way of proceeding that one might think is not only (1) more radical than that of Heidegger, and thus (2) shows up a certain subjection of Heidegger's gesture to a metaphysics of the *logos*—a metaphysics that would be vulnerable to some aggression or gesture of . . . destruction, precisely.

But also, thirdly, a way of proceeding that, going back up before the *Bedeutung* of the word *be,* would finally have a chance to account for its appearance, and its relation to the *Sinn* and the *Sein*, and to the *Seinssinn*.

If I have suggested some possible questions in the form of possible objections to Heidegger, this is of course—and out of a certain respect for the text—to give to Heidegger not even the opportunity to respond to them yet, but first of all the opportunity to show that these questions are precisely *his questions*.

87 How would Heidegger show this? One might reply to this question in two moments.

(1)[1] the moment of pure *formality*.

Before even determining it as the question *of* being, the question in general whose framework, whose formal structure, you will remember, Heidegger begins by sketching out, the question in general cannot arise before language in general. To object to Heidegger's procedure that it gives itself too much too soon, is to ask a question of it, or is even already to reply to a question which, itself, can appear only in this ether of language in which, precisely, Heidegger's question is being reproached with taking its breath too soon. The possibility of the question in general does not *give itself* language; it opens it purely and simply. However little it gives itself, even if it gives itself nothing, that nothing does not exclude the less than nothing that is here the opening of the question. To ask a question of Heidegger's question—in that it envelops language—is to concede that he is right.

However, one should not understand this schema in its formal logical value. The point is not simply to say: anyone who reproaches Heidegger

1. The numbering begun here is not continued in the manuscript.

with presupposing language in his question of being is also speaking and, in asking a question of Heidegger's question, in asking Heidegger *where does language come from?* also gives language to himself, so that the only way to destroy here or to shake up Heidegger's question would consist *not simply* in a violence (violence always going via language, and Heidegger would essentially link warfare to language, *polemos* to *logos* [*Einführung* . . .]), the only way to destroy or shake up Heidegger's question here would consist not simply in a violence of words that would destroy itself as speech proffering being, but in, distinguishing it from violence, what I would call the brutality, muteness and deafness of a library-burner or a thought-strangler pushing his brutish rage to the point of not knowing what a library is and that it is a library that he is burning, confusing it with a pastry shop or the *88*
Eiffel tower or something. And, after all, the explication of the question of being would be helpless before a phenomenon as *natural* as this brutality, a brutality I have evoked only grossly and in caricature, but the like of which one could find in events that have the external form of speech or writing.[2]

No, we are not just dealing with such a formal logical schema. But to pass beyond logical and discursive formality here, we have to take into consideration the fact that we are dealing with the question *of being* and that this question of being is not a question among others, a question coming, as an example, to illustrate the general formal structure of the question in general.

Indeed, the schema I have just rapidly described would be valid as a formal logical schema for any question. Any question implies language, therefore no question can arise, can *a fortiori* arise as an objective question with regard to this implication since, *de facto*, it would itself make the mistake that it was trying to denounce (namely, the *Faktum* of language). If one remained with this formality, it would be easy to show that one does not need to make intrinsic reference to language to pose questions concerning beings or forms of being that have nothing to do with language—that is, the totality of beings into which language has not yet emerged (i.e., almost the totality of the world: not only the rocks, the sun and the winds, but even a pre-logical zone of experience, this or that zone of affect in animals, children or even humans in general, a zone which one might think is older, more archaic than language). In this case—again at the level of formality—one might think that there are questions where the *Gefragtes* is not language, is not a being of language, that this *Gefragtes* is in fact anterior to language and thus that the question concerning it, the *Frage* of this *Gefragtes*, comes first with regard to the question of being; and consequently that on the basis of this instance

2. Marginal addition: "There is a text by Heidegger on brutality (cf. [illegible word])".

one has the right to object to Heidegger's question of being without logical
89 self-contradiction, without incoherence. And one has the right because one is staying precisely in the sphere of the *formal*—that is, in a sphere in which one is speaking only in general of the formal structures of the question in general, without yet distinguishing between *ontic* question and question of *being*, where the originality of the *Gefragtes* has not yet been taken into consideration. As long as one remains there, the questions concerning physics, mineralogy, the structure of the plant, of affect, of protozoa, the silence of infinite spaces or any other question of this type—these questions have an ontic anteriority over the question of being, over the explicit question of being, and one can address questions to this latter about its ontic origin. Which, be it said in passing, confirms the *already* and the historicity of the question of being.

But from the moment that the question of being is recognized and one sees that it is no longer a sample among others of this formal structure of the question in general, then everything changes.

Everything changes because one realizes that the presupposition of language in the question of being has a meaning it has in *no other case*; and that, if the question of being is an *example* of the question in general in its formal structure, it is an example not in the sense of an indifferent sample, but of the *teleological exemplar* that reveals to the question in general its origin, its model, and its horizon. It is in this sense that the question of being would be exemplary. Exemplary of the question [several illegible words].

Exemplary not only in that it is presupposed by every question on beings not linked to language: when one wonders what physical beings or psychological beings are, perhaps at the level of pre-logical affect, I must know what I mean in asking what it is and in wanting to respect it as what it is; but *exemplary* too through the type of link it has to language.

For indeed, although every question other than the question of being necessarily has language as its element, it is not intrinsically and totally linked to language; the object of the question, beings, exist in their meaning inde-
90 pendently of the *Bedeutung*.

Is it the same with being and the question of being? By replying to this question one departs from the purely formal problematic of the question in general and one justifies the *assurance* enveloped by the question: namely, that one has always pre-comprehended not the *Sinn* but precisely the *Bedeutung* of the word *be* (not the meaning but the signification).

Heidegger does not really reply to this question in *Sein und Zeit*.

Setting off from the pre-comprehension of the signification of the *word* "being," he concludes that this pre-comprehension must be guided by a *mean-*

ing that must be made explicit, and he looks for *what type of being* one must address oneself to, what type of being must be interrogated (*<B>efragtes*) to develop this question. And this is the analytic of *Dasein* to which we shall be returning in a moment.

The problem of the relations between the *meaning*, the *signification* and the *word* in the case of the word *be* is posed as such for the first time only in the *Einführung in die Metaphysik*, that is about eight years later. It is this development that gives to *Sein und Zeit*'s point of departure, the point of departure in the pre-comprehension of the *Bedeutung*, its true justification, a justification that was not simply lacking, but was reserved and implicit. So it is appropriate to take a byway to reach this justification before moving on; the more so in that the style of this justification sends us back to the historicity that is our theme here.

In chapter 2 of this book, raising the objection according to which the word *be* is an empty vocable and an evanescent signification, Heidegger deals with what he calls the *grammar* and the *etymology* of the *word being*. I am not going to follow Heidegger step by step here. I will simply take a few points of reference along his path, while inviting you to read this text. The "grammar" of the word *being* follows the process at the end of which being, *to einai*, *esse*, imposed itself in metaphysics, in the *form* of the infinitive, and more precisely of the verbal substantive. This grammatical process explains that the signification "being" should have come to make itself in-determinate, or if it does not explain it—in the *etymological* sense of the word—it is of a piece with this process of indetermination. A process of in-determination that one could not fail to be tempted to understand as a process of conceptualiza- 91
tion, as the genesis of a concept, of the concept that is the most abstract and poorest in comprehension, that is the broadest in extension. The grammatical sequence that liberates the infinitive mood from any complement, subject, and so on, makes possible, or is made possible by, is in any case of a piece with, the interpretation of the thinking of being as the concept of being. This was the first of the prejudices, as you remember, denounced by Heidegger. Next, the expression *Sein* is not only an infinitive but a *verbal substantive*, an infinitive preceded like every substantive by a definite article. The passage to the substantive and to substantivity—that is *ontologico-grammatically* to substantiality—this passage, to use Heidegger's expression, *consolidates as it were the void* that inhabits the infinitive. It consolidates it and makes it into something. It organizes the ontic limitation in a substantialist guise. Since one says *to einai, das Sein, l'être*, being must be something, a being, another being, a hidden or superior being, and so on. The conceptual dissimulation of the thinking of being, a dissimulation that was already an ontic dissimu-

lation, was produced through infinitization; the *ontic* dissimulation as such of the thinking of being is produced in the substantivation of the verb, as it appears in Greek, in German and in French, whereas the two forms of the same dissimulation are joined powerfully and indissociably in English, where one cannot put the article in front of the *be* of *to be*, and where one must say *being* [*étant*] for *être,* such that they dared, in the only translation that exists in that language, to translate *Sein und Zeit* as *Being and Time*.

Should we abandon a grammatical form that is so threatening for the right thinking of being, a thinking that is neither a concept nor a thinking of a being? Heidegger pretends to think so but only in order to show that simply renouncing this form, simply erasing this word that the verbal substantive is, would obscure the problem still further.

And then, in order to show that, he uses a schema that will be very useful to us in a moment or rather next time, when we come to what I called *the*
92 *second assurance* enveloped in the question of being.

The schema is as follows: What would happen if, giving up on the grammatical form of the verbal substantive in philosophical discourse, we had to limit ourselves to the other forms? That would be the very gesture of *empiricism*, of what is called empiricism (though Heidegger does not use the word here). In that case, one would say: *being?* — I know nothing about it. I do not know what that means, primarily because I've never come across it and no one will ever come across it. The pre-comprehension Heidegger talks about at the beginning of *Sein und Zeit* is in this case merely an incomprehension. I understand what *being* means only when being comes to determine something or is determined by something, when I say *I am*, and you are, and he or it is, and so on. And the nucleus or principle of intelligibility here is the first person singular or plural. We understand fully what being means in the phrase: *I am* or else, says Heidegger, since today the theme of the *we* is in fashion, in the phrase *we are.*

Now Heidegger makes an effort—a very brief effort in fact—to show ([French] p. 80) that in that case, by abandoning all reference to being, to what being means, we hear and understand [MS *entendons* written above *comprenons*] the proposition "I am" or "we are" even less clearly than before. Now what interests me here is the argumentative schema that is barely sketched out by Heidegger. What guides this very short demonstration is again, I would say, the destruction or at any rate the denunciation of the signification of *proximity* and self-identity, such as it might appear in the discourse of the one saying: *I am* is the proposition of being that is the clearest and the surest, because I know what being I'm talking about and I know what being I'm talking about because here the proximity of the one speaking to the being that he is seems absolute, absolute to the point of being not even a proximity but an identity. Now the metaphor of proximity, which underlies the proposition of identity, is here misleading. Heidegger does not explain why, and seems certain that we will follow him without difficulty when he affirms that there is no absolute proximity of the self to its being and that, on the contrary, "Here we must admit that everyone is the furthest from himself, as far as the I from the you in 'you are'" (*Introduction to Metaphysics*, 74). 93

Let me read a few lines. Read [French] pages 79–80.

> *Can it still be any wonder to us now that "Being" is so empty a word when the word form itself is based on an emptying [of meaning] and the apparent fixation of this emptiness? This word "Being" serves as a warning to us. Let us not be lured away into the emptiest of forms, the verbal substantive. And let us not entangle ourselves in the abstraction of the infinitive "to be." If we really want to arrive at the "to be" along the path of language, let us keep to forms like these: I am, you are, he, she, it is, we are, and so forth; I was, we were, they have been, and so forth. But then we gain no clearer understanding of what "to be" means here, or what its essence consists in. On the contrary! Let us simply make the attempt!
>
> We say: "I am." One can speak of this sort of Being only in reference to oneself: my Being. What does it consist of, and where is it situated? It would seem that this should be what we can most easily bring to light, for there is no being to which we are closer than the one that we ourselves are. All other beings we ourselves are not. All other beings still "are" even when we ourselves are not. It seems we cannot be as close to any other being as we are to the being that we ourselves are. Actually, we cannot even say that we are close to the being that we ourselves in each case are, since after all we ourselves are this being. Here however we must admit that everyone is the furthest from himself, as far as the I from the you in "you are."
>
> But today the We is what counts. Now it is the "time of the We" instead of the I. We are. What Being do we name in this sentence? We also say: the windows are, the rocks are. We—are. Does this statement ascertain the Being-present-at-hand of a plurality of I's? And how does it stand with the "I was" and "we were" with Being in the past? Is it something by-gone for us? Or are we precisely that which we were? Are we not becoming precisely just what we are?* (*Introduction to Metaphysics*, 73–74) 94

What appears here in particular is the *proximity*, and very specifically that proximity of self to self—which is trying to state itself in the *cogito* or the *ego sum, a proximity* that, in the form of absolute *proximity*—that is, of self-identity—grounds the signification of every other proximity, every proximity having meaning and appearing only on the basis of a *here* that is, precisely, absolute proximity of self to self, identity of self to self. Now, what Heidegger seems to mean here is that the meaning of this absolute proximity, in the form of the *I am*, can only be clarified on the basis of the meaning of being which is implied in *I am*; because the *I am* is a determination of being and this determination alone grounds the meaning of proximity in general, only the thinking of being, only the relation to the meaning of being can announce to me in non-metaphysical fashion the meaning of proximity in general, what the *near* and the *far* mean in general. So long as being, the meaning of being implied in the proposition of absolute proximity that the *I am* is, so long as the meaning of being that is implied in it is not made explicit, the proposition of proximity does not have its *proper meaning*. That is to say it is merely metaphysical. And the metaphysics that rests on the unquestioned evidence of the I am is also a *metaphorics*. And it is also an empiricism since it is the gesture of empiricism to dissimulate the transcendental horizon on the basis of which the determined is determined; here wishing to hear being only in its determination as I am, you are, he is, and so on, or he is this or that, and so forth. And this conjunction of empiricism and metaphysics is not surprising. Kant and Husserl always criticized or limited with one and the same gesture metaphysics and empiricism. [Illegible interlinear insertion]

If the I am, for example, remains a metaphorical proposition, borrowing its proper meaning from a thinking of being which remains hidden or silenced, if the proximity stated in it is there stated in the form of metaphor, it follows that it is when one speaks of the *proximity of being* that one destroys the metaphor and by the same token thinks of propositions such as "I am," and so on, as metaphors.

The direction I'm indicating here, I believe, faithfully extends Heidegger's indication in the passage I read just now. Faithfully, because it allows us to
95 understand —*and that is perhaps its operational efficacity*— what Heidegger means, not only (and we shall come back next time to this first point which for now I'm merely naming) when he chooses the strange expression *Dasein*, or the strange use he makes of it with regard to its conventional value in the German language, where it signifies simply existence, but also and especially what he means when, for example in the "Letter on 'Humanism,'" he speaks several times of the *proximity* of being (*Pathmarks*, 252, 253, 256, 257, 261, 268, 269).

Common sense—which feeds on metaphor to such an extent that metaphor is the last thing it can recognize except when it presents itself spectacularly in rhetoric—common sense would be tempted to hear the expression "proximity of being" as a nice metaphor or else as a dangerous metaphor, nice or dangerous because it would supposedly be modeled on the structure of other proximities that we believe we know well, the proximity of the neighbor, the proximity of the tool that is within my reach, the proximity of the future [illegible word] or the proximity of God spoken of by some believers [uncertain word]. Common sense knows what *near* or *far* means; it knows that the proper meaning of these expressions refers to space, or already to an already spatialized time or, in any case, to a being in its relation to another being, a relation already thought metaphorically when we're dealing with non-spatial beings (God, for example). [Several illegible words.] The fact that the *here* or the now necessary for any determination of proximity is not simply *in* space or *in* time does not bother it; how in any case could it be bothered? So when common sense hears talk of the proximity of being, it says: either being is a being and then one must know what it is for the expression to have a proper meaning; one must complete this incomplete expression; or else being is nothing, and then this expression is a pure and simple empty metaphor that must be clarified by something other than itself.

And yet, we have seen that without a relation of familiarity, of neighborhood or of proximity with being—which is nothing, which is not a being but which is the meaning of the being—I could never understand the proposition of absolute proximity: the *I am* or the I am here or the now or the 96
present, the presence of the present. It is therefore in proximity to the proper meaning of being or the light of being that every other proximity is clarified, it is in the proximity of this nothing that being is that the proximity or the distance of every being comes about.

What I've just said introduces us to a passage from the "Letter on 'Humanism'" which I will translate rapidly.

> Yet being—what is being? It "is" It itself. *Es "ist" Es selbst*. The thinking that is to come must learn to *erfahren* that [experience, go through] and to say it. "Being"—that is not God and not a cosmic ground. Being is essentially farther than all beings [and in *Sein und Zeit*: Being is the Transcendent] and is yet nearer to the human being than every being, be it a rock, a beast, a work of art, a machine, be it an angel or God. Being is the nearest. *Das Sein ist das Nächste*. Yet the near remains farthest from the human being. Human beings at first cling always already and only to beings. (*Pathmarks*, 252)

And if we follow the theme of this distant proximity throughout the "Letter . . . ," we see first of all that Heidegger calls it language itself. My translation:

> The one thing [*L'Unique* (*das Einzige*) and not "l'unique réalité" [the unique reality] as Munier translates it] thinking would like to attain and for the first time tries to articulate in *Sein und Zeit* is something [once again, not a reality] that is simple. As such, being remains mysterious [*Geheimnis*: hid-

> den in secret familiarity][3], the simple nearness of an unobtrusive prevailing (*unaufdringlichen Waltens*). The nearness *west* [not "se réalise" as Munier translates it, but . . . but what? The [French] translator of the *Einführung* translates *west* as *este* from *ester* and explains that this means "realizes itself
> 97 historically as essence (*Wesen*)"[4] without its model being given outside or before history; so este if you like, comes about, comes to *Wesenheit*] as language itself. (*Pathmarks*, 253)

What does this mean, that the proximity of being is produced as language? Being is nothing, is not a being; it does not belong to the totality of beings. Its meaning can appear only if beings come to be declared as what they are in their being (i.e., if being is said). But this does not mean that being belongs only to language in the sense in which one might speak of a linguistic being in a pejorative sense. A being that was only in and through the word would be nothing but a verbal phenomenon, and so it would not be Being. The co-belonging of being and language—to which we shall have to return—forbids us from making the being of language dependent, as a simple character or power among others, on a being that might be called man, for example.

So the essence of language must be rethought in the light of the meaning of being. In doing so, one will go beyond that philosophy of language that makes of language the original character of man. To the contrary, one will come ("Man thus speaks, but it is because the symbol has made him man,"[5] or, as has been said since, "The symbol's order can no longer be conceived of as constituted by man but must rather be conceived of as constituting him,")[6] to determine man on the basis of language as language of being, and this is not a simple nuance or a simple logical inversion of the procedure. This inversion is hugely important since it liberates being from the ontic determination and it allows one no longer to "tell stories"—that is, no longer to
98 think the question of being as the product, or the idea, or the character of a being already known, or that one believes one already knows: namely, man. Which would rule out the very possibility of a truth in general.

I think the best thing here is to continue my translation. So:

> The nearness [. . .] *este* as language itself. But language is not mere speech, insofar as we represent the latter at best as the unity of phoneme (or writ-

3. [Translator's note:] Derrida comments on the noun *Geheimnis*; Heidegger's word is the adjective *geheimnisvoll*.

4. "Index des termes allemands," in Martin Heidegger, *Introduction à la métaphysique*, trans. G. Kahn (Paris: Presses Universitaires de France , 1959), 239.

5. Jacques Lacan, "The Function and Field of Speech and Language in Psychoanalysis," in *Écrits*, trans. Bruce Fink (New York: W. W. Norton, 2006), 229.

6. Jacques Lacan, "Seminar on the Purloined Letter," in *Écrits*, 34.

> ten character), melody, rhythm, and meaning (or sense). We think of the phoneme and written character as a verbal body for language (*Wortleib*), of melody and rhythm as its soul, and whatever has to do with meaning as its spirit. We usually think of language as corresponding to the essence of the human being represented as [Husserl] *animal rationale*, that is, as the unity of body-soul-spirit. But just as ek-sistence—and through it the relation of the truth of being to the human being—remains veiled in the *humanitas* of *homo animalis*, so does the metaphysical-animal explanation of language cover up the *seinsgeschichtliches Wesen*, the essence of language in the history of being. (*Pathmarks*, 273–74)

Comment.

And now there appears what again resembles a pure and simple metaphor in the expressionist-romantico-Nazi style (which is perhaps—without a doubt even—*also* romantico-Nazi, but the problem, our problem, is that of knowing if it is *only* a metaphor and if its romantico-Nazi style exhausts it: and if, allowing oneself to be fascinated by this style, one is not missing, through another philological violence, the essential point). So, Heidegger continues,

> According to this essence [historico-ontological], language is the *house* of being, which is propriated by being and pervaded by being. And so it is proper to think the essence of language from its correspondence to being and indeed as this correspondence, that is, as the *Behausung* [shelter, habitation] of the human being's essence. But the human being is not only a living creature 99
> who possesses language along with other capacities. Rather, language is the house of being in which the human being ek-sists (*ek-sistiert*) by dwelling, in that he belongs to the truth of being, guarding it. (*Pathmarks*, 254)

Before pausing over the status of what looks like a romantic metaphor and rhetoric, I shall begin to justify it as follows. What Heidegger wants to show is that to the extent that there is language only in the clearing of being and to the extent that being cannot be a simple product of language, failing which it would not be and thus would not be what it is—to that extent the meaning of being is, let's say without metaphor and abstraction, the condition of possibility of language on which it nonetheless depends. Given which, man cannot possess language as a simple faculty among others, for otherwise the truth of being—what allows for truth in general—would depend on the determinate faculty of a determinate being and would therefore be relative, and so forth. There is no truth in anthropology. This is a facile schema on which I do not insist. So one must think language on the basis of being and the essence of man on the basis of the possibility of language. Which has never been done explicitly by the metaphysics that determines man as being composed of a soul and a body or as a type of being created on the basis of another being—God—or as a natural being endowed with the power of speaking the truth (i.e., having *the power of language*—and not only of animal language, but of a language stating the truth, i.e., *letting beings be* as what they are, i.e., liberating itself from the intra-ontic relation and thus having this power of language alongside other powers).

Now, assuming we agree that we have to think man on the basis of language and language on the basis of the truth of being, why translate these "on the basis ofs" and these "conditions of possibility" into house, shelter, habitat, and so on? Why this operation which seems to charge with obscure affectivities a cold necessity of thought or a simple order in the linking of
100 implications?

First, if one spoke the language of *conditions of possibility*, one would let it be understood—manifestly against Heidegger's intention—that being, as condition of possibility of language, is a *formal,* abstract, absent instance, the transhistorical condition of history; on this account, history would appear with language but the condition of language would not be historical. But it is precisely the opposite that Heidegger wants to show. The same schema would hold for the relations of language and the essence of man. In saying of language that it is the condition of possibility of man, one would hypostasize the *logos,* a pre-human logos, God's logos, just as one would have hypostasized being just now by making of it a prehistorical being. In the same way, one cannot translate the order of significations in question into the language of *chronology* or logic (moments that are earlier because they are primary) and the precedence of being and of language over the essence of man is not a chrono*logical* or *logical* anteriority for this simple reason that there is no *chronological* or *logical* relation between logic—the logos that makes possible a logic—and anything else at all.

So one must speak another language that respects this relation of *implication* that binds together being, language, and man. A concrete and historical relation of implication in a sense of the historical that will become clearer as we proceed.

In what way is this relation of implication more faithfully described as a relation of *dwelling*? To find out, we would have to determine the essence of dwelling. I am going to try to do so very schematically from the point of view that interests us but also very deliberately in a non-Heideggerian language, in a language stripped of German philology and the pathos that always might seem shocking, for example, in one of the texts on Hölderlin, or in that 1951 lecture called "Building, Dwelling, Thinking,"[7] which ends

7. Martin Heidegger, "Building, Dwelling, Thinking," in *Poetry, Language, Thought*, trans. Albert Hofstadter (New York: Harper Colophon Books, 1971).

by referring the housing crisis back to a dwelling crisis for which, ultimately, metaphysics is supposedly responsible (I'm caricaturing, but it's more serious than that). Read them if you like. We are going to speak in a different style. *101*

Because being is not a being, it appears only in language. It is in language. If language were to disappear, being and the difference between being and beings would also collapse. So language is the *shelter* of being, language guards being. This shelter is historical, that is to say it has not been constituted for all eternity (a historical determination [uncertain word]), it is history itself, which is to say it is a constructed shelter, one that is constructed, assembled: a dwelling. But the dwelling is not only that, it is also the originary place, the *here* starting from which I measure my movements; I go out of my house, I stay in my house. But there would be no movement possible for me without reference to an originary place outside of which I am exposed. Without reference to the here of the house, exposure, the adventure and the danger of going outside would themselves have no meaning. Of course, thinking the soul without the body is already to forget history, but to think, as with some modern philosophers, the *here* as being first of all that of my body, is perhaps also to give in to a metaphysics of the body upright and standing like a God, without origin other than itself, and to think outside any milieu.[8] The milieu opens here; it is originary; it is that in which one dwells, that within which man dwells, man prior to his being determined as *animal rationale*, body and soul, and so on. To dwell is not only to be *in* one's here in an entirely original fashion, as this *in* does not translate the being-in of a thing in a box, to dwell is also to have the *keep* of one's house and what is stored in it, and to have the keep of this always-already that is the meaning of my relation to the house. Historiality is being in an *always-already*, is to be unable to go back any earlier than the house, for to be born is to be born in a house, in a place that is arranged and ready before me; it is my *originary* here, *qua* here, that I did not choose but on the basis of which every explicit choice will make sense. Such is the relation that man has to language, and that language has to being. I will not insist. Heidegger says, then,

> But the human being is not only a living creature who possesses language along with other capacities. Rather, language is the house of being in which *102*
> the human being ek-sists by dwelling, in that he belongs to the truth of being, guarding it. (*Pathmarks*, 254)

If, now, we reflect that movements of going out (of ek-sistence, of being-in as speech-dwelling, of here or there, etc.) can determine ontic significations *in*

8. Derrida has the following, scribbled here in between the lines: "(no body in Heidegger ⇒ [two or three illegible words])".

truth only if their meaning is first fixed ontologically, then we will only find out what *house* and dwelling mean, in their *proper* sense, by meditating on the relation of man to language and of language to being. We do not know first what *house* means, even if this word seems very familiar to us and to refer to the most familiar thing in the world. In truth it is what familiarity and proximity mean that we do not know, before having made explicit the relation of man to language and of language to being. So that we must reverse the terms and the direction of the metaphor. [Sentence added in the margin: "The term, the hidden object of the metaphor, to remain with the Aristotelian definition, is not what one thinks"]. When common sense hears that language is the house of being, it understands the following: for me, the known is the *house* and by referring the unknown (language in its relation to being) to the known, one is trying to make the unknown known to me. In truth, it is the opposite that happens: as there is no house and dwelling without humans, no humans without language, and no language without being, it is the relation to being, to dwelling-being, that teaches me truly what dwelling is and what house is, and in the house what [illegible] is—and will be—which I cannot learn without meditating on language.

It is in the proper sense that one should say that language is the house of being in which man dwells. And one is speaking *metaphorically*—which tells us a great deal about the status of metaphor—when one speaks the house outside of this relation to being. The *housing crisis*—one could say, jumping over many intermediate steps—is the expression of this deportation in a metaphor that is no longer even thought as such (i.e., in metaphysics).
103 There is a metaphysical root to the housing crisis, in the historial sense in which Heidegger understands metaphysics—a historico-metaphysical root. Do not translate this as follows: Heidegger thinks it is enough to meditate on the relation to being to solve it. And that it is pointless in this regard to construct affordable housing or projects [illegible interlinear addition]. You would be more naïve than he is and you would not have understood him.

Before leaving this point, I will translate a few more lines from the "Letter on 'Humanism,'" lines that we should now be in a position to understand appropriately.

> Thinking builds upon the house of being (*baut am Haus des Seins*), the house in which the jointure of being, *die Fuge des Seins* in its destinal (*geschickhaft*) unfolding, enjoins, *verfügt*, the essence of the human being in each case to dwell in the truth of being. This dwelling is the essence of "being-in-the-world" ("in-der-Welt-sein") (cf. *Sein und Zeit*, 54).[9] (*Pathmarks*, 272)

9. [Translator's note:] This is Heidegger's own reference to *Sein und Zeit*.

Read [German] pp. 53–54, [French] tr. p. 75.

*3. Being-in as such: The ontological constitution of in-ness itself is to be analyzed (cf. chapter 5 of this division).

[. . .]

What does being-in (*In-Sein*) mean? We supplement the expression being-in right away with the phrase "in the world," and are inclined to understand this being-in as "being in . . . ." With this term, the kind of being of a being is named which is "in" something else, as water is "in" the glass, the dress is "in" the closet. By this "in" we mean the relation of being that two beings extended "in" space have to each other with regard to their location in that space. Water and glass, dress and closet, are both "in" space "at" a location in the same way. This relation of being can be expanded; that is, the bench in the lecture hall, the lecture hall in the university, the university in the city, and so on until: the bench in "the cosmos." These beings whose being "in" one another can be determined in this way all have the 104
same kind of being—that of being present as things occurring "within" the world. Being present "in" something objectively present and the being present together with something having the same kind of being (in the sense of a determinate relation to place) are ontological characteristics which we call *categorial*. They belong to beings whose kind of being is unlike Dasein.

In contrast, being-in designates a constitution of being of Dasein, and is an *existential*. Thus, we cannot understand by this the objective presence of a corporeal thing (the human body) "in" a being objectively present. Nor does the term being-in designate a spatial "in one another" of two things objectively present, any more than the word "in" primordially means a spatial relation of this kind. "In" stems from *innan-*, to live, *habitare*, to dwell. *"An"* means I am used to, familiar with, I take care of something. It has the meaning of *colo* in the sense of *habito* and *diligo*. We characterized this being to whom being-in belongs in this meaning as the being which I myself always am. The expression *"bin"* [I am] is connected with *"bei"* [at, near]; "Ich bin" [I am] means I dwell, I stay near . . . the world as something familiar in such and such a way. Being as the infinitive of "I am" *[ich bin]*: that is, understood as an existential, means to dwell near . . . , to be familiar with . . . . *Being-in is thus the formal existential expression of the being of Dasein which has the essential constitution of being-in-the-world.*

"Being together with" the world, in the sense of being absorbed in the world, which must be further interpreted, is an existential which is grounded in being-in.* (*Being and Time*, 54–55)

I continue:

This dwelling is the essence of *In-der-Welt-seins*. The reference in *Sein und Zeit* to *In-Sein* as "*Wohnen*" is not some *etymologische Spielerei*. The same

> reference in the 1936 essay on Hölderlin's word, "Full of merit, yet poetically, man dwells upon this earth,"[10] is not the adornment of a thinking that rescues itself from science by means of poetry. The talk about the house of
> 105 being is not the transfer of the image "house" onto being. But one day we will, by thinking the essence of being in a way appropriate to its matter, more readily be able to think what "house" and "dwelling" are. And yet thinking never creates the house of being. (*Pathmarks*, 272)

And so on (you can see why).

If I have detained you so long in this detour, this is because here, on the basis of a privileged example, we can follow the operation that Heidegger is undertaking when he seems to be using metaphors, an operation which in the eyes of many is essentially alchemical or illusionistic or mystificatory, and which in truth is not even an operation. It is not even an operation because the point here is not to use metaphors as instruments of rhetoric [illegible word] (didactic, heuristic, etc.) but to return to the origin of metaphor or metaphoricity, and thus to think metaphor as such before it is seized upon by a rhetoric or a technique of expression. Here, as you saw—and this schema would show up again wherever Heidegger's language seems metaphorical—the proper meaning of the word *house* or the word *dwelling* is out of reach for a speaking that does not speak on the basis of the truth of being. When we think we know what we're saying when we say "house" every day in common and not poetic language, we are in metaphor. Now the thinking of the truth of being is to come but to come as what was always already buried. It follows that metaphor is the forgetting of the proper and originary meaning. Metaphor does not occur in language as a rhetorical procedure; it is the beginning of language, of which the thinking of being is however the buried origin. One does not begin with the originary; that's the first word of the (hi)story.

This means in particular that there is no chance, that there will never be any chance for those who might think of metaphor as a *disguise* of thought or of the truth of being. There will never be any chance of undressing or
106 stripping down this naked thinking of being which was never naked and never will be. The proper meaning whose movement metaphor tries to follow without ever reaching or seeing it, this proper meaning has never been said or thought and will never be said or thought as such. We must not turn away from, but be wary of, the very opposition of proper meaning and meta-

10. [Translator's note:] See Martin Heidegger, "Hölderlin and the Essence of Poetry," in *Elucidations of Hölderlin's Poetry*, ed. trans. Keith Hoeller (Amherst, NY: Humanity Books, 2000), 51–66.

phor if we are tempted to think them as the opposition of two terms. It is in rhetorical derivatives, in the deportation far away from the poetic or from thinking, it is in philosophy that this opposition hides its meaning by presenting itself as a bipolar operation (rhetorical and philosophical).

If one considers that metaphor is interminable and that it is the ontic covering over of the truth of being, that metaphoricity is the very essence of metaphysics, then one becomes aware (1) that there is no possible overcoming, no *Überwindung* of metaphysics. If overcoming means overcoming, simple overcoming. And this is indeed what Heidegger often makes clear, particularly in the text entitled, precisely, "Overcoming Metaphysics" (1936–1946) in which one reads the following: "Above all, overcoming does not mean thrusting aside a discipline from the field of philosophical 'education.'"[11] Further on: "Metaphysics cannot be abolished like an opinion. One can by no means leave it behind as a doctrine no longer believed and represented" (85). Further on:

> [. . .] we may not presume to stand outside of metaphysics because we
> surmise the ending of metaphysics. For metaphysics overcome in this way 107
> [and here one can say metaphor instead of metaphysics: metaphysics is a metonymy for metaphor and only the thinking of being allows one to think this strange metonymy] does not disappear. It returns transformed, and remains in dominance as the continuing difference between Being and beings. (85)

It is therefore (2) because what is absolutely fundamental is neither being, which is nothing, nor beings, but the ontico-ontological *difference*; because metaphorical inauthenticity cannot be overcome and does not figure, any more than does inauthenticity in general for Heidegger, as a regrettable and avoidable accident. Dissimulation is as originary and essential as unveiling. Cf. *Vom Wesen <der Wahrheit>*. If this were not so, then the historicity of being would be derivative and secondary. [Illegible marginal addition]

How did we get to this point? We came to these anticipations—and Heidegger shows that the thinking in transcendence [two uncertain words] toward the truth of being is anticipation—on the basis of the grammar of the word *be* and of the thematic of proximity that Heidegger was developing at some point.

The grammar of the word *be*, which we interrogated in order to clarify the first of the two assurances taken by the question in language, left us in perplexity. The form of the verbal substantive—*being*—at once seemed to

11. Heidegger, "Overcoming Metaphysics," in *The End of Philosophy*, trans. Joan Stambaugh (Chicago: University of Chicago Press, 2003), 85.

lend its form, to lend itself as form to the (ontico-conceptual) dissimulation of the truth of being and yet seemed as though it should be saved, preferred to the empiricism of the non-infinitive forms, I am, you are, and so on, he is . . . .

For now at least, grammar alone (i.e., the formal morphological consideration of the word *be*) cannot help us. We must, then, move on to the material consideration, if you will, of the origin of the word *be* (i.e., to etymology).

108 [French] Pages 80–81:

> The examination of the definite verbal forms of "to be" yields the opposite of an elucidation of being. What is more, it leads to a new difficulty. Let us compare the infinitive "to say" and the basic form "I say" with the infinitive "to be" and the basic form "I am". In this comparison "be" and "am" show that they have different stems. Furthermore "was" and "been" in the past form are different from both of these. We stand before the question of the different stems of the word "to be." (*Introduction to Metaphysics*, 75)

And then in the second part of the chapter of the *Einführung* . . . that is entitled "On the Grammar and Etymology of the Word 'Being,'" Heidegger determines as it were the *threshold* on which etymology and, in a general way, philology, linguistics, and semantics, as such, will have to stop and reach exhaustion.

The word *be* in Greek, Latin or Germanic has three Indo-European roots. Not having time to dwell on this here, I refer you to [French] pages 81 and 82 of the *Einführung* . . . . The *three roots* refer to different significations which are *live, blossom, dwell*. The significations have been erased and the history of the word *be* is the history of this erasure. Linguistics can take note of this erasure and we attach the greatest value to everything that linguistics can tell us, can bring us by way of certainty concerning the history of this erasure. But as to what it signifies, linguistics is necessarily mute. This erasure inscribes—and it inscribes the difference between being and beings. What happens in this erasure is that *being* will liberate itself from the metaphysics of *living*, of *blossoming*, of *dwelling*, to such a point that it will be able to mean the non-living, the non-blossoming, the non-dwelling. The possibility of a liberation with regard to any possible metaphor—that is, any determined ontic signification—that's what semantics as such cannot account for. This liberation, this in-determination is the originary historical phenomenon of what one might call, in depth and in general, freedom; that which allows one
109 to let be, to let beings be what they are, is also what allows them to appear as what they are in the truth of being, once our signification "being" is no longer predetermined and constrained by an ontic limitation. This is why in *Vom Wesen des Grundes* Heidegger links the ontico-ontological difference to freedom as transcendence.

The philosopher-philologist (for example Renan, Nietzsche) is too hasty to register the results of philological science and believes he is merely registering them when he says, "Here's what *being* meant at the origin," and refers us to the roots in order to understand what it truly means. The erasure of this first signification is an *abstraction* and—as Nietzsche in particular will say—it is by banking on this semantic grammatical abstraction that Western philosophy, since Parmenides, embarked on the aberrant path with which you are familiar. (Nietzsche close to Heidegger although—.)[12]

This theory of conceptual abstraction is very widespread, but it is particularly interesting in these philologists Renan and Nietzsche, precisely because they were philologists and because they thought that by speaking of abstraction they were shielded from any metaphysical interpretation coming in along with the simple philological deciphering of the facts. I will, then, pause for a moment *in the margin* of the reading of Heidegger, who does not allude to these texts, especially not to that of Renan. The conjuncture of these two texts—I am referring to Renan's *On the Origin of Language* (first edition 1848) and Nietzsche's 1872 fragment "Philosophy in the Tragic Age of the Greeks,"—the conjuncture of these two texts is all the more . . . enigmatic for the fact that, as you are going to see, similar conclusions are reached from diametrically opposed premises.

In chapter 5 of *On the Origin of Language*,[13] Renan begins by advancing the following propositions that I can only sketch out here:

(1) At its birth language was as *complete* as the human thought it then
represented, which means that there is no pre-cession of thought over
language; language is not an instrument that adapts itself more or less 110
well by running after a thought that is already formed.

(2) "Sound psychology" guiding "the state of languages" attributes a major role to sensation in the origin of language. Which means that the primitive language knew nothing of abstraction, and whereas the grammatical system of ancient language contains, says Renan, "the highest metaphysics," one sees everywhere in its words a material conception become the symbol of an idea. There is here a first alienation that Renan describes by citing Maine de Biran and Leibniz.

But (3) precisely, Renan makes a clear distinction between grammar and lexicology. Only grammar is purely *human* and *rational*; it alone is not sub-

12. Thus in the manuscript.

13. Ernest Renan, "De l'origine du langage," in *Œuvres complètes*, vol. 8, ed. Henriette Psichari (Paris: Calmann-Lévy, 1958). [Translator's note: All translations from Renan are my own.]

jected to sensibility, and the logicity of language is the purely grammatical (this brings us back to our Husserlian theme from last Saturday, a theme that presented itself in truth as very classical). And you will see what the status of metaphor is in this interval between the *lexicological* and the *grammatical*, which is the interval between matter and form, nihilism and rationalism. Before posing this question of the status of metaphor, let me read a few lines from Renan where he defines the interval and the transcendence of the grammatical with regard to the lexicological, a transcendence that is really that of *reason* as an attribute of man and the logicity of language, the *logos* itself, p. 63 of volume 8 of the *Oeuvres complètes*.

> Primitive language was therefore the joint product of mind and world: envisaged in its *form*, it was the expression of pure reason; envisaged in its matter, it was but the reflection of sensory life. Those who derived language *exclusively* from sensation were mistaken, as were those who gave to ideas a purely material origin. Sensation furnished the variable and accidental element, which could have been quite otherwise than it is, i.e., the words; but the rational form without which the *words* would not have been a *language*, in other words grammar, is the transcendent element which gives the work
> 111 a truly human character. The error of the 18th Century was to take too little account of grammar in its analyses of discourse. Sounds do not form a language, any more than sensations make a man. What makes language, just as what makes thought, is the logical link that the mind establishes between things. Once one has reserved this superior element for experience, which constitutes the originality of the human mind, one can without scruple abandon to the lower world everything that, as it were, merely pours matter into the pre-existing molds of reason. (Renan, 63; Derrida's italics on "form" and "exclusively.")

The most immediately perceptible consequence of this metaphysics of grammar and lexicology is that the grammatical is ahistorical, as are the *pre-existing molds of reason*, and that the historicity of language, on the one hand, is only the movement of matter (i.e., words), and on the other is oriented by grammatical rationality or teleology. The history of language is the history of words progressively liberating themselves from matter or the secret mire, to be purified and spelled out and adapted to the purely rational categories of grammar.

Now the *force* of this history, what gets it moving—that is, what makes possible the passage from verbal matter to grammatical form, what makes possible *desire* (in the Aristotelian sense, since here the Desirable is pure form and immobility getting matter moving and pulling it towards itself), the place and the name of Desire as historicity of language—is *metaphor*.

Or else, as Renan would say, *transport*. It is transport that little by little delivered words from their determinate sensory origin, literally made them *travel*, uprooted them and thus made them more and more diaphanous and ready to be informed by pure grammaticality.

Following immediately from the passage I read a moment ago, Renan indeed continues: "*Transport* or metaphor was thus the great procedure in the formation of language. One analogy led to another and thus the meaning 112
of words traveled in *apparently* the most capricious manner [. . .]" (Renan, 64). There follows a series of extreme, interesting examples, for the most part drawn from Hebrew. And in the middle of this cohort of examples, the word *be*.

Being is simply a word, a verbal material for Renan. And here is what he says about it on the basis of the same philological content that Heidegger refers to, but adding a Hebraic or Semitic note (pp. 66–67):

> In all languages *breath* has become synonymous with *life*, for which it serves as a physical sign. It is something well worthy of reflection that the *most abstract* terms used by metaphysics should all have a material root, whether it be apparent or not, in the first perceptions of a highly sensitive race [reference to Locke, *Essay*, Book III, Ch. 1, §5]. The verb *be*, of which Monsieur Cousin said boldly in 1829: "I know of no language in which the French word *be* is expressed by a corresponding term that represents a sensory idea;" the verb *be*, say I, in almost every language is drawn from a sensory idea. The opinion of the philologists who assign as first meaning to the Hebrew verb *haia* or *hawa* (be) that of *breathe,* and seek signs of onomatopoeia in this word, is not without plausibility. In Arabic and in Ethiopian, the verb *ķâna*, which plays the same role, has as its primitive signification *to stand upright* (*extare*). *Koum (stare)* in Hebrew also passes in its derivatives into the meaning *being (substantia)*. As for the Indo-European languages, they composed their substantive verb from three different verbs: 1) *as* (Sanskrit *asmi, immí, eimi, sum*); 2) *bhû* (*phuô, fui*, German *bin*, Persian *bouden*); 3) *sthâ (stare, Persian hestem)*, become part of the verb *be*, at least as an auxiliary, in the modern languages of India and in the Romance languages (*stato,* été). Of these three verbs, the third is notoriously a physical verb and signifies *to stand upright*. The second very plausibly had the primitive meaning of *breathe*. As for the first, it appears to be attached to the third person pronoun [important for 113
> Heidegger]; but this pronoun itself, however abstract it be, seems to refer to a primitively concrete meaning. (Renan, 66–67)

This passage calls for several remarks (5).

(1) That Renan is probably unfair with regard to Victor Cousin who, when he said, "I know of no language in which the French word 'be'

is expressed by a corresponding word that represents a sensory idea," clearly did not intend to be responding to any problem of semantic derivation or genesis but merely to a problem of signification or intention of signification, one might say, in the present state of language in which the sensory origin has been buried. A remark that no doubt comes from Victor Cousin's Hegelian vein here latching onto, as did Hegel in a text I mentioned last time, the radical in-determination of this signification of being.

(2) Renan does not pose the question of the absolute liberation of the signification *being* with respect to these metaphorical anchoring-points—that is, the question of the meaning of being as history of the *truth* of being.

(3) By making the *word being* a word, a verbal material excluded as such from pure grammaticality and pure rationality, he doubtless recognizes that its signification, that the signification of this word has a *history,* but precisely an empirical history, external to the movement of rationality—which is itself not historical. Empirical history of the signification of being. But what can a rationality and a grammar without "being" be?

(4) It goes without saying that this theory of metaphor is essentially of a piece with a metaphysics, a dualistic metaphysics that in particular determines man as *animal rationale*. Metaphor rests in its possibility on the parallelism, of which man is the link, between the physical world and the psychic or rational world, between the outside and the inside, and so forth. It is in particular through this metaphor and this analysis
114 between two domains that Renan explains the possibility of writing. Read quickly:

> The parallelism between the physical world and the intellectual world was the distinctive feature of the first ages of humanity. Whence those symbols, transporting into the domain of religious matters the procedure that had served for the development of language; whence that ideological writing, giving body to thought and applying to the written representation of ideas the same principle that presided over their representation by sounds. Indeed, is the nomenclature that we have described anything other than a symbolism, a continual hieroglyph, and do not all these facts come together to bear witness to the close union that originally existed between soul and nature? (Renan, 67–68)

Now although it is thought as *composition* and in the metaphysical horizon of dualism, this idea of the close originary union between soul and nature and so forth, might have permitted Renan to escape, at least when dealing precisely with the origin of language, from this dualism of the lexicological and the grammatical. And in fact there exists in Renan a scarcely elaborated and timid theory[14] of the primitive word that supports such an intention. But this theory is, precisely, timid; it presents itself as a sort of appendix concerning exceptions to the rule and, in any case, for what interests us, the word *be* is not concerned by it. This theory concerns only certain pronouns and simple particles, and the word *be* belongs to the matter of language subject to an empirical history that never transgresses metaphorics.

Let me read pp. 68–69:

> However, as such a state [the close union that originally existed between soul and nature] was far from excluding the exercise of reason, but simply held it enveloped in concrete images, we believe that one must admit as primitive in their significations a number of the words that correspond to 115
> essential categories of mind, and *without which the data from sensation would themselves be incomplete, as are some pronouns and some simple particles*. We are not claiming that the origin of these words is absolutely immaterial and that there is not hidden in them a sort of subjective onomatopoeia, so to speak; we are simply saying the reason for their formation might have been in man and not outside. *Indeed, these words belong as much to grammar as to lexicology; now grammar is entirely the work of reason; the outside has no part in it*.[15] The distinction between *full* words and *empty* words that dominated ancient grammar [here Renan is alluding to the *General Grammar* of Port-Royal and to Aristotle's poetics] here finds its perfect application. The former, which could be called *objective words*, designating things and forming a meaning by themselves [*categoremata* ≠ *syncategoremata*] all had as the cause of their appearance an external phenomenon; the second, which one could call *subjective words*, designating only a relation or a view of the mind, must often have had a purely psychological cause [rational grammar here then depends on a psychology of reason]. Once this reservation—or better, this distinction—has been made, the general law we have established conserves its perfect truth. (Renan, 68–69)

In spite of its naïveté, this theory of primitive words points the way in which Renan might have posed the question of the word *being*, wresting it away from pure natural lexicology. By going behind the opposition of the grammatical and the lexicological, he could have encountered in the signification of the word *being* what makes it escape from this distinction, since the meaning of *being*, as Heidegger questions it, is anterior, as their common focus, to the distinction between being as essence and as existence, or the use of the

14. [Translator's note:] There is an interlinear addition in the ms. at this point: "But perhaps—."

15. Derrida's emphasis here and earlier.

word *be* as *copula* in attributive judgment or as existential judgment, before even judgment and predication in general. This last reason, added to the
116 others, explains why Renan, along with so many others, letting himself be guided here by rational grammar itself guided by the judicative sentence, could only let these questions lie dormant.

(5) You have seen that Renan talks of *abstraction* as process of liberation from metaphor and especially in the case of being. This abstraction is guided by *logic* and the metaphor is pulled out of itself by the call of an ahistorical—and therefore always pre-existing—rationalizing grammar, and it is because man is a *metaphysical* animal that he can liberate himself in this way from metaphor and let himself be guided by grammar. Abstraction and logic are the *good* of Metaphysics. Well, you will see that Nietzsche arrives at the same result by describing this process as *illogical* and by accusing metaphysics of feeding off this *illogicism*.

As it is late, here I shall simply read Nietzsche's text without commenting on it. It is moreover as clear as day ([French] page 89).

> And if Parmenides could permit himself, in the uninformed naiveté of his time, so far as critique of the intellect is concerned, to derive absolute being from a forever subjective concept, today, after Kant, it is certainly reckless ignorance to attempt it. Now and again, particularly among badly taught theologians who would like to play philosopher, the task of philosophy is designated as "comprehending the absolute by means of consciousness," even in the form of "The absolute is already present, how could it otherwise be sought?" (Hegel) or "Being must be given to us somehow, must be somehow attainable; if it were not we could not have the concept." (Beneke) The concept of being! As though it did not show its low empirical origin in its very etymology. For *esse* basically means "*to breathe*." And if man uses it of all things other than himself as well, he projects his conviction that he himself breathes and lives by means of a metaphor, i.e., a non-logical process, upon all other things. He comprehends their existence as a "breathing" by analogy with his own. The original meaning of the word was soon blurred, but enough remains to make it obvious that man imagines the existence of other things by analogy with his own existence, in other words anthropomorphic-
> 117 ally and in any event, with non-logical projection. But even for man—quite aside from his projection—the proposition "I breathe, therefore being exists" is wholly insufficient. The same objection must be made against it as must be made against *ambulo, ergo sum* or *ergo est*.[16]

16. Nietzsche, *Philosophy in the Tragic Age of the Greeks*, trans. Marianne Cowan (Washington: Regnery, 1998), 83–84.

Basically, the differences I've pointed out between Nietzsche and Renan come down to the fact that Renan believes that metaphor liberates us from metaphor and etymology, and that transfer guided by reason liberates us from earlier and more secret metaphorical linkings (⇒ rhetoric). Nietzsche thinks that there is no meta-metaphor and thus no logical metaphor. No pure grammar (cf. *Will to Power*, §97; [French] p. 65 (I on grammar) et §151 [locate]).[17] But both of them make of the signification "being," a signification *abstracted* from an empirical signification. *118*

It is this abstractionist interpretation that, as you know, Heidegger tirelessly destroys. Primarily because in the first place one would have to know what abstracting is, and because to conduct this operation called abstraction satisfactorily, one would have to be guided by a pre-conceptual pre-comprehension of the meaning that commands this concept (tree, [French] pages 89–90).[18] As Heidegger notes, Aristotle had already understood that

17. The parenthesis is an interlinear addition. Derrida marked these two passages with brackets in his copy of Nietzsche's *La volonté de puissance* (trans. G. Bianquis [Paris: Gallimard, 1938], 65 and 83), which is his usual way of marking a quotation to be read out in class, even though here he writes "cf." So we provide the passages here: "The last thing in metaphysics we will rid ourselves of is the oldest stock, assuming we can rid ourselves of it—that stock which has embodied itself in language and the grammatical categories and made itself so indispensable that it almost seems we would cease being able to think if we relinquished it. Philosophers, in particular, have the greatest difficulty in freeing themselves from the belief that the basic concepts and categories of reason belong without further ado to the realm of metaphysical certainties: from ancient times they have believed in reason as a piece of the metaphysical world itself—this oldest belief breaks out in them again and again like an overpowering recoil." [Translator's note: This passage does not appear to figure in any of the different English compilations of *The Will to Power*, but does appear in a translation of late fragments (Nietzsche, *Writing from the Late Notebooks*, ed. Rüdiger Bittner, trans. Kate Sturge [Cambridge: Cambridge University Press, 2003], 124–25). The second reference, §151 of the French translation Derrida used, page 83, corresponds to §581 of the Kaufmann edition of *The Will to Power*: "*Being and Becoming*.—'Reason,' evolved on a sensualistic basis, on the prejudices of the senses, i.e., in the belief in the truth of the judgments of the senses. / 'Being' as universalization of the concept 'life' (breathing), 'having a soul,' 'willing, effecting,' 'becoming.' / The antithesis is: 'not to have a soul,' 'not to become,' 'not to will.' Therefore: 'being' is *not* the antithesis of non-being, appearance, nor even of the dead (for only something that can live can be dead)." Friedrich Nietzsche, *Will to Power*, trans. Walter Kaufmann and R. J. Hollingdale, ed. Walter Kaufmann (New York: Random House, 1968), 312.]

18. *Introduction to Metaphysics*, 85: "It is questionable, to begin with, whether the generality of Being is that of a genus. Aristotle already suspected this. Consequently, it remains questionable whether an individual being can ever count as an example of Being at all, as this oak does for 'tree in general.' It is questionable whether the ways of Being (Being as nature, Being as history) represent 'species' of the genus 'Being.'"

being is not a genus nor the most general of genuses (theory of the *pollakhōs legomenon*).

It follows, and here we are closing our loop for today, that word, signification and signified are in the case of being linked in a way that is completely original and unique; which explains that the <first> *assurance* that roots us in the *Faktum* of the pre-comprehension of the *Bedeutung* "being" is itself quite singular. Referring to the well-known (and in particular Husserlian) distinction between physical sign, signification, and thing itself, Heidegger shows in the *Einführung* that in the case of being the thing *seems* not to exist. When I say "clock," there is the (physical) word, the signification and the clock itself. And so long as one conducts analyses of the word and the signification, one is not speaking of the thing itself. And similarly, one could not explain *being itself* on the basis of a simple study of the word or of its signification. This would be an error as unpardonable as wanting to study the movements of the ether or of matter or subatomic processes by giving grammatical explanations of the words *atom* and *ether*, instead of conducting the necessary experiments.

But the fact is that here the *thing itself is not a being*, even if by *being* one designates the being of this or that being. The being of the building is not the
119 building or a part of the building, the roof or the cellar. And *a fortiori* being in general is not the totality of beings. Must one conclude from this that being consists in the signification and in the word? No, for this would be as inept as saying that the being of the building consists in a signification of the word. The signification of the word being signifies precisely that it has to do with more than signification; otherwise it would not be in conformity with the signification (see St. Anselm). If there is only one thing in the world the analysis of which is not exhausted by an analysis of signification, it is indeed *being*.

It follows that *being*, without existing outside the signification "being," is not to be reduced to the signification "being." So that the link between *being* and the signification "being" is of an absolutely unique type. [French] p. 99 of the *Einführung* . . .

> From this it follows that ultimately, in the word "Being" and its inflections, and in everything that lies in the domain of this word, the word and its signification are bound more originally to what is meant by them—*but also vice versa*. Being itself relies on the word in a totally different and more essential sense than any being does.
>
> *The word "Being," in every one of its inflections, relates to the Being itself that is said, in a way that is essentially different from the relation of all other nouns and verbs in language to the beings that are said in them*. (*Introduction to Metaphysics*, 92–93)

This is what justifies, after the fact and retroactively, the <first>assurance and the *Faktum* that, in *Sein und Zeit*, install the question of being in the element of language and the pre-comprehension of the *Bedeutung ist*. This is a *retroactive* justification because these themes are only implicit in *Sein und Zeit*.

We will never finish justifying this *Faktum* in which we recognized last time the sign of the historicity of the question of being. For beyond etymology and grammar and historical linguistics, it will turn out in particular
that our pre-comprehension of the meaning of being, in so far as already it 120
escapes from the hold of historical or structural sciences of language, at this point where it resists them, is nonetheless already marked, limited by its already *historial* provenance, a historial provenance from which one must not liberate oneself as from a simple metaphor, but that one must repeat and understand as such.

Heidegger does indeed show, still in the *Einführung* . . . , that our current pre-comprehension of the meaning of being still privileges, deep down, the third person singular, the *is*. And that this privilege is *Greek*. This limitation, which will bring with it a whole other cortege of limitations, must be, if not criticized, at least shaken, solicited in its historial import. Which one can do only by posing historially the question of being. This announces the *Durchstreichung* of the notion and of the word *being* that I was speaking about last time.

Before concluding, I shall read, then, a few lines from the *Einführung* . . . , in which this *crisis of limitation* is announced ([French] page 103):

> The definite and particular verb form "is," *the third person singular of the present indicative*, has a priority here. We do not understand "Being" with regard to the "thou art," "you are," "I am," or "they would be," although these all represent verbal inflections of "Being" that are just as good as "is." We take "to be" as the infinitive of "is." To put it the other way around, we involuntarily explain the infinitive "to be" to ourselves on the basis of the "is," almost as if nothing else were possible.
>
> Accordingly, "Being" has the meaning we have indicated, which recalls the Greek conception of the essence (*Wesen*) of Being—a definiteness, then, which has not come to us from just anywhere, but which has long ruled our historical Dasein [*geschichtlich*: *proventuel*, in G. Kahn's [French] translation]. At one blow, our search for the definiteness of the meaning of the word "Being" thus becomes explicitly what it is: a meditation on the provenance of our *concealed history* [*Geschichte: provenance*, translates Kahn]. The question, "How does it stand with Being?" must maintain itself within the history [the provenance] of Being if it is, in turn, to unfold and preserve its
> own historial import. (*Introduction to Metaphysics*, 100–101) 121

I think we are now better prepared to pose the question of the second assurance, i.e., to repeat the question I posed in closing last time. Why does the question of the history of being begin with the question about a specific *Befragtes*, i.e., with the exploration of a specific being, in the form of *Da-sein*, i.e., of the being that *we are insofar as we are questioning*? And what is the value *of this second assurance*, which is justified by this *proximity* of ourselves to ourselves, of our question to itself, of our speech to itself? Taking into account that we have questioned, with Heidegger himself, this enigmatic, metaphorical, signification of *proximity*—proximity of speech to itself so long as it is not yet thought on the basis of the essence of being. So long as the *Da* of *Dasein* is not thought on the basis of *Sein*.

How to justify anticipatorily the argument of proximity that risks being based on metaphor, i.e., metaphysics, so long as the essence of being has not clarified it in return? In other terms, is setting off into the analytic of the historicity of Dasein and the Da of Sein not justified by Heidegger in the style and within the limitations of metaphysics still? Heidegger would no doubt not deny it, and would not deny that the Da of Da-sein has a certain metaphorical meaning; and when the Da is metaphorical, when absolute proximity is metaphorical, of what can it be a metaphor? Of another proximity? Or of a distancing, and is not the other proximity, the other Da, a fort? Is not the difference between fort and Da the first metaphor of Sein, the first metaphysical occultation of the question of Being? Heidegger would no doubt not deny it, but then what? Then . . . we can do nothing other than keep talking about it and talking with in it.

SESSION FOUR

11 January 1965

Last time we dwelt at length in the problematic field of what I called the 123
first assurance of the question of Being, namely the Faktum of the pre-comprehension of the signification of the word *be*. The original Faktum of a language, of language, in which the presence of being has always already operated if this language is a language.

Along the way, and especially in conclusion, we wondered about the enigmatic signification of proximity, proximity to self in the I am, proximity of the Da in Da-sein: everything we said about this—and that I cannot go over again here, even schematically— prepared, as I announced, the problem of the second assurance that we are broaching now. Second ≠ other assurance / common root of the two assurances. Let me recall briefly however that we are developing this question of the two assurances under the aegis of the general question I posed during the session before last, namely: Why, what necessity justifies that the question of Being as History, of Being/History should pass via the preliminary moment of an analytic of the historicity of Da-sein? And what does this preliminary signify here?

The Faktum of language sketched out the response—with the difficulties that we encountered. Since Being is not, nor comes forth, nor appears, outside language, it is history, yes, but it comes forth through (and I leave this *through* to all its enigmatic power) a speaking being, a speaking being who poses or to whom or by whom or through whom the question of being 124
precisely poses itself. And posing itself thus immediately constitutes thereby the originality of the being to which or through which or for which it poses itself. The reflexivity of "poses itself," here, which seems to make Being the subject of the question, must not be, through another falsification, a pretext to think that Being is another Being, a subject, a God who addresses it to such and such a being, as it happens the being in the form of Dasein, and that in so doing it constitutes it as Da-sein. [Illegible sentence added in the margin.] Because Being is not a being, there is no chance for such a meta-

physical hypostasis of the initiation of the question to come about, except of course if it is given the opportunity by some misrecognition function.

Other ways of proceeding—that one would not expect to see here compared to those that are occupying us at the moment and that I mention only for . . . amusement—are indeed threatened by metaphysical hypostasis, just when one would expect it least, and this is because of a failure to pre-criticize philosophically the notions in question. These ways of proceeding are familiar enough to us for me to be content with three quotations in which the grammatical function of what Heidegger would call the language of being is occupied in these propositions by symbol or myth and in which the (speaking) Dasein becomes man, as if one knew at that point already what one was speaking about under these three names (symbols, myths and men).

I believe I read the first two quotations very rapidly last time. So let me re-read these sentences.

(1) "The symbol's order can no longer be conceived of as constituted by man but must rather be conceived of as constituting him." (Lacan, *Écrits*, 34)

(2) "Man thus speaks, but it is because the symbol has made him man." (Lacan, *Écrits*, 229)

(3) "I therefore claim to show, not how men think in myths, but how
125 myths operate in men's minds without their being aware of the fact."[1]

I return to Heideggerian prudence and, finally, to the second assurance taken in this text which is almost forty years old.

Let us remind ourselves of the structure: *Gefragtes, Befragtes, Erfragtes.* Being is the questioned, the *Gefragtes* of the *Fragen.* If Being is the Being of a being, the *Befragtes,* the *interrogated* of the question can only be a being, a being interrogated as to its being. But in order that, when interrogated, it reveal the questioned appropriately to us, it must be *appropriately* interrogated and our access to the interrogated must be the right access.

Beings are interrogated, but beings are everything that is and anything at all. Being comes forth in all the forms of beings. The forms of beings—which must not be confused with the regions of being—are very numerous: there are beings in the form of what is called existence, the fact that something is, the *that* (*Dass-sein*), beings in the form of essence (of *what* the thing is, of the *such* that it is—*So-sein*). In the form also of the *Res (Realität)*, in the form of permanent object-being before us (*Vorhandenheit*: "subsistent

1. Claude Lévi-Strauss, *The Raw and the Cooked: Mythologiques*, vol. 1, trans. John and Doreen Weightman (Chicago: University of Chicago Press, 1983), 12.

being," as <the> Gallimard <edition> translates it),[2] in the form of content, or constancy (*Bestand*), in the form of Being-there (*Dasein*), in the form of value (*Geltung*), in the form of the *there is* (*es gibt*).[3]

The very fact that Heidegger wonders to what form of being he should address himself, the fact that he remarks that the question is worth posing, however rapidly and discreetly he does so here, is the sign of a vigilance that has never appeared as such in the history of ontology. All ontologies (with the sole exception of what one could, with caution, call Husserl's ontology) implicitly chose as their guide such and such a type of being without making a theme or a question of their choice. And according to Heidegger it is most often in the form of *Vorhandenheit* (of the object, if you like, and by what is merely an alternation in the form of the subject) which has served as the *exemplary* form of being. Cf. §6 on Kant and Descartes ([French] p. 45, *Being and Time*, 23–24).

Now it is precisely the problem of exemplarity that Heidegger does not want to dodge here. He writes in §2, [French] p. 22, I translate: *126*

> On *which* being is the meaning of being to be read (*An welchem Seienden soll der Sinn von Sein abgelesen warden*), from which being is the opening up (*Erschliessung*) of being to get its start (*soll ihren Ausgang nehmen*)? Is the starting point arbitrary, or does a certain being have a priority (*Vorrang*) in the elaboration of the question of being? Which is this *exemplary* being and in what sense does it have priority? (*Being and Time*, 6)

A problem, then, of exemplarity, a *de jure* problem, of the justification of exemplarity, of privilege.

A remark on the passage I have just read. Heidegger says "*on* which being is the meaning of being to be *read*" (reread the German). And Heidegger does not pause over this notion of reading that is functioning here in a muted way . . . .

So one might wonder: to what extent is this metaphor of reading innocent? To what extent innocent the definition of a question that makes—*at least by metaphor*— of the questioned *Gefragtes* a *meaning* (*Sinn*, the meaning

2. [Translator's note:] By "Gallimard," Derrida appears to refer here to the Boehm-De Waelhens translation of Division 1 of *Being and Time* (Paris: Gallimard, 1964). But see also p. 96, below, referring to the selections from *Being and Time* translated by Henry Corbin and included in the 1937 volume entitled *Qu'est-ce que la métaphysique?* also published by Gallimard.

3. [Translator's note:] Derrida is paraphrasing *Being and Time*, 5–6: "Being is found in thatness and whatness, reality, the objective presence of things, substistence, validity, existence, and in the 'there is.'"

of being) and of the *Befragtes*, of the interrogated, a text *on* which the meaning is deciphered? Which transforms, at least metaphorically—but what a metaphor—the *Sinn* into a *Bedeutung*. And it is *Da-sein* (often too rapidly translated as man) that will be determined as the *right text*, without the use of this metaphor being as naïve as that of Hobbes in the introduction to the *Leviathan*, where it has one think "That *Wisdome* is acquired, not by reading of *Books*, but of *Men*";[4] the other forms of being will, then, be determined as bad texts for the deciphering of the meaning of being, as *apocryphal* texts: that is, as bad *crypts*, as crypts which conceal by distancing (*apo-kruptein*), whereas *Dasein* will be the good crypt that still hides, of course, but in such a way that it does not *distance* us but *brings us close* to the meaning it gives us to read. And this metaphor of reading that makes of being a meaning legible in a text—as if the text or the book were not itself a form of being much more
127 determinate still than *Dasein*—this metaphor of reading, however discreet its appearance here, is in no way an accident of Heidegger's style, any more than it has ever been, I believe, wherever it has functioned, which is to say, I believe, everywhere, everywhere in the entirety of Western discourse at least, from Plato to Heidegger (Plato, *Phaedrus*). Freud recommends in the *Traumdeutung* ([German] p. 98)[5] that we beware the metaphor of the text, of the metaphor making of the unconscious an *original text* of which conscious-

4. [Translator's note:] Thomas Hobbes, *Leviathan*, ed. Richard Tuck (Cambridge: Cambridge University Press, 1996), 10.

5. We were unable to check the edition that Derrida references here: page 98 of the German edition of *Die Traumdeutung*— in the *Gesammelte Werke*'s double volume 2–3 (Frankfurt: Fisher, 1942)—does not seem to be the one meant by Derrida here. [Translator's note: It appears that Derrida is thinking of the following passage from Freud's *The Interpretation of Dreams*, a passage he cites in "Freud and the Scene of Writing" (in *Writing and Difference*, trans. Alan Bass [Chicago: University of Chicago Press, 1978], 211) : "So let us try to correct some conceptions which might be misleading so long as we looked upon the two systems in the most literal and crudest sense as two localities in the mental apparatus—conceptions which have left their traces in the expressions 'to repress' and 'to force a way through.' Thus, we may speak of an unconscious thought seeking [, after being translated,] to convey itself into the preconscious so as to be able then to force its way through into consciousness. What we have in mind here is not the forming of a second thought situated in a new place, like a transcription which continues to exist alongside the original; and the notion of forcing a way through into consciousness must be kept carefully free from any idea of a change of locality" (Freud, *The Standard Edition of the Complete Psychological Works of Sigmund Freud*, vol. 5, ed. and trans. James Strachey [London: Hogarth Press, 1951], 610; Freud, *Gesammelte Werke*, vols. 2–3 [London: Imago, 1991], 615). I have inserted the phrase "after being translated," omitted in Strachey's English version.]

ness would be merely the *Umschrift* (transposition, translation, falsification). He seemed in so doing to refuse the metaphor of the text only when it is a question of one type of writing (phonetic). For in some later texts (comment: FS?).[6] In the *Notiz über den "Wunderblock"* (vol. 14, [German] pp. 3–8),[7] he does not fail to compare the unconscious to those blocks of wax with which you are perhaps familiar, which are protected by a transparent plastic film. One writes with a stylus on the transparent film, the signs are inscribed on the grey wax, and it then suffices to pull back the transparent film for the visible writing to be erased. But the invisible traces remain inscribed in the depth of the wax. Here inscription and not text.

This metaphor of the text does not appear by chance in Heidegger; one can almost say that he resolutely takes it on in spite of all the later Nietzschean-style protests against grammar and writing. He takes it on, since a little later, when he is defining, as you know, his method as *phenomenology*, phenomenological ontology, and as apophantic phenomenological ontology, repeating history and reactivating the history of *phainesthai* and *logos*, Heidegger specifies that phenomenology as science of the being of beings, as ontology, and specifically insofar as it takes as its theme the privileged being that is *Dasein*, has as its methodological meaning *Auslegung*, which is translated [into 128
French] as "*explicitation*" [and into English as "interpretation"]—which is indeed what it means.[8] It is indeed the action of unfolding that spreads out and turns over what is enveloped—but it is also the word used to designate exegesis—for example of sacred texts—and interpretation: *hermēneuein*. An act of deciphering reading. And this is indeed how Heidegger understands it, [German] p. 37, §7:

> The *logos* of the phenomenology of Dasein has the character of *hermēneuein*, through which the proper meaning of being and the basic structures of the very being of Dasein are *announced* (*kundgegeben*) to the understanding of being that belongs to Dasein itself. (*Being and Time*, 35)

And Heidegger goes further in this direction: not only does he feel that he is not transposing into a more originary order an operation (the interpretative reading of a text) that would be proper to a quite particular and quite determined field of science, but, on the contrary, it is the hermeneutics he

6. [Translator's note:] Derrida's "FS" presumably refers to "Freud and the Scene of Writing."

7. [Translator's note:] *Standard Edition*, vol. 19, 227–32.

8. [Translator's note:] I have translated Derrida's "explicitation" as "explication" throughout.

is talking about that he thinks is hermeneutics in the proper sense, from which would be derived what is called more complacently, and with a sense of security, hermeneutics—namely, the method of deciphering by reading documents in other fields, in the other humanistic disciplines: for example: history, literary history, theology, and so on, [German] p. 38:

> To the extent that this hermeneutic elaborates the historicity [*Geschichtlichkeit*] of Dasein ontologically as the ontic condition of the possibility of the discipline of history [historical science: *Historie*], it contains the roots of what can be called "hermeneutics" only in a derivative sense: the methodology of the historical humanistic disciplines. (*Being and Time*, 35)

Here we encounter a schema that will interest us on its own account later:
129 since there would be no historical science without the historicity of *Dasein* (no *Historie* without *Geschichte*), the hermeneutics that gives us to read or think the historicity of *Dasein* is the condition of possibility of hermeneutics as the method of historical science. Of course this gesture is very heavy with consequences and it is a discreet if not fragile link in the chain of Heidegger's propositions, and one on which those interested in anti-Heideggerian strategy or tactics would have every reason to put some pressure.

The point is indeed to find out if the reversal of the metaphor, the legitimacy of which we tried to prove last time around the notion of dwelling, can be justified here. Is hermeneutics as reading of a text, in the sense in which this operation is familiar to us, a gesture that not only can be transposed when we are dealing with the meaning of being, but one that is itself rooted in the first reading of that same text? *Da-sein,* first letter to Being [*première lettre à l'Être*]. Can one say that *Da-sein* is itself a text, when one would be tempted to think that since in fact it alone writes texts, it is not itself text? Can the meaning of being in general be deciphered in a text, if one not only doubts that *Da-sein* is a text, but if one further thinks that the text is a highly particular form of being, which is in the world and does not even have the privilege of *Da-sein*? Even supposing that the analytic of *Dasein* is legitimately a phenomenology and an apophantics (a pre-judicative apophantics, let us be clear, with Heidegger)—legitimately because *Da-sein* is language, has as its proper essence the fact of being structured as the possibility of language—it still remains to be ascertained if from speech to text the consequence follows; and whether this passage poses no problem as to the method of reception (i.e., allows no decisive and essential difference to emerge between hearing and reading meaning); and whether one can speak without risk of a reading of spoken meaning (*Dasein* language only [several illegible words in the margin]).

Heidegger seems to think so and one can imagine his response here. On the one hand he would judge us unduly sure of our knowledge of what a text is, and what a reading is, when we say that the text in general is in the world, that it is a highly determinate and derivative form of being and that it calls *130*
for a quite particular operation [illegible interlinear phrase]. He would also say that we do not know what a text is without reference to the possibility of speech (which is no doubt, we would reply, to limit oneself to models of alphabetic or in any case phonetic writing—that is, ones whose structure is controlled by the representation of speech. But here it must be confessed that the problem is too complex for one to be able to untangle clearly what, even in ideo- or pictographic writings, is interpretation of speech). Then, Heidegger would add that to speak of a writing independent of speech is to think it "independent" of voice and not of speech in general, which designates the possibility of signification and of language in general. *Gesagtes ≠ Gesprochenes*. So much so that one could not speak of deciphering a text—however determinate this notion may be—without the possibility of deciphering, of the hermeneutics of signification in general already having conditioned it. Finally, for Heidegger, the passage from vocal speech to inscription is not the emergence of an essentially new mode of language. For two reasons.

(1) Because Heidegger, in a very traditional manner—here I mean Platonic—thinks that the emergence of writing, the modification of speech into writing is more of a degradation, a lethargy, and thus already a dimming, a forgetting of living speech. And already the beginning of chatter (forgetting and Plato, *Phaedrus*).For example, in *Was heisst Denken?,* p. 47 of the French translation, Heidegger mentions the becoming-chatter that threatens Nietzsche's *scream* [cri] once it has to become *written* [écrit]:

> Even so, a man who teaches must at times grow noisy. In fact, he may have to scream and scream, although the aim is to make his students learn so quiet a thing as thinking. Nietzsche, most quiet and shiest of men, knew of this necessity. He endured the agony of having to scream. [. . .] But riddle upon riddle! What was once the scream "the wasteland grows . . . ," now threatens to turn into chatter. [. . .] Script easily smothers the scream, especially if *131*
> the script exhausts itself in description, and aims to keep men's imagination busy by supplying it constantly with new matter. The burden of thought is swallowed up in the written script, unless the writing is capable of remaining, even in the script itself, a progress of thinking, a way. About the time when the words "The wasteland grows . . ." were born, Nietzsche wrote in his notebook (GW XIV, p. 229, Aphorism 464 of 1885): "A man for whom nearly all books have become superficial, who has kept faith in only a few people of the past that they have had depth enough—not to write what they

> knew." But Nietzsche had to scream. For him, there was no other way to do it than by writing. That written scream of Nietzsche's thought is the book which he entitled *Also sprach Zarathustra*.[9]

To think writing as a chattering degradation of the scream or of speaking thought is thus to be wary of *grammar* and the grammatical model. And this is indeed what Heidegger does—Heidegger who, just like Nietzsche, here, accuses (if I can say that, improperly, for it is anything but an accusation), reawakens the quasi-somnambulistic gesture by which Western metaphysics let itself be guided without knowing it by the grammatical model—that is, by what it gave, in the strong sense of the words, to living speech, its *status*, its *station*, its *stance*—while attempting to listen without body and without substance. The fixity of grammar (i.e., its *inscriptibility*), has fascinated philosophy, which has thought the possibility of language on the basis of the possibility of grammar and therefore the possibility of thought on the basis of the possibility of grammar. Whence the tendency to think being in grammatical categories and . . . you know this problem. See p. 74 of the [French] translation of the *Einführung* . . . :

> We said that language, too, is conceived by the Greeks as something in being and thereby as something in keeping with the sense of their understanding of Being. What is in being is what is constant and as such, something that exhibits itself, something that appears. This shows itself primarily to seeing. The Greeks examine language optically in a certain broad sense—namely, from the point of view of the written word. In writing, what is spoken comes to a stand. Language is—that is, it stands in the written image of the word,
> 132 in the written signs, in the letters, *grammata*. This is why it is grammar that represents language as something in being, whereas through the flow of talk, language drains away into the impermanent. And so the theory of language has been interpreted grammatically up to our time. The Greeks, however, also knew about the oral character of language, the *phōnē*. They founded rhetoric and poetics. (Yet all of this did not in itself lead to an adequate definition of the essence of language.) The standard way of examining language is still the grammatical way. (*Introduction to Metaphysics*, 67–68)

This wariness with regard to the written and to grammar often shows up elsewhere in Heidegger, in prefaces where he says, for example, that "what was spoken no longer speaks in what is printed," (*Introduction to Metaphysics*, xxix) (*Einführung*), and so on. With this wariness Heidegger is more than Platonic. I said a little while ago that he was Platonic. In fact, it would

9. Martin Heidegger, *What Is Called Thinking?* trans. J. Glenn Gray (New York: Harper & Row, 1968), 48–49.

be easy to show that Plato, like all the Greeks that the Heidegger text I just quoted talks about, submits in spite of the protestations of the *Phaedrus* to the model of writing; he submits to it without realizing it and here too in the metaphorical register since he says he prefers to sensory writing, to the invention of the God Thot, the writing of the truth inscribed in the soul. True discourse is, he says at 276a, "a discourse that is written with knowledge (*hos met' epistēmēs graphetai*), in the soul of the learner"[10] (fixity of knowledge).

Now Heidegger here indeed seems to be wary of the grammatical model in general. Through this wariness (the first of the two reasons I announced, for which Heidegger would not accord any original dignity to the written form), one might believe that Heidegger ought to abstain also and especially from the idea of *hermeneutics*, which appears to be rigorously dependent on it.

But the second reason I announced will remove this objection.

(2) Writing is indeed not the irruption of something new in speech, it is not a mode of essential rupture with speech, even if it is its first degradation, because living speech, *legein*, saying, was always already a text, even if *133*
it was not an inscribed text, engraved in solid exteriority. A *text,* as its name indicates, is a *tissue*, written or not, printed or not. A tissue means a synthetic multiplicity that holds to itself, retaining itself [*se retenant elle-même*]; there is text as soon as there is phrase—that is, a synthetic and significant unity of several organized words. The *logos* is thus always a text in this sense; it links and gathers significations and retains them. (The *retaining* [*retenir*] must be thought before the distinction between soul and body on the basis of which the difference between text and logos is commonly thought.)

Retains them—what does that mean? It means first of all holds them together, gathers them (*legein*). And there would be no phrase, thus no discourse, without that. The text, here, is the tissue of the *sumplokē*, of the interweaving of nouns and verbs, that Plato says is the constitution of the logos. But *retain them* also means, *and by the same token*, retains them in a memory, in a retention that properly constitutes the condition of the text. There would be no sentence if at the end of the spoken sentence I did not retain its beginning, and the anticipation thus made necessary would not be possible without this retaining and gathering of past meaning. This essential and originary necessity of the *Trace*, of the engramme, one might say, in non-written language itself, this necessity of the trace means that speech is always already writing, always already text, that the text does not make an irruptive appearance, does not surprise speech, and thus *may possibly* also translate and

10. Plato, "Phaedrus," in *Euthyphro, Apology, Crito, Phaedo, Phaedrus*, trans. Harold North Fowler (Cambridge, MA: Harvard University Press, 1914), 567.

express it in writing properly so-called. If speech were not already text, no text could transport any speech. (The text is the union of soul and body not thought of metaphysically as suture, but originarily.)

What I am thus calling the *second reason* does not contradict the first and does not disallow the initial wariness with regard to *graphein*. It simply signifies, and this is coherent with all of Heidegger's thought, that degradation, forgetting, chatter, the moment of the text, are all essential possibilities that are always already present at the heart of speech, that inauthenticity does
134 not supervene on authenticity, does not surprise it from the outside but is its essential, permanent and necessary accomplice. It is the complicity or the duplicity that is fundamental; difference, and not virgin and mythical authenticity.

This second reason that could, then, come to ground and legitimate the hermeneutical scheme, also explains the occasional praise of the letter that one can find here and there in Heidegger, and which one might think at first blush contradicts the passages I read a moment ago. So, in the "Letter on 'Humanism,'" speaking of the chatter that threatens language on the *truth of being* and on the history of being, Heidegger, apparently contrary to what he seems to say elsewhere, sees in the return to a craftsmanship, to a patience of writing, a guard-rail against over-hasty expression. The truth of being, he says ([French] p. 109, [*Pathmarks*, 272]) would in this way be withdrawn from mere opinions and conjectures and be handed over to the craftsmanship of writing become so rare today (*rar gewordenen Hand-werk der Schrift*). Or else again, at the end of the "Letter on 'Humanism,'" appealing to the humility of the slow-footedly traced furrow, Heidegger writes:

> What is needed in the present world crisis is less philosophy, but more attentiveness in thinking; less literature, but more cultivation of the letter. (*Pathmarks*, 276)

That is why Heidegger could legitimately speak of "reading" the meaning of being in a privileged and exemplary being. I here close my remark on this word *reading* and this hermeneutical *method*.

How does Heidegger reply to the question of the exemplary being? The point is to choose the exemplary being in a way that is not metaphysical or philosophical, which implies *no presupposition of any sort.* The only thing we have the right to have at our disposal when we choose this exemplary being is the question itself: the question of being itself and its first assurance: namely,
135 language that allows the question to be spoken. The exemplary being from which we will set out will have to be determined in its exemplarity by the sole possibility of the question. The being—guiding thread and transcendental

guide of the question of being—will have to be prescribed by the question alone. This is why Heidegger determines the *Befragtes*, the *interrogated*, as a *questioning being*.

The only *presupposition* of the question is that it be *posed* and the privileged being of the question of being will be the questioning being, posing the question of being; this being determined in its relation to its being by the possibility of the questioning—and of questioning concerning being—is we *ourselves*.

> [. . .] *the* being we inquirers ourselves in each case are (des *Seienden, das wir sind, die Fragenden, je selbst sind*). Thus to work out the question of being means to make a being—one who questions—transparent [make clear (*durchsichtigmachen*), bring to light] in its being. (*Being and Time*, 6)

What Heidegger wants to avoid is letting a gap open between the meaning of being and the privileged being, between the question and the example, a split through which some presupposition or metaphysical option could slip and, by dictating the choice of example, predetermine the whole enterprise. For there to be a suturing of this split between the question and the example, which is the first beginning of the response, the example must not simply [uncertain word] be *chosen* but prescribed on the basis of some absolute *proximity*. This is where we again come across this enigmatic signification of proximity that gave us food for thought last time.

Here the proximity can appear to be *double*.

(1) On the one hand, it is the immediacy of the passage from the question to the questioner. Nothing is closer to the question than the being that is questioning. It is the question itself that is interrogated; it is in the question and in the proximity of the question to its questioning origin that the 136
questioned meaning is sought. The response will never take the form of an object coming to fill or satisfy an expectation or a desire, coming to *espouse* (the *responsa* being a promise of marriage) the hollowed-out form of the question. One must stop hoping, from the question here in question, for a response in the form of an object that one could grasp hold of and of which one could say: *voilà, eureka*, that's the formula we can write on the board. Here the question lets us expect nothing of the sort, nor expect anything in general, except its own awakening that has never ceased to wake up to itself. By choosing as exemplary the being in which the question is spoken and produced, Heidegger is thus claiming to remain as close as possible to the meaning of the question and never bury it in the slurry of the response.

(2) On the other hand, the absolute proximity we are speaking about is our proximity to ourselves. "This being, which we ourselves in each case are and

which includes inquiry among the possibilities of its being [. . .]" (*Being and Time*, 7). This is where the second assurance is taken out. This is what I will call the *Faktum* of the *we are*. The *we are* is here still totally in-determinate. We do not yet know *what* we are. The *we* does not designate any human community, any sociality determined in one sense or another. It is not yet even determined by the category of the *Mitsein* that will be discovered later. The *we are* is determined only by the proximity of the question. We are in the process of questioning and dialoguing in the question. "We are" means here: we are questioning. We are questioning, we are in the question, we are *in question*. We are in the proximity of the question. But in so doing *we are* and the *we are* is the expression of proximity of the question as proximity to ourselves. "We are" means we are close to ourselves.

Now, at the beginning of chapter 2 of the introduction to *Being and Time*,
137 §5:

> True, Dasein is ontically not only what is near or even nearest—we ourselves *are* it, each of us. Nevertheless, or precisely for this reason, it is ontologically what is farthest. (*Being and Time*, 15)

What does this mean? Literally, it means the ontic proximity of *Da-Sein* to itself, to ourselves, is ontological distancing. Comment. [Illegible marginal sentence.] This identity in a different relation of *distancing* and *proximity*, introduces us to the problem of the hermeneutic *circle*.

I would not fix on the hermeneutic circle, whose problematic accompanies what we are here calling the second assurance, if it were not to install us definitively in the heart of that historicity of the question of being that is here our theme. The hermeneutic circle could by this fact take for us the following form: I can access the meaning of Being-History only by setting off from the structures of historicity of a being determined as *Da-Sein*. But I can determine these structures only on the basis of the meaning of being and the anticipation of this meaning of being. But before the circle is determined in this way, it takes a much more general form, which would be the following.

In fact, ontically, we are absolutely close to what we are, we, questioning beings, but our point of departure can only be justified retroactively, when we will have replied to the question of the meaning of being. Or, conversely, does not claiming to begin by determining *Da-sein* in its being before knowing and in order to know what being means, lead a demand that was supposed to be absolutely radical and without presupposition into a vicious circle?

This impression could appear to be all the more justified in that the *name* Heidegger gives to the questioning being that we are is introduced in the most abrupt way, without the least show of explanation. Heidegger, who

in general is careful to guarantee patiently every one of his moves, never explains in this opening of *Sein und Zeit* the choice of the expression *Da-sein*. 138
And moreover he will never explain it as a concept but as a mysterious and enigmatic focal point, with complex inflexions, separating more and more *Da* from *Sein*, making *Da* not simply determinative of *Sein,* adjective or adverb, but a sort of noun-verb as originary as *Sein* (Being-the-there: Beaufret).

In *Sein und Zeit* this denomination intervenes like a *decree.* Several times Heidegger says this is what we shall call this exemplary being that we are: *Da-sein.* See [German] p. 7: "This being, which we ourselves in each case are and which includes inquiry among the possibilities of its being, we formulate terminologically as *Dasein*" (*Being and Time*, 7).

And Heidegger goes on without explanation. Beginning of §4: "We define this being terminologically as *Dasein*" (10).

This apparent arbitrariness hides a profound necessity even if the necessity does not absorb into itself all the arbitrariness. A necessity not to determine being-there too soon by another category. "No arbitrary idea of being and reality," says Heidegger, "no matter how 'self-evident' (*selbstverständlich*) it is, may be brought to bear on this being in a dogmatically constructed way; no 'categories' prescribed by such ideas [comment] may be forced upon Dasein without ontological deliberation" (*Being and Time*, 16). The *there* of *Da-sein* would be the only difference between an *X* and the first category of *Dasein*. And it is the only one that determines the exemplary being from the sole point of view of the question that it is the possibility of posing; namely, the question of being. In this question, being comes forth, is *there*, in the being that we are, being comes forth as such, enigmatically (i.e., as a question), it is there, without the there yet being clearly understood, without it being 139
decided whether this *there* of the being that we are is a proximity or a distancing, it being highly probable that this *Da*, which does not have any spatial sense, designates rather a movement, the transcendence that, moving from the being to the being of the being, delivers the meaning of being itself. The question is there. Being in question is there.

In any case, the initial indetermination and its apparent un-justification guarantees against any anthropologistic precipitation in the determination of being-there. It must be said that this precipitation has rarely been avoided, and it is tempting. It is what gets Heidegger accused of anthropologism by Husserl (in his annotation to *Sein und Zeit*—which is dedicated to him—but also in his *Nachwort*). It is what got *Dasein* translated by that properly catastrophic locution *human-reality*[11] and which spread its damage far beyond the

11. [Translator's note:] This is the translation originally proposed by Henry Corbin and adopted by, among others, Jean-Paul Sartre.

first true translation of Heidegger, but into *Being and Nothingness* and into the whole problematic current in the same intellectual circles after the war.

Da-sein is not man. What does that mean? It does not mean that *Da-sein* is something other than man but that one does not gain access to *Da-sein*, to the being of the being called *Da-sein*, on the basis of what one thinks one knows under the name of man, on the basis of what common sense and metaphysics have already determined as man: *animal rationale, zōon politikon*, or whatever you will.

The question of knowing what we are and what *man* means is thus held in reserve when we are talking about *Da-sein*. And when Heidegger on two or three occasions lets it be understood that for him *Da-sein* is man, he shows that the illumination of the definition goes from *Dasein* to man and not the other way around. When, for example, on [German] page 11 he writes, "this being's (the human being's) kind of being" (*Being and Time*, 10), the function of the parenthesis is both to show that on the one hand, the humanity of *Da-*
140 *sein* is bracketed for now, or on the other to say: *Da-sein* (or, if you will, what we call *man* without yet knowing what that means). When, to take another example, Heidegger writes, [German] p. 25: "Dasein , that is, the being of human being," (*Being and Time*, 24) the *that is* has two functions: on the one hand, the point is to specify in the context in which this sentence is inscribed what being-there was for Greek ontology:

> The problem of Greek ontology must, like that of any ontology, take its guideline from Dasein itself. In the ordinary and also the philosophical "definition," Dasein, that is, the being of human being, is delineated as *zōon logon echon*, that creature whose being is essentially determined by its ability to speak. (*Being and Time*, 24)

On the other hand, the *that is*, inasmuch as it carries beyond the Greek context, clearly shows the direction of the passage: even if man is another name for *Dasein*, the true meaning of this name is said only as *Dasein* and after the explication of *Dasein*. This *order* of implication, in its formal and methodological aspect, must be rigorously maintained, failing which, in practice the most serious and most undetectable flaws of reasoning are to be feared. One could become aware of this very rapidly by delving into what many pre- and post-Heideggerian philosophies are made of. Philosophical anthropology, necessary though it is, must lean on this analytic of *Dasein* and come after it if it wants to rest on a satisfactory philosophical base, as Heidegger notes on [German] p. 17 (*Being and Time*, 17).

See also the important §10, which deals with the relations between the analytic of being-there and anthropology, biology or psychology.

After having indicated what still remained non-questioned, non-criticized in the notions used by these sciences, and in particular in that of the subject (even when it is determined with Cartesian/Husserlian rigor), Heidegger
writes, 141

> Thus we are not being terminologically idiosyncratic when we avoid these terms as well as the expressions "life" and "human being" in designating the beings that we ourselves are. (*Being and Time*, 45)

What, then, of the accusation of a circle? This accusation is from the start and as a matter of principle invalidated, once one considers that it refers to a logical model, to a logic of proof and a deductive structure of reasoning that are not the ones we must follow here. They are not the ones we must follow here, not because we are going to follow an in-coherent logic that spurns every deductive path and affirms what cannot be proved. What cannot be proved, if it emerges, will not be what, "within" a logic of proof, contradicts norms, but what, prior to the deductive procedure and to logic in general, asks questions in particular about the origin of logic, of logos (i.e., about the being that makes it possible). And this interrogation is pre-deductive because it is phenomenological or apophantic. "Such 'presupposing,'" says Heidegger,

> has nothing to do with positing a principle from which a series of propositions is deduced. A "circle in reasoning" cannot possibly lie in the formulation of the question of the meaning of being, because in answering this question it is not a matter of grounding by deduction, but rather of laying bare and exhibiting the ground (*aufweisende Grund-Freilegung*). (*Being and Time*, 7)

[Perhaps that is the beginning of a response to the question you were asking the other day, Tort,[12] speaking about the "logic of proof."]

This response to the objection that there is a circle is a response of principle, a formal response to a formal objection. Now, more concretely, why 142
is there no circle in Heidegger's way of proceeding, or if there is a circle, in what way is the circularity of this circle something other than an error, and in fact the very process of hermeneutic explication? "Beings can be determined in their being without the explicit concept of the meaning of being having to be already available" (*Being and Time*, 7). The anticipation, which is not the conception, the implicit anticipation of this meaning of being, the pre-comprehension of the meaning of being, is not only sufficient for this but is necessary, as we have seen, for the question of being in general, and of

12. Michel Tort, then a student at ENS-Ulm, was attending Derrida's course.

the being of *Da-sein*, to emerge. Every *ontology* must *presuppose*, must have *presupposed*, this implicit meaning of being in order to look for an explicit concept. And this presupposition or this pre-comprehension, far from being a logical error, belongs to the very being of *Da-sein*, what makes it precisely an *ontological* being as Heidegger also says, but it is even what allows this logical question to be posed. This pre-comprehension or this pre-supposition is *precisely* what constitutes the privilege of being-there. Being-there is to have *already* begun to understand the meaning of being and thus to be able to pose the explicit question of the meaning of being. That is a clarification, at least, of the expression Being-there: in being-there, the meaning of being is already there, announces itself in the possibility of the question that concerns it explicitly.

If there is a circle, this circle is thus not the iterative sterility of "going round in circles" in a syllogism, but the very movement whereby we are already caught, surprised, drawn into the question of the meaning of being. Given this, as Heidegger says elsewhere, I forget where,[13] one must not try to break the circle but try to find out how best and precisely to enter into and move in it, to situate oneself in it and get one's bearings in it.

The circularity is historicity: that is, the gravity of an already-there that weighs down and gives its place, its center, to the question of being that has always already begun to provoke us, that surprises us not like the unforeseeable caprice of a new fashion, of a new or simply future mode [*d'une nouvelle mode, d'un mode nouveau ou simplement futur*] of posing questions, but
143 surprises us because it is not at our disposal, because it has already begun, because we cannot get around it, because we are caught in it and it has us at its disposal without subjecting us. This circle and this commencement in the pre-ontological, which is neither the non-sense of being nor the explicit concept of the meaning of being, account for this unity of the near and the far, of a *Da* which is a here and an over there, and first of all the movement that gathers them, and of what metaphysical logic can no longer think as other than contradictions. The contradictions are historicity: that is, the impossibility of a *pure* point of departure in the absolute proximity of the ontic or the ontological, the impossibility of such a point of departure and the necessity, therefore, of setting off from the *pre-ontological*; this—apparently methodological—necessity of setting off from the pre-ontological indeed refers to, and confirms, the ontico-ontological difference, the difference between being and beings as more "fundamental" (in quotation marks because it is not a fundament) than being and than beings, more fundamental than both

13. [Translator's Note:] *Being and Time*, 148.

proximity and distancing. There is proximity and distancing only through difference. Which is why, before leaving this question of the circle, I am going to translate two brief passages from *Sein und Zeit*.

First this, §5:

> The ontic-ontological priority of Dasein is therefore the reason why the specific constitution of the being of Dasein—understood in the sense of the "categorial" structure that belongs to it—remains hidden from it. Dasein is ontically "nearest" to itself, ontologically farthest away; but pre-ontologically [*onta/on*] certainly not foreign to itself. (*Being and Time*, 16)

That is the circle and that is why there is no *logical* circle.

And now here is the second passage. End of §2, [German] p. 8. 144

> "*Circular reasoning*" does not occur in the question of the meaning of being. Rather, there is a notable "*Rück oder Vorbezogenheit*," a retro- or pre-reference [pre-ference][a retrospective or anticipatory reference] of what is asked about [*Gefragten*] *(Sein)* to asking as a mode of being of a being. The way what is question*ed* essentially engages our questioning belongs to the innermost meaning of the question of being. But this only means that the being that has the *Charakter* of *Dasein* has a relation to the question of being itself, perhaps even a distinctive one. (*Being and Time*, 7–8)

I'm closing here the development concerning the second assurance: namely, the point of departure in *Da-sein*. It is time now, since we must begin with the analytic of *Da-sein*, to wonder what the historicity of *Da-sein* signifies and how it introduces us into the meaning of Being-History. Well, following the thread of this question, we are going to see reappear, in an apparently surprising way, at a certain decisive turn in our path, grounded in necessity, a connotative signification of what a moment ago I called the text or the originary texture. Texturology, as J. Dubuffet says. We are going to wait for it and see it coming, coming back.

The historicity of *Da-sein* appears as a theme in *Sein und Zeit* at only two points, of unequal importance. First of all, very rapidly and quite briefly in §6 (i.e., in the introduction). Then, taking up again systematically and at length the introductory outline, throughout the whole of chapter 5 of division 2 of *Being and Time* in its five sections—chapter 5 entitled "Temporality and Historicity." In these two series of developments, §6 of the introduction and chapter 5 of division 2 of *Being and Time*, and as is signified by the title of chapter 5 ("*Zeitlichkeit* und *Geschichtlichkeit*"), the theme of historicity is 145
grafted onto the theme of temporality. Section 5 had just taken on the theme of temporality as the transcendental horizon of the problem of being, before

§6 takes up that of the historicity of Dasein. And the third and fourth chapters of division 2 were devoted to authentic and inauthentic temporalization, before the fifth chapter takes on the relations of temporality and historicity. The problem of historicity is *grafted* onto that of temporality—that signifies, of course, that historicity is not temporality, and that the confused concept of *becoming* should not obscure their specificity, but this graft signifies above all that historicity can be thought in its root only on the basis of the movement of temporality, of an ontological interrogation into what the temporality of *Da-sein* signifies.

You know that *Sein und Zeit* does not claim to provide a complete or even definitive analytic of being-there. Relative to the *subsequent* project of a philosophical anthropology resting on an adequate philosophical base, *Sein und Zeit*, says Heidegger, presents merely a few "fragments" (*Stücke*), "even if these fragments are essential" (*Being and Time*, 17). Now the most essential "fragment" is here the explication of the meaning of the being of the being named being-there as *temporality*. The explication of being-there as temporality does not suffice to provide a response to the principal question, that of the meaning of being in general, but it is an ontological point of departure to this response. If, precisely, being-there is a pre-ontological being—that is, a being that has as its being to understand being and to be able to pose the question of being—an important step will have been taken if one shows, as Heidegger intends to show in *Sein und Zeit*, that that on the basis of which, the horizon on the basis of which being-there pre-comprehends being is what is called *time*.

It follows that the very project of *Sein und Zeit* takes the following form: originary explication of time as the horizon of the understanding of being, an explication that sets off from temporality as the being of the being that understands being.

For this explication to be originary supposes in particular that the concepts
146 of time as they are inherited from metaphysics, from Aristotle to Bergson via Kant and Hegel, must be reduced or destroyed. This is what, directly or indirectly, through historical references or through descriptions, the first part of *Sein und Zeit*, the only one published, tries to do. For reasons of economy and by reason of our initial choice, we are going to have to operate an *abstraction*; our attention is going to have to extract from *Sein und Zeit* this theme of history that I said was *grafted*. Naturally the image of the graft would be very infelicitous if it made you think of an implantation or an importation, of the domestication of a foreign concept. By graft, we here must think of a secondary branch that has grown with a relative autonomy and that we are here obliged to consider a little to the side. But we shall see how the graft necessarily sends us back to the root.

The root is the condition of possibility. The being of *Dasein* has its meaning in temporality. Temporality is, I quote §6, "the condition of the possibility of historicity as a temporal mode of being of Dasein itself" (*Being and Time*, 19) (temporal mode of being: *zeitliche Seinsart*). That means historicity is a mode, a certain mode of temporality, which explains in particular that this mode is modified, modalized according to structures that are those of temporality itself, in particular that the significations of authenticity and inauthenticity will be found again in it.

And then, here is the first gesture that appears necessary when one wants to gain access to the originary historicity of *Da-sein*.

This gesture is one of re-duction or re-gression: reduction or regression to a point earlier than two *histories*, than two significations of the concept of history that are too often considered as primary and foundational, whereas they are derivative and ought to refer to the historicity of *Da-sein* as their condition of possibility.

(1) These are, first, *universal history*, the history of the world (*Weltgeschichte*). One can speak of a history of the world only if one already knows what history and world mean and on what conditions a history and a world 147
are possible and can appear. Now one of the essential features of the most important analyses of *Sein und Zeit* (chapter 3 <of division 1>) is to show what world means, what the being of world is, the worldhood of the world which is constituted in *Da-sein*'s relation to being-in-the-world. I cannot get into those important analyses here. I simply point out that on the pretext of describing historicity, one is describing the history of the world, the history of the universal totality of the events of the world, one is already presupposing knowledge of what totality and world and the being-world of the world mean. This presupposition is never criticized by universal histories or philosophies of history that claim to say the whole of what is happening in the world before even having asked questions about world-being (Hegel?). Now this question about *Weltlichkeit* can be developed only on the basis of an analytic of *Da-sein* guided by the question of being. Now this analytic of *Da-sein* shows that the world *is* not, that it is not a container or a total content but that it worlds (*weltet*) on the basis of the transcendence and freedom of *Da-sein* in its power of projecting itself toward the whole, of anticipating beyond the totality of beings, therefore toward the Nothing; this movement of anticipation being linked to the very movement of temporalization. You can find this linking in *Sein und Zeit* as well as in *Vom Wesen des Grundes* (1929), an essay translated by Corbin and collected in *Qu'est-ce que la métaphysique?* [in English in *Pathmarks*].

(2) The historicity of *Dasein* is also prior to history in the sense of historical *science*. It is pointless to go to the historian *qua* historian and ask him

what historicity is. The historian is the scholar who is already dealing with a delimited scientific field that is, precisely, called historical reality, *Historie* as a field that is *Geschichte*, and the historian has an object he deals with and that he calls the historical object. But as to the origin and the conditions of possibility of this field of objectivity, the historian *qua* historian, in his historical practice, can tell us nothing. But that does not mean that it is enough [illegible interlinear addition] to take a simple reflective and critical step back, a transcendental regression in the classical sense toward the con-
148 ditions of historical objectivity in order to discover this origin of historicity toward which Heidegger is trying to bring us back. Indeed, Heidegger is not here following everything one could call the critiques of historical Reason, such as flourished in Germany before and around Heidegger, in Dilthey (Dilthey is an author as present in the wings of *Sein und Zeit* as Husserl), in Simmel, in Rickert, critiques of historical Reason that wanted, as it were, in neo-Kantian style, to reawaken the question, On what conditions is historical science possible? Reawaken it in a *neo*-Kantian style—that is, not by asking in the scientifically dispiriting form that is Kant's in the *Conflict of the Faculties*: "But how is it possible to have a history *a priori*? The answer is that it is possible if the prophet himself occasions and *produces* the events that he predicts."[14] But in a more fruitful form, one more in tune with all the progress and historical optimism of the nineteenth century: On what conditions have historical knowledge and objectivity been possible, with people like Dilthey, Rickert, Simmel, and so forth, being or believing themselves to be with respect to historical science in the situation of Kant with respect to physico-mathematical science?

But these questions, which are of the order of historical epistemology, and which are marked by the stepping back of a theory of historical knowledge, leave us as helpless as is the historian before the question of historicity itself. For these questions, *qua* epistemological questions, are guided by the idea of science and of scientific object. They emerge when the historical can begin to be thematized by science. One could say, to take up the Husserlian schema used in *Formal and Transcendental Logic* and that seems to me to function here in a perfectly *analogous* way: history and the epistemology of history deal with the objective thematic face of science but they do not think to go
149 definitively searching for the pre-scientific origin of science. In the same way, to take up again another analogous schema: just as Husserl wants to redo a transcendental aesthetic that does not let itself be guided by already

14. Immanuel Kant, "The Contest of Faculties," in *Political Writings*, ed. H. Reiss, trans. B. Nisbet (Cambridge: Cambridge University Press, 2003), 177.

constituted science, by geometry and mechanics, as was the case with Kant, but to come back to the space and the prospective time of perception, in the same way, Heidegger wants to get back before the question of historical objectivity that would already give itself the historical object and that predetermines the historical as object. On [German] page 375, §72 (*Being and Time*, 358), he plays on the difference between *Objekt* and *Gegenstand* in order to sketch the interval that separates his questions from those of history and epistemology. These latter, in their *Fragestellung*, concern themselves only with the *Objekt qua* accessible to a science, *qua* theme (and like Husserl, Heidegger says "theme" here, object of an absolutely scientific theme). But in dealing with the *Objekt*, they do not ask themselves how history can at a certain moment—for it is not so from the outset and always—become what stands opposite, the *Gegenstand*, the objective thematic face of science. They cannot ask themselves this, and they cannot reply to it, for the response can only come from the side of a pre-scientific, pre-epistemological analytic of the historical and of historicity and of its rootedness in temporality. There is in the structure of historicity something that allows it at a certain moment to become a scientific *object* and one must descend below the scientific project to know this.

We have just distinguished two levels of superficiality or rather of derivation with regard to what is in question for Heidegger. The level of *Weltgeschichte or of the philosophy of history* and the level of *historical science* which itself was differentiated into the scientific activity of the historian and the critical reflection of the epistemologist. Let's note that the level of *Weltgeschichte* and the philosophy of history is that of the greatest naïveté since they both rely or at least claim to rely on a *historical truth* delivered by science. They are both certain that something like *historical truth* is possible, that an opening that gives us access to the historical past is possible, whatever the critical work one then proceeds to carry out on documents, signs, monu- 150
ments, archives, and so on. The critical work presupposes the very thing it is trying to protect: namely, the possibility of historical truth. What is being aimed at here is the type of construction or reconstruction of the historical world carried out by Dilthey. Using the very words of the title of a book by Dilthey, Heidegger writes that thematization—that is, historical unveiling, unveiling by historical science (*die historische Erschliessung*) of history (*Geschichte*)—is the presupposition of any possible "*Aufbau der geschichtlichen Welt in den Geisteswissenschaften*"[15] (*Being and Time*, 359).

15. Heidegger is alluding to Dilthey's *Der Aufbau der geschichtlichen Welt in die Geisteswissenschaften* (Frankfurt: Suhrkamp, 1970), first published in *Abhandlungen der*

We shall have to encounter again, in the proper place of its derivation, the problem of objectivity and of historical science, which, besides many remarks here and there, is treated for its own sake in §76 of *Sein und Zeit*. For the moment, we have to come back to the historicity of *Da-sein* as a structure grounded in temporality as the meaning of the being of *Da-sein*. We shall follow a few indications from §6 and the analyses of the whole of chapter 5 <of division 2>.

Historicity as the constitution of the being of *Da-sein* is what Heidegger calls *Geschehen*. Here we are going to have some difficult translation problems. In the Gallimard edition,[16] Corbin sometimes translates it as *historial*, sometimes, as do Boehm-de Waelhens, as *accomplissement*; these two translations are equally unsatisfactory, but one must admit that it is very difficult to replace them. We shall not translate it and we shall try to clarify it, to translate it by analysis and not by definition, by analysis and by the play of its functioning in Heidegger's discourse, and by the system of significations associated with it: *Geschichte* and *Geschick* (Fate). The *Geschehen* is the originary movement, the emergence of what is subsequently called *history, Geschichte*. It is the supervening, advening, to-coming [*à-venir*], all these words being dangerous insofar as they run the risk of being contaminated
151 by the notions of event or advent that are *in* history. The most neutral but not the least ridiculous would be *historying* [*historier*], which would have the advantage of keeping the verbal form and consequently the synthetic operation that is produced in the *Geschehen* which is precisely a *gathering* (*Ge-*), a sketch of a totalization that has its possibility in the synthesis of temporalization, precisely. [Illegible interlinear sentence.] The *Geschehen* as structure of *Da-sein* is recognized by the following *fact*: "In its factical being Dasein always is how and 'what' it already was" (*Being and Time*, 19). This formula of Heidegger's, "*Das Dasein ist je in seinem faktischen Sein, wie und 'was' es schon war*" (*Being and Time*, 19), this formula, which the translators are right to suggest is trying to allude to the enigmatic past that inhabits Aristotle's definition of quiddity (*to ti ēn einai*), needs to be understood prudently. This presence of the *past* in the present being, in the *ist* of *Dasein*, obliges us to shake the naïve confidence we have in our language when we say "I was," "he was," when we put a verb referring to *Dasein* into the past tense. Unless

Preussichen Akademie der Wissenchaften. Philosophisch- Historische Klasse, Jg. 1910, pp. 1–123 [translated as *The Formation of the Historical World in the Human Sciences*, trans. Rudolf A. Makkreel and Jon Scanlon, in *Selected Works*, vol. 3, ed. Rudolf A. Makkreel and Frithjof Rodi (Princeton, NJ: Princeton University Press, 2002).]

16. [Translator's note:] See above, p. 77, n. 2.

we re-comprehend what *past* means in this case, we would be closing off for ourselves the possibility of history itself. Obviously, here too, it is not grammar that can teach us what the past of the verb *be* is.

So what is meant by the sentence that says, "Being-there *is* what it was, it is its past, *seine Vergangenheit*" *(Being and Time*, 19)?

Naturally, any category coming from the world of nature and of *vorhanden* or spatial objects would miss the meaning of being-past as the being of *Da-sein. Dasein* is its past: that means that its past is not passed by [*dépassé*], that it is not *behind* it like another place or another force that would still have causal efficacy and would maintain an influence on the present. The past does not follow the present like a ball and chain dragged along by *Dasein*'s ankle. *Dasein* is intrinsically its past: the *ist* is intrinsically constituted by *Vergangenheit*, without which *Da-sein* would not be essentially historical (formal I think). The past does not follow, that means that in every *Geschehen* that "historizes" by projecting into the to-come—and there is history 152
only through this exiting of the past, of ek-stasis toward the to-come—every *Geschehen* opening the future is already not followed but pre-ceded by the past that my being is. The *Pre-ceded*. Comment.

There is here an irreducible elementary structural nucleus within which the movement of the *Geschehen* appears to be isomorphic with the movement of temporality. Irreducible nucleus because if one undid its synthesis, *Zusammenhang*, tissue (Text, texture, fundamental phrases) one would lose all chance of understanding history other than as an empirical accident foreign to the movement of truth (Kant and time).

Of course, it belongs essentially to this elementary structure not only to be indefeasible but—and because it is always already operative—to be able to pass unnoticed, as it does not only in everyday life and the vulgar conception of history but even in some philosophies of history or some philosophical conceptions of historicity.

What does this mean and what can one be thinking in saying this? Before giving examples—which Heidegger does not give—I am first going to translate two sub-paragraphs of §6.

> This elemental historicity of Dasein can remain concealed from it. But it can also be discovered in a certain way and be properly cultivated. Dasein can discover, preserve, and explicitly pursue tradition. The discovery of tradition, and the disclosure of what it "transmits" and how it does this, can be undertaken as a task in its own right. Dasein thus assumes the mode of being that involves historical inquiry and research (*historischen Fragens und Forschens*). But the discipline of history [historical science, *Historie*]—more precisely, the historicity underlying it (*Historizität*)—is possible only as the

> kind of being belonging to inquiring Dasein, because Dasein is determined by historicity (*Geschichtlichkeit*) in the ground of its being. [So *Historizität* is only possible as scientific research undertaken by Dasein because Dasein
> 153 is determined by *Geschichtlichkeit*. Comment.] If historicity (*Geschichtlichkeit*) remains concealed from Dasein, and so long as it does so, the possibility of historical (*historisch*) inquiry and discovery of history is denied it. If the discipline of history (*Historie*) is lacking, that is no evidence *against* the historicity of Dasein; rather it is evidence for this constitution of being in a deficient mode. [A passage very badly translated in the Gallimard edition.] Only because it is *geschichtlich* in the first place can an age be *un-historisch*. (*Being and Time*, 19–20)

Paraphrasing, one could say that engaging in historical science and not engaging in historical science, posing historical questions and not posing historical questions, being aware of the tradition as such and not being aware of it, [three illegible words] *historisch* or not, supposes in both cases historicity (*Geschichtlichkeit*); these two behaviors are both modes of *Geschichtlichkeit*, the one as much as the other deficient and inauthentic. This is the claim I would like to comment on more patiently, but before coming back to it, I am going to translate the next few lines that link this claim to the question of the meaning of being.

> On the other hand, if Dasein has seized upon its inherent possibility not only of making its *Existenz* transparent, but also of inquiring into the meaning of existentiality itself, that is to say, of provisionally inquiring into the meaning of being in general; and if insight into the essential historicity of Dasein has opened up in such inquiry, then it is inevitable (*unvergänglich*) that inquiry into being [questioning toward being: *Das Fragen nach dem Sein*], which was designated with regard to its ontic-ontological necessity, is itself characterized by historicity. The elaboration of the question of being must therefore receive its directive [*die Anweisung vernehmen*] to inquire into its
> 154 own history (*seiner eigenen Geschichte nachzufragen*) from the most proper ontological sense of the inquiry itself, as a historical one (historisch) [. . .]. (*Being and Time*, 20)

Here the Gallimard translation has taken no account of the very calculated use of these two words, and it is more free and approximate than ever. So I'll paraphrase: The very meaning of the question of being demands interrogation of its *Geschichte* (i.e., the becoming *historisch*). I continue my translation:

> [. . .] that means to become historical in a disciplined way in order to come to the positive appropriation of the past, to come into full possession [*Aneignung*] of its most proper possibilities of inquiry. The question of the meaning

> of being is led to understand itself as historical [*historische*] in accordance with its own way of proceeding, that is, as the provisional explication of Dasein in its temporality and historicity. (*Being and Time*, 20)

I now return, then, as I said I would a moment ago, to this problem of the absence of historical science or consciousness as a proof, not against, but of historicity, and as a deficient mode of historicity rather than a mode of non-historicity. This claim is laden with consequences and in conclusion today I would like to emphasize how original it is by beginning to confront it with claims by Hegel and Husserl that are close, but radically different once one pays attention.

Hegel first. I shall begin by proposing a very general point of comparison. Both of them, Hegel and Heidegger, insisted on the fact that historical science (*Historie*) presupposes, that historical truth *presupposes Geschichtlichkeit*. I have just said *presupposes* and already a difference is showing up between Hegel and Heidegger. For Heidegger the possibility of *Historie* presupposes the possibility of *Geschichtlichkeit*, but, as we saw, non-history, the absence of historical consciousness, presupposes it no less; it is simply an inferior or 155
deficient mode of it. For Hegel, though, the possibility of history (*Historizität*) does not presuppose but *merges with Geschichtlichkeit*, in such a way that the absence of historical consciousness or of historical science is the absence of *Geschichtlichkeit* pure and simple. Non-historicity as *Un-historizität* is for Hegel non-historicity as *Geschichtslosigkeit*. The difference is important and we are going to see how and why.

Let's start by putting two passages side by side: the one, very well known, by Hegel, and the other, less well known, by Heidegger. They seem to mean the same thing. Before reading them, I recall that the word *history*, in its Greco-Latin root, goes back to *historia*, which comes from *historein*, which means to inquire, to inform oneself, to learn. And this is one of the branches of an etymological tree whose root nourished another branch which is *episteme* (science). So the word *history* was first determined on the basis of the idea of historical science and not of historical experience. Only later was the *content* of the narrative called history, the content that could be the object of a historical narrative. And these two significations are bound together in the word *history* that designates both event and narrative at once. So the Greco-Latin concept pulls toward science, pulls toward *Historizität* a signification that should not be reduced to it. It determines history on the basis of historical science, whereas, according to Hegel, they are inseparable and have no privilege of originarity, are not derived one from the other, while according to Heidegger it is historical science that is derived, that presupposes

in its possibility a history that is not yet science. In other words, the Greco-Latin concept of *historia either* (according to Hegel) illegitimately privileges one of the two co-originary significations, *or else* (according to Heidegger) inverts the true relations and makes the *derivative originary*. This operation is not only a linguistic accident, it harbors a fundamental metaphysical operation and an operation that is, precisely, historico-metaphysical. The privilege accorded to historical science in the determination of history is itself a historical adventure that has a historical meaning, which is none other than
156 the *philosophical or metaphysical* conception of history: that is, a scientific conception, philosophy thinking itself from the start with Plato as *episteme*.

Now the Germanic notion of *Geschichte* escapes of itself from this scientifico-philosophico-metaphysical determination of history; it escapes from the *historical* determination of history. "Escape the historical determination of history" can be heard two ways because "historical determination" means two things. (*A*) It means a determination that took place historically: it is a feature of the history of thought that history was determined as it was on the basis of Greek philosophy. (*B*) It also means that this determination remains historical (in the sense of *historisch* as opposed to *geschichtlich*), and then the content of the determination is historical science. Of course the history of this historical determination escapes historical science as such; it is deeper and older than that science.

The German notion of *Geschichte* has *come* to designate history as science, has come to function as synonymous with the Greco-Latin term *history-historia*. But originarily, it designates not the narrative but the *gathering of what befalls*, of what is dispensed as a present and as a destining. Which means that the notion of *Geschichte* as such unites the two significations without *a priori* privileging the one or the other.

And by the same token it brings out the essential and necessary, in no way fortuitous, character of the unity of the two senses of the word *history*. Hegel and Heidegger both are conscious of this and before coming back to the difference I just announced, I will read, then, the two passages that echo each other.

Hegel: This is in the *Lectures on the Philosophy of World History*, in the introduction, [French] p. 62 in the Gibelin translation:

> In our language the word "history" (*Geschichte*) combines both objective and subjective aspects and signifies the *historia rerum gestarum* as well as the *res gestae* themselves, the historical narrative (*Geschichtserzählung*) as well as the events (*Geschehene*), deeds, and happenings themselves—aspects that in the strict sense are quite distinct. This conjunction of the two meanings

> should be recognized as of a higher order than that of external contingency: we must assume that historical narrative appears simultaneously with the actual deeds and events of history, that they are set in motion together from 157
> an inner common foundation.[17]

Heidegger (beginning of §73 of *Sein und Zeit*, not translated):[18]

> The most obvious ambiguity (*Zweideutigkeit*) of the term *Geschichte* has often been noted and it is by no means "vague." It makes itself known in the fact that it means "historical effectivity" (*geschichtliche Wirklichkeit*) as well as the possibility of a science of it. (*Being and Time*, 360)

Having brought the two texts together, let's come back to Hegel's and let's see what it means and how the intention animating it is different from Heidegger's. Knowing how it is different means knowing how the non-fortuitousness, the essential necessity that is hiding behind this linguistic phenomenon, is thought differently by Hegel and Heidegger. Neither of them thinks it is a linguistic accident and Heidegger would no doubt even subscribe to a remark of Hegel's, delighted, not about the term *Geschichte*, but *Aufheben* that unites in itself two contradictory significations (to suppress and to conserve), delighted then that the German language should have the privilege of this properly untranslatable—because contradictory—concept, and should thus be a language that is immediately speculative (in the Hegelian sense of this word).

For Hegel, this word *Geschichte* is not a linguistic accident, because historical effectivity appears at the same time as the possibility of narrative, and therefore of historical science. *Historizität* is not only one mode, a later and important modification of *Geschichtlichkeit*, it is contemporary and consubstantial with it. Living historically is possible only if one has language and if one has consciousness and if consequently one can gather—sum up—one's
experience. Memory, in the profound and productive sense that Hegel gives 158
to this word, is spirit itself, *Mnemosyne* and *Geist*: that is, the power to gather oneself, to inherit from oneself. This power of gathering and summation and re-citing [*ré-cit*] is the ground common to historical experience and historical science. An individual, a consciousness or a people are historical (*geschichtlich*) from the moment they are in a position to form the project of the narrative of their experience, once their experience is in a position to recite

17. Hegel, *Lectures on the Philosophy of World History*, vol. 1, trans. and ed. Robert Brown and Peter Hodgson (Oxford: Oxford University Press, 2011), 115.

18. [Translator's note:] Derrida is referring to the fact that no French translation of division two of *Sein und Zeit* had appeared at the time of this course.

itself, to produce signs of itself (and in the *Encyclopedia* Hegel explains that *Mnemosyne*, memory, is the producer of the sign) and thus to produce signs, works, to produce itself in works—that is, in an objective *a priori* without which there would be neither *Geschichte* nor *Historie*. Which implies by the same token that there is no strictly individual history but only at the level of the people constituted as a state (i.e., a reasonable, rational and concrete institution), the individual being abstract. Which also confirms what Hegel says in the *Phenomenology*—namely, that animal *life* has no history even if the species evolves: the evolution of the species, incapable of summing itself up, of keeping the thematic memory of its becoming and its progress, is not historical. Only spirit and Reason have a history, only the state has a history and the individual separated from the state has the same status as the animal. The notions of history, spirit and culture, or of politics, and of objective morality (*Sittlichkeit*) rigorously entail one another. As a consequence, a people that does not constitute itself *thematically* and *expressly* as a rational State that is a guardian of institutions and of historical patrimony, a people that does not have the politics of its historical science—such a people has no history, is not *geschichtlich*. You see the Heideggerian difference dawning. Such a people for Hegel is not living in a deficient mode of *Geschichtlichkeit*: it is not *geschichtlich* at all. Its culture is not a culture; it is animal and it is nature.

In order to show this and make it more specific, I shall rely once more on the introduction to the *Lectures on the Philosophy of World History* (pp. 62–63
159 of the French translation). First point: the origin of history as origin of the state. "Family memorials and patriarchal traditions are of interest within the family or tribe. Their repetitiveness is no object worthy of memory" (115). Here, no memory at all, since on the one hand the course is uniform (i.e., repetitive, quantitative), and on the other hand, no project arises to carry through to rational universality, in the eyes of the world, the testimony of this becoming. Memories are still habits—that is, animal sedimentations not thinking themselves as such.

Hegel continues:

> [. . .] although distinct deeds or turns of fate may inspire Mnemosyne to retain those images, just as love and religious feeling impel the fanciful imagination to confer shape upon such initially shapeless urges. But it is the state that first supplies a content that not only lends itself to the prose of history but also helps to produce it. (115)

This means that the State furnishes a material that is already universal and objective in its signification and to this extent already able to nourish the universal form of narrative and historical science.

Not only is the State able to gather up signs in monuments, libraries, depositories, not only does it organize rationally the circulation of signs and historical works, but it produces these signs and signs able to circulate in a fashion that is rational, transparent and universal and univocal (general will). I continue:

> Instead of the merely subjective dictates of the ruler, which may suffice for the needs of the moment, a community in the process of coalescing and raising itself up to the position of a state requires commandments and laws, general and universally valid directives. It thereby creates a *discourse* [of 160
> its own development], and an *interest* in intelligible, inwardly determinate, and—in their results—enduring deeds and events, ones on which Mnemosyne, for the benefit of the perennial aim that underlies the present configuration and constitution of the state, is impelled to confer a lasting memory. (115–116 [Derrida's italics: the phrase in brackets is an interpolation by the English translator])

So the state is the origin of both historical reality and the historical account. Only the state is the origin of complete history. This is why, reciprocally, there is no state without history. A State cannot do without its own history, the consciousness of its own past. It is incomplete in itself without that. Whereas pre-State experiences (love, religion, etc.) are complete in themselves without needing the consciousness of their own past. They are actual in themselves, whereas the actuality of the State is incomplete without the consciousness of the past.

> All deeper feelings such as love, as well as religious intuition and its forms, are wholly present and satisfying in themselves; but the external existence of the state, with its rational laws and customs, is an incomplete present, the understanding of which calls for incorporating the awareness of its past [history]. (116)

So much for the State as origin of historicity in general.

Now (2) peoples without a state, cultures without a state are not living in a deficient historicity but in a non-historicity. This is no more than the converse of what we have just been saying, but Hegel illustrates it with an odd and curious example that is worth our pausing over a little, if only as a contribution to the still burning question of societies said to be without history, which are often assimilated without further ado to people said to be without writing. The example that illustrates Hegel's intention here is the difference 161
between China and India. I quote (it is what follows in Hegel's text).

Read [French] pp. 63–64, and comment.

> *It is obvious to anyone who begins to be familiar with the treasures of Indian literature that this country, so rich in spiritual achievements of a truly profound quality, nevertheless has no history. In this respect, it at once stands out in stark contrast to China, an empire that possesses a most remarkable and detailed historical narrative going back to the earliest times. India has not only ancient religious books and splendid works of poetry but also ancient books of law, something already mentioned as a prerequisite for the formation of history, and yet it has no history. But in this country the original organization that created social distinctions immediately became set in stone as natural determinations (the castes), so that, although the laws concern the civil code of rights, they make these rights dependent on distinctions imposed by nature, and they specify, above all, the position (in terms of injustices more than of rights) of these classes toward one another, i.e., only of the higher vis-à-vis the lower. The ethical element (*Sittlichkeit*) is thereby excluded from the splendor of Indian life and its realms.
>
> Given this bondage to an order based firmly and permanently on nature, all social relations involve a wild arbitrariness, ephemeral impulses, or rather frenzies, without any purposeful progress and development. Thus, no thoughtful memory, no object for Mnemosyne presents itself, and a deep but desolate fantasy drifts over a region that ought to have had a fixed purpose—a purpose rooted in actuality and in subjective yet substantial (i.e., implicitly rational) freedom [. . .]* (Hegel, 116–17).

Of course this petrification and this naturalization of spirit or historicity is not an accidental phenomenon that has happened here or there, at one moment or another (in India for example). This is the threat that lies in wait for every community, people or nation, in the form of de-politicization or the natural or biological or organicist or even technicist conception of the political.

162 Next time we shall be concerned with an analogous but already different intention in Husserl, concerning the origin of historicity and peoples said to be without history. Then we shall see how Heidegger breaks with this Hegelian-Husserlian metaphysics of history, this spiritualist metaphysics, this metaphysics of *Geist* too rapidly determining history on the basis of the possibility of knowledge and self-knowledge, of science and consciousness, and allowing itself to be dictated to by the categorial difference between nature and culture behind which Heidegger intends to go back, interrogating the historicity of a *Da-sein* that is not yet determined either as spirit, or as subject, or as consciousness, but as temporality, this temporality being for now the only transcendental horizon prescribed for the question of being from which we must not let ourselves be distracted.

SESSION FIVE

25 January 1965

Let me remind you that at the end of the last session we were getting ready to consider from the point of view of the origin of historicity and from the point of view of peoples said to be without history, from the point of view of a hypothetical zero degree of historicity, a Husserlian intention that I said was analogous to that of Hegel, such as we identified it especially on the basis of the introduction to the *Lectures on the Philosophy of World History*. An analogous intention—that is, a different one within one and the same system of relations, within one and the same structure. This confrontation, I was saying, had to give a place, give place to a certain "destructive" rupture by Heidegger, a rupture with the Hegelian-Husserlian metaphysics of history, a spiritualist metaphysics, a metaphysics of *Geist* and *Ratio* determining historicity still too rapidly on the basis of knowledge and self-knowledge, of science and consciousness, letting itself be dictated to by the categorial difference, held to be originary and irreducible, between nature and culture. That difference has, however, supervened as an event in metaphysics, and Heidegger intends to go back behind it when he interrogates the historicity of *Dasein* at a depth of originality at which it has not yet been determined as spirit or reason, subject or consciousness (nor conversely, which comes to the same thing—although these notions have meaning only through their properly metaphysical differences and oppositions—body or affect, object or unconscious). But as temporality, this temporality being in *Sein und Zeit*, as we saw, the only transcendental horizon prescribed to the *question of being*.

Before speaking—very rapidly, as I have just been doing, for the *164*
Hegeliano-Husserlian metaphysics of history—it is necessary to recall that in Husserl's mind, every time phenomenology encounters history and makes it a theme, it is not a matter of metaphysics and *a fortiori* not Hegelian metaphysics. Of course, Husserl intends to break with all metaphysics—"We are

the true positivists"! . . . . [1] He intends that phenomenology be at least the delaying reduction of metaphysics. Metaphysics, every metaphysical proposition, will be deferred until phenomenology has accorded it its rights. This reduction of metaphysics—on which I do not wish to dwell here—takes aim especially at Hegel. Hegelianism is for Husserl—who did not know Hegelianism well, it has to be said, but that is nothing original—the very type of speculative thought, of dialectics running wild as it breaks with the description of experience and of the things themselves, right from the *Phenomenology of Spirit* itself. The reduction of metaphysics by phenomenology takes aim especially at Hegel and still more especially at Hegel's metaphysics of history. For him, Hegel is responsible for that awakening of dogmatic metaphysical idealism that covered with its heavy and powerful systems the Kantian transcendental question: dogmatic re-slumber. And what he reproaches him with more specifically is a sort of historicism. By tying the movement of truth to the historical figures of spirit, he supposedly reduced truth-value to a *Weltanschauung*, an expression indeed used by Hegel to designate the figures of spirit in the phenomenology, and taken up in the sense with which you are familiar by Dilthey, precisely. When Husserl criticizes the historicism or the relativism of Dilthey in *Philosophy as Rigorous Science*, he reproaches him precisely with not knowing the meaning of truth, the meaning of truth-value which properly, which intrinsically implies a claim to an infinite and unconditioned universality, with no grounding link to
165 a place or a time.[2] Philosophy as rigorous science belongs to a moment in Husserl's itinerary when the point is above all to show the independence of truth-value, of normativity, with respect to any empirically determined moment in history, even if that means later making explicit the original and non-empirical historicity of truth. Now, in Husserl's view, if Hegel manages to avoid at least the appearance of relativism, this is thanks to a metaphysical speculation that comes in alongside the empirical description and that, instead of describing the things themselves, supposedly involves an act

1. [Translator's note:] This is a quotation from Edmund Husserl, *Ideas Pertaining to a Pure Phenomenology, First Book (General Introduction to a Pure Phenomenology)*, trans. F. Kersten (The Hague: Martinus Nijhoff, 1983), 39.

2. At this point in the manuscript there is a large blank space with the following words written in the middle of the page: "here see Cerisy text." This is perhaps a reference to the essay "'Genesis and Structure' and Phenomenology," delivered as a conference paper at Cerisy-la-Salle in 1959 and published in the volume *Genèse et structure*, edited by de Gandillac, Goldmann, and Piaget (Paris: Mouton, 1964), subsequently appearing as an essay in J. Derrida, *L'écriture et la différence* (Paris: Le Seuil, 1967), 238. [*Writing and Difference*, 154.]

of faith within the teleology of Reason and Spirit which allows for the recognition of universal truth marching toward itself in the labor of history. But precisely when faith in this metaphysics of history was lost, after Hegel, by all the post-Hegelians, all that remained was the historicism that was the very nucleus of Hegelianism.

So it is—of course—out of the question to make Husserl purely and simply an inheritor of the Hegelian metaphysics of history.

Nevertheless, when around the time of the *Krisis* historicity becomes a theme for phenomenology, the teleology of Reason reappears and with it some very Hegelian accents. I do not want to go here into the heart of this problem, and repeat everything that has been said about the *Krisis* and about history in Husserl. I would simply like, as I have done for Hegel, to broach the problem of historical science and of people said to be without history, always placing as an epigraph to these considerations the sentence from Heidegger that I read last time, asserting that the absence of *Historie* (of historical science or consciousness), far from proving the absence of *Geschichtlichkeit*, is but a mode—a deficient mode, to be sure—of the *Geschichtlichkeit* of *Dasein*.

In the *Krisis*, as you know, Husserl begins by asserting that the peoples
and civilizations in which the idea of science or philosophy has not emerged *166*
have only an empirical historicity. Why empirical historicity? And what does that mean? It means that so long as the idea of science as idea of an infinite tradition, of an infinite opening of the horizon in the acquisition and transmission of truth (i.e., universal validity)—so long as this Idea or this task has not emerged, a community cannot think of itself as historical. It cannot think of itself as historical because it does not form the project of a tradition, of a pure, univocal, transparent transmission, as ideally speaking a scientific transmission must be. There is no pure historicity without consciousness of that pure historicity—that is, without the conscious ideal of this pure traditionality which can be nothing other than the traditionality of truth, since truth in its being-meaning [*sens d'être*] implies unconditional and infinite universality. Now, so long as a society is not inhabited by this project—a project that has determined the Greco-European *eidos*—it is merely an empirical aggregate. This is what Husserl says of China and India, for example. It is merely an empirical aggregate because it does not think its unity on the basis of the idea of a universal project and on the basis of a pure (i.e., infinite) historicity. It still thinks its unity as an accidental, fortuitous, natural unity (remember the passage from Hegel I read last time), a geographical, political, social unity, and so on. Naturally all the peoples touched by the European idea of science and philosophy are *also* finite empirical unities, but their spiritual essence has been marked in its interiority by the idea of science as

infinite task, and Europe thinks itself in the horizon of a historicity without limit, in the ideal of a pure historicity and traditionality. Conversely, once this idea of the infinite task—which is not European in the empirical sense but which is universal—is opened to so-called non-European peoples, they gain access to this ideal of pure historicity.

The *empirical historicity* I have just been talking about is also designated by Husserl, notably in a letter to Lévy-Bruhl (1935) as *non-historicity* (*Geschichtslosigkeit*). In it, he speaks of so-called primitive societies with which ethnology
167 was then concerned. *Non-historicity* meant here: finite historicity, made finite by *closed off horizons*, says Husserl.

In other words, and this is the first point I wanted to emphasize here, the possibility of historicity (*Geschichtlichkeit*) depends on the possibility of science or philosophy [three illegible interlinear words], and these latter are themselves possible only if the idea of the infinite has appeared, the idea of the infinite as indefinite opening. There is no pure historicity before Reason and the ideal possibility of the infinite transmissibility of meaning. There is no pure historicity; that means that there is no properly historical (*geschichtlich*) becoming and no properly historical (*historisch*) object for a science of history.

[Cf. Hegel but culture more than nature]

In other words, reason and the infinite are here on the side of history. As in Hegel and, it would seem, against the great pre-Hegelian metaphysics, for which there was no historicity other than empirical and for which the movement of truth, if there were one, was anything but historical. So that, be it said in passing, if, against these great rationalisms and great infinitisms of the *historicity of meaning* that Hegel and Husserl still are, one wished to re-affirm the finitude of meaning in order to free oneself from the theologico-metaphysical horizon that still remains that of Hegel and Husserl, one would, very curiously, have to reinstate, at a certain level and in a certain sense, a certain foundational a-historicity of meaning. I say "very curiously" because one might seem thus to be going back to a-historicisms of a classical type—those of the seventeenth century—at the very moment one was supposedly shaking in this way the very foundation of metaphysics. The ahistoricity in question, then, would then no longer be an eternal theological foundation, but a certain silent permanence of non-meaning, or rather an absence of meaning that precedes the opposition between meaning and non-meaning, an origin of meaning and history that would precede any alternative between Reason and unreason, between a truth and an untruth, and without which these alternatives could not emerge, no more than could
168 any historicity. I close this parenthesis here. Perhaps we will need to reopen it on another occasion.

It is not necessary to dwell for long on Husserl's teleology to perceive its Hegelian resonance. This resonance would appear still more clearly if one were to note that, like Hegel and like Heidegger later, Husserl refuses (1) historicism—that is, the reduction of meaning and truth to their empirical becoming—<and> (2) the historian any privilege in determining the meaning of historicity and the origin of the historical truth about which he is speaking. I do not want to get too close to Hegel here—these are texts we'll be commenting on in the second-semester seminar on Hegel.[3] But I shall show how these two gestures come together in Husserl, on the one hand his refusal of historicism, and on the other his withdrawing from the historian the right to define the origin of historicity and historical truth.

Historicism—in its essential schema—consists in saying that every epoch, every community, in its originality and its irreplaceability and its historical irreversibility, has *its* truth, its logic, its norms, and so on. So there is no universal meaning, and so forth. I shall not insist.

To which Husserl retorts that of course all that is true and that it would be absurd to deny it. But that very affirmation, precisely because one takes it seriously, presupposes the following.

(1) That in truth, historico-empirical, ethnologico-empirical facts can, precisely, be legitimately invoked only if they are determined by a science that establishes them in truth. Which supposes that a science of these historical facts is possible. Historicism is an attribute of the historian who believes in the possibility of his science and therefore in the opening and the horizon of a historical *truth*.

This historical truth must itself escape from the historicist reduction for *169*
historicism itself to be possible and at a certain level legitimate. Thus there is a layer of truth that it cannot contest without contradicting itself. We have a scientific project that is called history or ethnology, and so forth, which presupposes that different epochs and communities can open themselves to the truth of other epochs and other historical or ethnic communities.

(2) This presupposes, then, secondly, that the historian or the ethnologist has some *a priori* certainty concerning the possibility of this truth and the universality of the structures of historicity or culture or being in community that

3. Derrida might be here referring to a seminar entitled "Hegel and History," also mentioned by him later (see below, p. 215). All that remains in the record, however, is another 1964–65 course Derrida gave at the ENS entitled "The Theory of Signification in the *Logical Investigations* and *Ideas I*"—a course consisting of twelve (written out) sessions, given as part of the *agrégation* curriculum. See above, "General Introduction," p. x.

allows him to define his own field and undertake his enquiries. He already knows what history means, just as he knows what human community means, what language and historical fact mean, when he enters into contact with other epochs or communities, however different they may be from his own. Without the apodictic and unconditional unity of this *a priori* field and of these universal structures, he could not even point out the differences and the relativity in the name of which he is taking an empiricist and historicist position. By definition, this field and these universal structures of historicity, this origin or this essence of historicity, cannot be the object of a historical science or of the historian's work. First because they are in no case *objects*, and then because this essence and this origin are always already presupposed by the historian. So Husserl can say in the *Krisis* that he does not even need to seek to oppose historical facts to the facts invoked by the historicist historian: the very assertion of the facticity of these facts by the historicist historian proves the historical *a priori* Husserl is talking about. Given this, one can say both that historicism, as an unconditional systematic proposition, as claiming to be an unconditional systematic proposition, is thus untenable, and at the same time that the historian and historical science cannot, as such, determine the meaning and the origin of historicity.

These affirmations are common to Hegel, Husserl and Heidegger. Rather than develop banalities about this, I prefer to determine the point where a
170 decisive break already takes place between Hegel and Husserl. Heidegger's break with both of them will be all the more decisive.

We saw last time that, for Hegel, a society without historical science was purely and simply a society without history. Now Husserl, in particular in one of the texts appended to the *Krisis* (1934, *Beilage* 26, [German] p. 502–3), a text entitled, precisely, *"Stufen der Geschichtlichkeit. Erste Geschichtlichkeit,"*[4] tries to distinguish between several levels of historicity. And this distinction is going to allow him to recognize a historicity in cultures to which the idea of science and notably the idea of historical project have yet remained foreign.

The lowest level is that of the historicity common to *every* society, every speaking community (i.e., every one that has a culture)—in that case, the simple bond of the generations, community activity, the unity of the surroundings as informed by culture and empirical techniques, the transmission of tools, the oral traditions of important events, all that ensures that there is a

4. Husserl, *Die Krisis der europäischen Wissenschaften und die transzendentale Phänomenologie*, ed. Walter Biemel (La Haye: Martinus Nijhoff, 1954), 502–3. [Beilage 26.] [Translator's note: *The Crisis of European Sciences and Transcendental Phenomenology*, trans. David Carr (Evanston, IL: Northwestern University Press, 1970). Beilage 26 is not in fact included in the translation.]

certain historical signification to community life. Historicity is here synonymous with community of culture and humanity.

Historicity in this most universal sense, says Husserl, has always already begun, it is a universal that belongs to the *menschlichen Dasein*. It is the unity of a personal becoming and, as *Umwelt*, what can be considered as the unity of an "organism." Naturally, as Husserl makes clear, insofar as humans participate only in this first level of historicity, they do not yet have the idea or the project of a historicity that goes beyond the finitude of their group or of a certain finite number of generations, and so forth. But without this first level or this first stage, the idea of the infinite task itself could not emerge. Now, the lower limit toward which this first historicity as finitude of meaning tends is the non-historicity of which Husserl speaks in his letter to Lévy-Bruhl. *171*

The *second level* is marked by the emergence of philosophy or science and of the humanity capable of the idea of philosophy or science, and thus of the project of the infinite task. There, Reason as power of universality has emerged, but it could not have emerged if it were not already slumbering in inferior historicity and even in non-historicity, in nocturnal obscurity, as he says elsewhere. In "Philosophy as Mankind's Self-Reflection: The Self-Realization of Reason," he writes,

> Thus philosophy is nothing other than [rationalism], through and through, but it is rationalism differentiated within itself according to the different stages of the movement of intention and fulfillment; it is *ratio in the constant movement of self-elucidation*, begun with the first breakthrough of philosophy into mankind, whose innate reason was previously in a state of concealment, of nocturnal obscurity.[5]

You can see where the difference between Hegel and Husserl is situated, against the same background of rationalist teleologism. Husserl recognizes that there is a historicity in communities in which universal Reason and the project of the infinite task is still sleeping, has not yet happened, in which it is still only a possibility.

At the first level, there is historicity without rationality or any project of scientific rationality. Whereas for Hegel, so long as rationality is only a possibility, there is not yet any history worthy of the name. On [French] p. 61 of the *Lectures on the Philosophy of World History*, he writes,

> The only fitting and worthy mode of philosophical reflection is to take up history at the point where rationality [*Vernünftigkeit*] begins to appear in *172*

5. Husserl, *The Crisis of European Sciences and Transcendental Phenomenology*, appendix 4 ("Philosophy as Mankind's Self-Reflection: The Self-Realization of Reason"), 338.

> worldly existence—not where it is first merely an *implicit* possibility [. . .]. (*Philosophy of History*, 114)

So you see that from the first to the second level there is indeed a rupture, the irruption of something radically new and the appearance of another type of historicity, and a historicity that is more historical, closer to its full essence, since it includes the idea of an infinite growth, and therefore the transmission of meaning as truth. It is the culture of truth that appears, whereas before there was only culture without universal truth. And in another *Beilage* (Beilage 27, [German] p. 507, Husserl writes,

> Human life is, in the broadest way and as cultural life, necessarily historical in the strictest sense. But scientific life, life as life of scientists in a community of scientists, signifies a new kind of historicity.[6]

And in the *Crisis of European Humanity and Philosophy*, Husserl also speaks
173 of a "revolution at the heart of historicity."[7] But precisely, the originality of this revolution, that in no way moreover contradicts its revolutionary and irruptive character, is the fact that it merely unfolds, makes explicit, brings up to date a reason and an intention, a *telos* hidden in the earlier stage.

This is what happens when the third stage appears. The third stage is obviously marked by the moment when philosophy as science, as it has been lived and practiced since its Greek origin, understands its own project, makes it explicit and thinks it as such (i.e., converts itself into *phenomenology*). I'll translate the last lines of this very short fragment (1.5 pages).

> *Die dritte Stufe* [the third step or the third stage: it can be translated as "step" or "stage" since it is both a structural and a genetic description] is the

6. [Translator's note:] This *Beilage* is not included in the English translation of Husserl's *Crisis*. Here and in other such cases I have translated from Derrida's French.

7. [Translator's note: The Husserl passage Derrida appears to have in mind is from the Vienna Lecture, appendix 1 of David Carr's translation (p. 279: "It [scientific culture under the guidance of ideas of infinity] also means a revolutionization of its historicity"), and appearing in the German edition as the third *Abhandlung* (p. 325: "Sie [wissenschaftliche Kultur unter Ideen der Unendlichkeit] bedeutet auch eine Revolutionierung der Geschichtlichkeit [. . .])."] The table of contents in Derrida's own copy of Husserl's book is labeled in such a way that clearly a translation of it was meant to be divided between a team of which Derrida was a part (J. Bouveresse, J. Derrida, Y. Duroux, Fischer, J.-L. Tristani, among whom at least the latter is known to have attended the present course). Françoise Dastur, who did not attend this course but had Tristani's notes from it, was also meant to be included in the team as she herself says in an interview with Dominique Janicaud: "When I came back to Paris, Derrida asked me to join him and five other advanced students in order to translate Husserl's *Krisis*. I was meant to translate about a hundred pages or so" (*Heidegger en France*, 64). This translation never in fact came about.

> *Umwandlung*, the mutation, the conversion of philosophy into phenomenology, with humanity's scientific consciousness in its *Historizität* [Husserl often says interchangeably *Historizität* and *Geschichtlichkeit*] and the function of converting itself into a humanity allowing itself to be guided by philosophy as phenomenology. (*Krisis*, Beilage 26, p. 503.)

That is a new rupture as explication. Naturally, these three *Stufen* are at once steps [*étapes*] and stages [*étages*]—that is, phases [*stades*] that are both structured and genetic, strata that are not *de facto* mutually exclusive. So that the lowest stratum is always present in the societies that have gained access to the two higher strata, and the second stratum is still present in any society that has gained access to phenomenology.

In any case, you see that by the determination of the first stratum, the lowest stratum as an *already historical* stratum, even though scientific reason has not yet appeared in it, Husserl takes his distance from Hegel and looks forward to Heidegger who will say, as you remember, that the absence of *Historie*, of science and of historical consciousness, is not the sign of non-historicity (*Geschichtslosigkeit*) but only of a *deficient* mode of historicity. And 174
we shall have to ask ourselves whether, speaking of a *deficient mode*, Heidegger does not also imply a teleology, all the while denying it.

To tell the truth, my language is improper: the texts on which I have just been relying to talk about Husserl and to show that they supposedly *look forward* to Heidegger by taking their distance from Hegel—these texts all date from later than 1934, and thus significantly later than *Sein und Zeit*. Without wishing to decide the question of a possible retro-influence of Heidegger on Husserl (in the *Krisis*), and without denying, any more than does Heidegger himself, the impetus that Husserl gives to Heidegger's thought, here in any case it is on the theme of historicity that Heidegger owes least to Husserl.

This is what I need to show now. I need to show in what way the point of departure of Heidegger's reflection on historicity, at the precise place where we are at this moment, is radically discontinuous with Hegelianism and Husserlianism and entails their prior destruction.

This will not be easy to show. I am going to insist primarily on the relation to Husserl, (1) because the destruction of the Husserlian metaphysics of history will imply *a fortiori* the destruction of Hegelian metaphysics for the reasons I was just giving; (2) because, quite simply, I intend to return at another time to the relationship of Heidegger to Hegel around the introduction to the *Phenomenology* and Heidegger's text entitled "Hegel's Concept of Experience."[8]

8. Martin Heidegger, "Hegel's Concept of Experience," [1942–43], in *Off the Beaten Track*, 86–156.

By what right, then, first of all, and in spite of Husserl's precautions with respect to metaphysics, can one speak of a Husserlian metaphysics of historicity, and how does it lend itself to a destruction in the Heideggerian sense? To reply to this question I shall try to tie into a bundle five themes, it being understood that their unity, what allows them to be gathered into a bundle, is not an external ligature but a common origin.

175 (1)[9] Husserlian teleology is a transcendental idealism. That means it presupposes, it gives itself notions, significations, forms of *egoity* and *subjectivity* as its ultimate foundation. Even if in some fragments, in meticulous, ambitious and difficult analyses, in more or less completed projects, Husserl promises himself that he will go back down before the ego or the subject to have us see its genesis and its history, that is not a fundamental and systematic theme of phenomenology. Of course Husserl, as I pointed out at one of our Saturday sessions, does not avoid, as Heidegger reproaches Kant with doing, the problem of the link between temporality and the I think (contradictory affirmation). But even when—in the last texts—he follows through to the end his respect for historicity, even when he rediscovers historicity in the depths of meaning, his final affirmation consists in recognizing that *subjectivity* is historical, and historical through and through. For example, in a letter of 1930, he writes this: "For, with the transcendental reduction, I attained, I am convinced, concrete and real subjectivity in the ultimate sense in all the fullness of its being and life, and in this subjectivity, universal constituting life (and not simply theoretical [comment] constituting life): absolute subjectivity in its historicity."[10]

Radical historicity is thus that of subjectivity—transcendental subjectivity it is true. Now you know—I have already said so and many texts by Heidegger develop this theme—that for Heidegger this notion of subjec-

9. The numbering that begins here is not followed in the manuscript.

10. [Translator's note:] Letter to Georg Misch, November 16th, 1930, in *Husserliana: Edmund Husserl Dokumente 3 (Briefwechsel)*, Band 6, ed. Karl Schuhmann (The Hague: Kluwer Academic Publishers, 1994), 282–83. There is no English translation of Husserl's correspondence. This letter is also quoted in a footnote by Derrida in his *Introduction à l'Origine de la géométrie de Husserl* (Paris: Presses Universitaires de France, 1962), 160, n. 1, trans. John P. Leavey Jr. as *Edmund Husserl's Origin of Geometry: An Introduction* (Lincoln: University of Nebraska Press, 1978), 145, n. 173: "For, with the transcendental reduction, I attained, I am convinced, concrete and real subjectivity in the ultimate sense in all the fullness of its being and life, and in this subjectivity, universal constituting life and not simply *theoretical* constituting life, absolute subjectivity in its historicity": quoted from A. Diemer, Fr. trans. Alexandre Lowit and Henri Colombié, in "La Phénoménologie de Husserl comme métaphysique," *Les Etudes Philosophiques*, n. s. 9 (1954), 36.

tivity remains a metaphysical notion, designating not the being of beings in general, but the being of a highly determinate being: the subject is a type of being that is determinate. Of course when Husserl speaks of transcendental subjectivity, he does intend to designate by that not a determined being in the world, but the absolute origin of the appearing of the meaning or the being of every being in general. The dimension of transcendental subjectivity designates that without which no meaning of being in general, no being 176
of beings, could appear, could phenomenalize itself and give rise to a discourse. Every meaning of being in general, must, if one wishes to speak of it, appear, and this appearing is appearing to, appearing for, and that is what Husserl calls consciousness.

Nevertheless, in spite of this gesture and in spite of all the gestures through which one could show how transcendental subjectivity offers the last and strongest resistance to the Heideggerian destruction of metaphysics, nevertheless, this origin of meaning and of the world (Fink) is nonetheless determined by Husserl as consciousness and as subjectivity. And the choice or acceptance of these traditional notions of metaphysics is not fortuitous; these words are not algebraic *X*s. In claiming to designate the absolute origin of the meaning of being in general, they designate at the same time at least by metaphorical adherence a determined form of being: namely, *substantiality*. And the history of meaning that links the phenomenological notion of subjectivity to Hegelian subjectivity, to Cartesian substantiality, to Aristotle's *hupokeimenon*, is, precisely, never interrogated by Husserl. You know that in many texts Heidegger brings out the fact that the notion of *subjective substantiality* as *ground* responds to a project of security or certainty (*Sicherheit*) that was first made explicit by Descartes and brought to its full accomplishment by Hegel, but which inhabits, animates, the whole of Western philosophy that determines being as a being-pre-sent, as a being before me, subsisting in its firm stability, lending itself to a mastery, remaining the same, like the Platonic *eidos* or the Aristotelian *hupokeimenon* as a thing at my disposal, as *zuhanden*, handy, and *vorhanden*, objectively present. The notion of *Vorhandenheit* is justifiably translated as "subsistence" by Boehm and de Waelhens. The *hupokeimenon*, subsistence, what holds steady under the becoming of accidents and attributes, is not first of all the subject, the *subjectum* as self or as man, but it is precisely the sense of the Cartesiano-Hegeliano-Husserlian gesture to transform substantiality into *subjectum*, this transformation keeping within itself, in spite of the protestations that have gone along with it, something of the *hupokeimenon* as thing in front of me, as subsistence and 177
Vorhandenheit, as object. The complicity between the notions of subjectivity and objectivity is irreducible. We are going to pause a little on this point but,

before that, I am going to read a few lines from the 1938 text called "Die Zeit des Weltbildes," collected in *Holzwege*. During a characterization of what he calls *modern times*, Heidegger writes this ([French] pp. 79–80):

> Of the essence here is the necessary interplay between subjectivism and objectivism. But precisely this reciprocal conditioning of the one by the other refers us back to deeper processes.
>
> What is decisive is not that humanity frees itself from previous bonds but, rather, that the essence of humanity altogether transforms itself in that man becomes the subject. To be sure, this word "subject" must be understood as the translation of the Greek *hupokeimenon*. The word names that-which-lies-before (*das Vor-Liegende*), that which, as ground [which is under, *hupo*] (*Grund*), gathers everything onto itself. This metaphysical meaning of the concept of the subject has, in the first instance, no special relationship to man, and none at all to the I.
>
> When, however, man becomes the primary and genuine *subjectum*, this means that he becomes that being upon which every being, in its way of being and its truth, is founded. Man becomes the referential center of beings as such. (Heidegger, "The Age of the World Picture," in *Off the Beaten Track*, 66–67)

This would be the fundamental gesture of modern metaphysics since Descartes, a modern metaphysics linked to the essence of technology that one can understand only via the project of *Sicherheit*.

Instead of following the analysis of this project as it appears in so many texts of Heidegger's, I prefer to show, staying close to this Husserlian idea of
178 the historicity of subjectivity, how this "destruction" of subjectivity is articulated upon the notion of the historicity of *Da-sein* in *Sein und Zeit*.

It would obviously be more than frivolous to say that the transformation of *Da-sein* into *Vorhandensein*, into an object before me or into a *hupokeimenon*, a subsistent being, that this metaphysical transformation—which followed the reduction of the meaning of being, of *ousia* into *hupokeimenon,* was due to a regrettable accident, a fault of philosophy, which could have avoided it. The threat of transforming *Da-sein* (the ek-sistence of *Dasein*) into substance on the model of objects available in the world, and of *Vorhandenheit*— this threat is not extrinsic to *Dasein*. It belongs to the very structure of *Dasein*. The inauthentic understanding of its being does not befall Dasein like an accident; it is a possibility and even an essential necessity inscribed in the very heart of its being. It is not even a decline into something low, in the moral sense. I refer you for this to §9 of *Being and Time*, [German] p. 43: "[. . .] the inauthenticity [I do not know why the [French] translators have here translated *Uneigentlichkeit* as "alienation" when two lines earlier they translated it as "inauthenticity"] of Dasein does not signify a "lesser" being or a "lower" degree of being (*Seinsgrad*)" (*Being and Time*, 42). Which explains that metaphysics, which is essentially substantialist (in the sense of *hupokeimenon* or in the sense of subjectivity), is not a fault or a sin of which one should rid oneself, of which one could purify oneself by "overcoming" metaphysics. Metaphysics, like inauthenticity, cannot be overcome.

Let's approach an important passage from *Sein und Zeit* (§25) where precisely this question of the *subjectum* is broached in relation with the structure of *Dasein* and its everyday inauthenticity. I'm choosing this §25 because Husserl is visibly targeted, if not by name.

The question that orients this paragraph is the point of departure of the "existential" question [comment]: who is being-there? (*Frage nach dem Wer des Daseins*)? In §9 the being of being-there [*l'étant-là*] was determined as 179
mine (*je meines*):

> The being which this being is *concerned about* in its being is always *my own* (*je meines*). Thus, Dasein is never to be understood ontologically as a case (*Fall*) and instance of a genus of beings *Vorhandenem* (subsisting before me). To something objectively present (*Vorhandenem*) its being is "*gleichgültig*" (indifferent), more precisely, this being (*Vorhandenem*) "is" in such a way that its being can neither be indifferent nor non-indifferent to it. In accordance with the character of always-mineness (*Jemeinigkeit*), when we speak of Dasein, we must always use the *personal* pronoun along with whatever we say: "I am," "you are." (*Being and Time*, 42)

This *Jemeinigkeit* of *Dasein* is not yet determined—this is important—as subjectivity. And the problem of knowing whether this *Jemeinigkeit* ought or not be determined as subjectivity is, precisely, posed in §25 that I wanted to broach. So the question is that of the who of *Dasein*, the *who* of *Jemeinigkeit*. It must be noted that the determination of this *who*, as *subjectum*, will appear in the analytic of Dasein's everydayness (*Alltäglichkeit*). It is in seeking for what everyday and inauthentic being-there is that we will encounter the theme of the *subjectum*. It will be brought out then that the inauthenticity of everydayness consists in understanding *Dasein* on the model of *Vorhandensein*, in understanding the origin of the world—the transcendence of eksistence of *Dasein* which makes the world world—in understanding this origin of the world, then, on the model of the things that are *in* the world and that offer themselves, in everyday life, to my activity as subsistent things and causes. Which, once again, is not a sin but a structural necessity of *Dasein* as being-in-the-world, a necessity that pushes it to act in the world and to transpose illegitimately the model of the beings it deals with in its labor. And

Heidegger is concerned to show that in spite of the deep protests of all the philosophers of subjectivity who, from Descartes to Husserl, obstinately try to mark the difference between subjectivity and objectivity, obstinately try
180 to avoid any thingification of consciousness and so forth, any naturalization of lived experience, in spite of that, the very idea of subjectivity remains in its principle contaminated by the schema of *Vorhandenheit*.

And indeed to the question: *who* is this being named *Dasein*, the I itself replies, the *subject*, the self (*Selbst*). Heidegger says,

> The who is answered in terms of the I itself, the "subject," the "self" (*Selbst*). The *who* is what maintains itself as an identity throughout changes in behavior and experiences, and in this way relates itself to this multiplicity. (*Being and Time*, 112)

(Remember what we were saying the other time about the Husserlian ego as transcendence in immanence.) Let me pursue my translation.

> Ontologically, we understand it as what is always already constantly present (*Vorhandene*) in a closed region. (*Being and Time*, 112)

(Even if, one might say here *contra* Heidegger, we are dealing with consciousness as *Ur-Region*, and here closure does not signify non-intentionality but the specificity and the untransgressable originality of the region. This obviously supposes that Heidegger is neglecting the noeme—that is, the meaning that, as we have seen, Husserl says does not really belong to consciousness. But if Heidegger can neglect this *explosive* affirmation—explosive because the an-archy of the noeme that is recognized in it blows open the closure of the region, i.e., what makes it a region—if Heidegger can, then, neglect this explosive affirmation that wrests the appearing of meaning from the closure of subjective consciousness, this is because Husserl himself did not consider it to be explosive and introduced it into his description as an inoffensive and discreet affirmation that did not disturb the regionalist themes of phenom-
181 enology). So, let me take up my translation again:

> Ontologically we understand the *Selbst* as something subsistent (*Vorhandene*), as what is always already constantly present in a closed region as that which lies at its basis (*zum Grunde liegende*) in an eminent sense, as the *subjectum*. As something self-same (*Selbiges*) in manifold otherness (*Andersheit*), this subject has the character of the *Selbst*. (*Being and Time*, 112)

And here are the allusions to the protestations of the subjectivists against substantiality:

> Even if one rejects a substantial soul, the thingliness of consciousness, and the objectivity of the person, ontologically one still posits something whose

> being retains the meaning of *Vorhandenheit* [substantiality], whether explicitly or not. Substantiality [*Substanzialität*, here] is the ontological clue for the determination of beings in terms of which the question of the who is answered. Dasein is tacitly conceived in advance as *Vorhandenes*. In any case, the indeterminacy of its being always implies this meaning of being. However, *Vorhandenheit* is the mode of being of beings which are not *daseinsmäßig*. (*Being and Time*, 112)

It will be protested that this identity of the *subjectum* is not a metaphysical thesis and that, by referring to it, one is merely describing what is *given*. That's what Heidegger is trying to do: describe what is *given* as it *is given*. And Heidegger addresses to himself for a whole paragraph a Husserlian-type objection to which he wishes to respond. Here is the Husserlian-type objection: I'll read it quickly in the Boehm-Waelhens translation:

> But does it not go against the rules of a sound method when the approach to a problematic does not stick to the givens that are evident within the thematic realm? And what is less dubious than the givenness of the I? And, for the purpose of working this givenness out in a primordial way, does it [this very
> manner of being given] (*Gegebenheit*) not direct us to abstract from every- *182*
> thing else that is "given," not only from an existing "world," [transcendental reduction] but also from the being of other "I"s? [Solipsistic hypothesis that accompanies the transcendental reduction at the beginning of the *Cartesian Meditations*.] Perhaps what this kind of giving gives—this simple, formal, reflective perception of the I—is indeed evident. This insight even opens access to an independent phenomenological problematic which has its fundamental significance in the framework known as "formal phenomenology of consciousness" [in quotes]. (*Being and Time*, 112–13)

Such would be the objection. To which Heidegger replies that the *Gegebenheit* is perhaps here the *Verführung* itself, that the being-given is perhaps the *ruse*, the *seduction* that se-duces, that leads off the path (*Verführung*), that seduces (i.e., that separates one from the right path, that dupes me); the so-called self-evidence of what is given is perhaps here the dissimulation and the evasion itself. An essential evasion that has its basis precisely in the being of *Dasein* as the power to hide or alienate itself, to say "I" even and perhaps especially when it is not the "I" that has itself in its sights or is speaking itself.

Let's translate:

> In the present context of an existential analytic of factical Dasein, the question arises whether the I's mode of givenness (*Gebung*) which we mentioned discloses Dasein in its everydayness, if it discloses it at all. Is it then *apriori* self-evident that the access to Dasein must be a simple perceiving reflection [*vernehmende* = translated as "spéculation" by Boehm and de Waelhens. It

> means a reflection in theory, that looks or listens or attends . . .] of the I of acts [*das Ich von Akten* = as the pole or actor of its acts]? What if this kind of *Selbstgebung* [of givenness of self: a Husserlian notion] of Dasein were to be a *Verführung* of the existential analytic [a seduction, a tempting distraction for the existential analytic, and in truth a transcendental seduction] and to
> 183 do so in a way grounded in the being of Dasein itself? Perhaps when Dasein addresses (*Ansprechen*) itself in the way which is nearest to itself, it always says "I am it" (*ich bin es*), and finally says this most loudly when it is "not" this being. What if the fact that Dasein is so constituted that it is in each case mine [its *Jemeinigkeit*] were the reason for the fact that Dasein, initially and for the most part, *is not itself*? What if, with the approach mentioned above, the existential analytic fell into the trap, so to speak, of starting with the *Gegebenheit* of the I for Dasein itself and its obvious self-interpretation? What if it should turn out that the ontological horizon for the determination of what is accessible in simple giving should remain fundamentally undetermined? We can probably always correctly say ontically of this being that "I" am it. However, the ontological analytic which makes use of such statements must have fundamental reservations about them. The "I" must be understood only in the sense of a noncommittal [*unverbindlichen*: nonbinding, neutral] *formal indication* of something which perhaps reveals itself in the actual phenomenal context of being as that being's "opposite" [i.e., as the opposite of the very thing it gave itself or said itself to be]. Then "not I" [the opposite] by no means signifies something like a being which is essentially lacking "I-hood" (*Ichheit*), but means a definite mode of being of the "I" itself; for example, having lost itself (*Selbstverlorenheit*). (*Being and Time*, 113)

Two brief remarks about this important passage.

(1) What is remarkable about it is that the *Jemeinigkeit* itself, far from leading to the security of I-hood, is shown to be the very thing that makes possible the *Verführung* and that, saying "I" when the I is given to me in self-evidence, I should have in my sights a non-I that would not be a non-I-hood (a thing of nature), but an other-me and that, even as I shout "I am" and "I am me," I should be in *Selbstverlorenheit*. ["Hume" added in the margin.]

(2) It is quite clear that this is the precise place of the precise question that what is called psychoanalytic theory must pose to the whole of classical
184 metaphysics in its most modern and highest form: namely, transcendental phenomenology, if at least psychoanalytic theory wishes to or must dialogue with philosophical thought at long last.

I'll break off here the reading of this passage after which Heidegger shows that the reduction to the pure ego and to the solipsistic sphere of the mine, in the sense that Husserl—who is still not named—understands it, is forbidden by the very structure of *Dasein*, that an ego without world and without others is never given to us, and that my relation to the other is not established by an *Einfühlung* bridging two subjectivities but has always already come about. These are difficult problems that perhaps presuppose a simplification of Husserl's intentions and especially of the methodological meaning of the reduction and of the non-worldliness of the ego. But I cannot and do not wish to get into that here. Moreover I spoke about this at some length two years ago in the course on the fifth *Cartesian Meditation*,[11] and last year around a presentation on *Mitsein*.

What I wish to hold onto for the moment, while inviting you to read the whole of §25 at least, is only this: the notion of subjectivity is still thought on the model of substance (*Vorhandenheit*). As regards Husserl, this means that Heidegger reproaches him as it were with things that are only apparently contradictory. He reproaches him for the method of transcendental reduction and the transcendental idealism that supports it, since the Reduction claims to give access to an egological lived experience that is absolutely independent, in its essence, from the existence of the world (cf. §49 of *Ideen*). This absolute independence of subjectivity, says Heidegger, is never *given*. On the one hand. On the other hand it leads, like it or not, to an ahistorical concept of the *ego*. Whence all the difficulties that Husserl indeed has in doing anything more than affirming the historicity of the *ego*. An ahistorical concept of the ego, 185
and even an a-temporal concept of the *ego*. And although Husserl recognizes very rapidly that the *ego* is temporal, that pure subjectity is pure temporality (≠ Kant: I think), he has the greatest difficulty in thinking the unity of cosmic time and lived time in the problematic of the reduction. Whence the admirable but so very awkward efforts in texts most often later than *Sein und Zeit* to describe the temporal *Ur*-constitution of the *ego*. *Ego*: eternal and temporal, intemporal and temporal. First reproach, then: an ego uprooted from the world, therefore not historical. Non-historical because abstract.

But at the same time, an *apparently contradictory reproach*: the transcendental reduction is not radical enough, not transcendental enough. Why? Because the lived experience which is claimed to be not of the world but origin of the world is still determined as subjectal—that is, as substantially substantial, as a substrate, as *Vorhandenheit* (i.e., we saw this earlier, as an object in the world, an object available in my *Umwelt*). Given this, the transcendental sphere of lived experience, instead of being faithfully described and made explicit, is determined by the speculative concept of *subjectum*

11. From February 16 to May 4 of 1963, Derrida gave a course at the Sorbonne—held in five (written out) sessions—entitled "Husserl's Fifth Cartesian Meditation" (see above, "General Introduction," p. ix).

that skews the description of the transcendental and subjects it to a worldly model. A perfectly radical reduction—the one Heidegger is claiming to be doing, without the now equivocal name "reduction"—ought also to place in brackets the subjective and egological dimension of lived experience, which is not absolutely originary, which is constituted on the basis of a transcendence more originary than that of an intentional egological consciousness and that is the transcendence of the *Da* of *Dasein*. There is something of this gesture (*mutatis mutandis*! . . .) in the text by Sartre I was talking about the other Saturday, in which he makes of the ego a transcendental object in the world, constituted on the basis of a transcendental field that is originally without subject.[12]

In thus radicalizing the transcendental reduction, Heidegger is claiming
186 to reduce even what Husserl calls the irreducible: namely, the egological form of experience, the form of the living present and everything that I have on occasion called transcendental archi-facticity. Comment.

Once phenomenology determines a transcendental source supposedly outside the world according to an intra-worldly model, it cannot rigorously think transcendental historicity. *Vorhandenheit* pure and simple can no more have a history than can a being foreign to the world. Neither the intra-worldly nor the extra-worldly can have a history. History is situated in that in-the-world, that *In-der-Welt-sein* of *Dasein*, an *In-der-Welt* that is not an immanence of the *Vorhandenheit* type.

Of course, these reproaches addressed to Husserl can affect only Husserl's explicitly and systematically elaborated project in the broad phases and great treatises, those that precisely make subjectity and egoity unassailable. But we know that in many unpublished fragments, Husserl tries, via radical and non-systematic descriptions, to get back to that pre-egological and anonymous stratum of lived experience where temporality is constituted and constitutes the *ego*.

So I have shown—schematically—why Heidegger did not feel able simply to be satisfied with the Husserlian description of historicity, insofar as it remained governed, I would say oppressed, by the metaphysical ancestry of the concept of the *subjectum*. This was the first of the five themes I announced. I'll be briefer with the four others, which are in profound solidarity with it.

Second, Husserl's teleology of history is not merely a subjectivism; it is a humanism. Although Husserl is forewarned and is the first to forewarn us

12. [Translator's note:] Perhaps a reference to Sartre's text *La transcendance de l'ego* (1937), trans. Forrest Williams and Robert Kilpatrick (New York: Noonday Press, 1957).

about a confusion between the transcendental *ego* and anthropology, every time he moves from transcendental phenomenological description to a sort of teleological interpretation of becoming, the notion of man reappears, and even man as *animal rationale*. It is precisely every time that Husserl must abandon the description of the given to interpret it that metaphysical presuppositions that have resisted the reduction appear, as though, once the reduc- *187*
tion is lifted, one had to forget what it showed us—for example, something that was not what one blithely calls by the name "man," and which was anterior—because it gives it its meaning—to what is called man (i.e., a being in the world, an animal being endowed with this strange power called reason).

Of course, the point is not to reduce the whole of Husserlianism to this gesture, but this gesture exists and it always intervenes at the moment when historicity is to be interpreted. This gesture presupposes *on the one hand* a radically original essence of man, from the Papuan to the phenomenologist, which means that even the revolutions introduced into the heart of historicity by the irruption of philosophy as infinite task, then by that of phenomenology as another understanding of philosophy—these revolutions take place *within* the unitary field of *the same humanity*, and the same history of the same humanity.

> But just as man and even the Papuan represent a new stage of animal nature, i.e., as opposed to the beast, so philosophical reason represents a new stage of human nature and its reason. (*Crisis*, 290)

And earlier he had said,

> Reason is a broad title. According to the old familiar definition, man is *das vernünftige Lebewesen*, the rational animal, and in this broad sense even the Papuan is a man and not a beast. He has his ends and he acts reflectively, considering the practical possibilities. The works and methods that grow out of this go to make up a tradition, being understandable again by others in virtue of their rationality. (*Crisis*, 290)

Thus, the move from the finitude to the infinity of the task is understood within an essence of man as animal endowed with reason. *188*

"Do we not," says Husserl in Beilage 3,

> stand here before the great and profound problem-horizon of reason, the same reason that functions in every man, the *animal rationale*, no matter how primitive he is?[13]

13. Derrida translated and wrote an introduction to the aforementioned "Beilage 3," published under the title *L'Origine de la géométrie* (Paris: Presses Universitaires de

We have seen how Heidegger was trying to get back behind a metaphysics that is always in his eyes not merely an onto-theology but a humanism. In the "Letter on 'Humanism,'" he shows precisely that the link between metaphysics and humanism is an essential, and not accidental, link. We have seen the necessity that Heidegger claimed to be obeying by not setting off from a definition—even one that was *selbstverständlich*—of man. He would oppose all these reasons to Husserl here, showing that a history that would be only a history of humanity (i.e., not of the meaning of being but of a determinate type of being), would not be a history or would in the end be merely an empirical history and not a history of truth. On the other hand, can one speak of historicity when the becoming described is merely the unfolding and explication of an essence of humanity as rational animality?

Third. The content, and not the form, of this teleology is evidently recognized on the basis of a guiding thread that is *science*. Philosophy is traditionally determined as *episteme* and it is by the possibility of science that man is defined, and by the revolutions of science that the stages and ruptures within humanity are recognized.

Historicity is determined on the basis of scientificity and—and here we are back with Hegel—historicity is determined in its teleology on the basis of scientificity, which means two things in one.

It means, first, as I have just noted, that the history of science, its origin
189 and its ends, are the indices of historicity in general. And it means, secondly, that only science or scientific humanity, the scientific community, has a *pure* historicity. The model and the *telos* of historicity, what allows its *eidos* to be defined, is the history of the sciences, the history of science as a history of *objectivity*. What does that mean?

According to Husserl—and his concept here again is extremely classical—there is no history without community, of course, but first and above all without *transmissibility*, without traditionality. Now only the scientific object is able to ensure a pure, unique, transparent tradition; only the language of scientific objectivity—of which mathematics and the exact sciences in general have given us the model. Only the exactitude of the object—of the ideal object, of course, for only the ideal object can be exact—ensures the univocity of expression, as Husserl assures us in *Ideen I*. Therefore it alone ensures a purity of historicity, a purity of the historical *ethos*, a transparency of the historical tradition and therefore of historicity. The serious consequence is that everything in science that is not exactitude can give rise

France, 1962), 213. [Translator's note: Husserl, "The Origin of Geometry," in *The Crisis of European Sciences and Transcendental Phenomenology*, appendix 6, 378.]

only to a *dubious* historicity. What in science *in general* is not exactitude is, of course, on the one hand the empirical scientificity of the vague sciences of nature and spirit, but it is also the scientificity of rigorous science which is not exact science; the concepts of phenomenology are not, cannot and must not in their essence be exact concepts [illegible word in parentheses[14]] but primarily and only rigorous. I am supposing that you are aware of this distinction (*Ideen I,* §§74–75). It follows that the language of phenomenology will never be perfectly univocal like that of mathematics. And the question of the historicity of phenomenology, of the transmission of its discourse, will be posed, in such a way that this [illegible word] at the heart of historicity will no longer be sure of arriving, like [illegible word] at a taking-possession of the meaning of history by history itself. A classical thought, I was saying. Yes and no. Yes, to the extent of the privilege of mathematical scientificity. No, to the extent that the existence of mathematics is conceived no longer, as *190*
in classical metaphysics, as the locus or the example of an eternal truth, but indeed as the purest historicity of truth. In both cases obviously it is empirical history that is, precisely, reduced.

History is therefore the transmission of ideal objects, the only ones that can be transmitted with their meaning, as such, without alteration as the same, and this to infinity; without essential limitation of any sort (free and not bound ideal objects). Historicity is thus objectivity and scientificity themselves, and the purity and progress of all three go together and increase at the same time.[15]

Of course, here too one must be extremely prudent and avoid schematizing too quickly. Although history is always guaranteed by the objectivity of objects, Husserl did worry about the origin of these objects and the subjective acts that constituted them. And he did take pains to root and ground scientificity in a pre-scientific life-ground that was itself historical. The whole thematic of the *Lebenswelt* which, *qua* systematic thematics is, moreover, later than *Sein und Zeit,* indeed concerns a stratum of language-community life and therefore of historicity prior to that of scientific life and supporting it. The only thing is, it turns out to be teleologically inferior, less purely historical, enclosed in the finitude of ends and horizons, and in any case the description of it, whatever its richness and powerful novelty, still remains

14. This word in parentheses might be "Geo."

15. At the bottom of page 17 of the manuscript, Derrida adds this: "next p.18, following class." In fact, Derrida adds more to the end of session 5, where a Husserl quote seems to break off at the words "any such surrounding world," only to be again picked up at the opening of the sixth session (cf. below, session 6, p. 128, n.2]).

guided by the subject-object correlation and the metaphysics of the *animal rationale*. The sphere of the *Lebenswelt* is the sphere of what Husserl calls the relative-subjective which does not yet create pure and purely objective idealities, that stratum of the relative-subjective having moreover universal structures that can and must be described as such by phenomenology. This
191 is what Husserl explains in particular in a short passage from the *Cartesian Meditations* that I will read because it appears to allude to Heidegger's analyses of *In-der-Welt-sein* in order to show their dependency and filiation with regard to Husserlian phenomenology. It is in §59 (*Cartesian Meditations*, 29)[16] (*Sein und Zeit*, 27):

> One consequence of the beginning phase of phenomenology was that its method of pure but at the same time eidetic intuition led to attempts at a new ontology [. . .]. As regards this, nothing prevents starting at first quite concretely with the human life-Umwelt around us, and with man himself as essentially related to this our Umwelt, and exploring, indeed purely intuitively, the extremely copious and never-discovered Apriori of any such surrounding world [. . .][17]

16. "29" refers to the year 1929 (Feburary 23–25) when Husserl delivered four lectures corresponding to his *Cartesian Meditations*; the following "27" refers to the publication date of *Sein und Zeit*, at the beginning of 1927.

17. Husserl, *Cartesian Meditations: An Introduction to Phenomenology*, trans. Dorion Cairns (The Hague: Martinus Nijhoff, 1960), 138. Derrida does not seem to use the Lévinas-Pfeiffer translation published by Vrin in 1947. Husserl's *Cartesian Meditations*, the main subject of a 1962–63 course given by Derrida, is unfortunately not (or no longer) to be found in Derrida's library in French or in German. This quotation is picked up in what follows (see below, session 6, p. 128, after the ellipsis).

SESSION SIX

8 February 1965

> If the discipline of history is lacking, that is no evidence *against* the historicity (*Geschichtlichkeit*) of Dasein; rather it is evidence for this constitution of being (*Seinsverfassung*) in a deficient mode. Only because it is "historic" (*geschichtlich*) in the first place can an age lack the discipline of history (be *unhistorisch*). (*Being and Time*, 20)

It is in the opening of this assertion, rather than by convoking the assertions of historians or ethnologists — who in their considerations on the subject of so-called historical societies or so-called societies without history presuppose at least that clarity has been reached on the essence of historicity and all the problematics attached to it — it is in the opening of this assertion of Heidegger's, and the better to understand it, that we tried to determine the place where it might "destroy" the Hegelian-Husserlian metaphysics of historicity. This last expression merited the precautions and the scare-quotes I spoke of last time, before tying together five Husserlian themes about which, each time, the Heideggerian difference was repeated.

The first four, the only ones I had time to develop, were the following:

(1) Husserl's teleology of historicity is a transcendental idealism organized
around a concept of subjectity that Heidegger shows is both foreign to the 194
world (i.e., non-historical) and intra-worldly (i.e., thought according to the model of a *Vorhandenheit*, of the object subsisting in the world), which is another way of missing any history that is not empirical. Remember, too, what we said about Husserl's transcendental reduction, that it was both illegitimate and insufficiently radical. Transcendental phenomenology is presented as having transformed into an intra-worldly thing the very thing it was claiming to protect against worldization, or reification or naturalization. I forgot on this subject to point out the fact that the word *consciousness* (*Bewusstsein* ≠ *Gewissen*) is not used in *Sein und Zeit*.[1]

1. [Translator's note:] In fact the word *Bewusstsein* does appear several times in *Being and Time*, but never in Heidegger's own name: see page 427 of the English lexicon of the Stambaugh translation.

(2) Husserl's teleology remains a humanism.

(3) The content of this teleology is recognized on the basis of the idea of science (historicity = absence [uncertain word] of the past).

(4) The description of the *Lebenswelt*, a theme that is, however, very close to Heidegger's intention, allows to circulate in it concepts such as those of nature and culture that import into it numerous latent and derivative metaphysical significations that, in any case, come in much later when seen from the historical originality of *Dasein* that Heidegger is trying to thematize.

We developed these four themes at length, taking many precautions and trying not to be unduly schematic.

195 <Page skipped in the manuscript.>[2]

> < . . .> surrounding world whatever, taking this Apriori as the point of departure for a systematic explication of human existence and of world strata that disclose themselves correlatively in the latter. (*Cartesian Meditations*, 138)

A genealogical claim, a claim of paternity to which, in advance as it were, Heidegger had thought he should respond with a claim of independence that I quote for its anecdotal interest. In the section devoted to the everydayness of the *Umwelt*, on [German] page 72, Heidegger writes in a note,

> The author would like to remark that he has repeatedly communicated the analysis of the surrounding world and the "hermeneutic of the facticity" of Dasein in general in his lecture courses ever since the winter semester of 1919–20. (*Being and Time*, 71)

That is an element in the historico-politico-university background of our problem.

196 In any case, to close this third point,[3] you see that for the very reasons that push Heidegger to go back behind the subject-object correlation and any history that would stick with it, he cannot be satisfied with a thematization of history that takes science as its guiding thread and scientific knowledge as its *Telos*.

Not that he judges Husserlian-type descriptions to be false and useless.

2. The preceding pages correspond to the first manuscript sheet of session 6 (recto plus one-third of verso). Then, after a page skipped, sheet 2—which carries on the session—also becomes sheet 18. Recall that, at the bottom of sheet 17 (recto) of session 5, we find: "next p.18, following class" (see above, p. 125, n.15). The quote being picked up here—at the beginning of sheet 2 of session 6—is thus the continuation of the quotation in sheet 17bis (above, p. 126). Derrida had apparently written twenty sheets for session 5 and, perhaps being unable to finish, left sheets 18–20 to session 6.

3. This "third point" had begun to be developed in session 5 (see above, p. 124).

Quite the contrary. Simply, they remain locked in the closure that we have been reconnoitering from the start.

(4) The other form of the same closure on which I shall not linger is, this time even if one stays within the descriptions of the *Lebenswelt*, the slightly precipitate opposition, of uncertain origins, between nature and culture—not that this opposition is useless, but it is so derivative, so laden with historical and metaphysical alluvia that one cannot seriously claim to discover the originary historicity of *Da-sein* by using these tools.

(5) Finally—and here I think we are getting to what is most important and most difficult—Husserl's thematics of historicity remains, to put it bluntly, a *worldview*. The accusation is serious and it has a meaning that does not immediately betray itself. What does it mean? To understand the gravity and the scope of the accusation, one must keep clearly in mind the whole Husserlian critique of the idea of worldview, of Dilthey's theory of *Weltanschauung*. This critique is developed in *Philosophy as Rigorous Science* (1911) and it is a centerpiece of phenomenology. In a word, Dilthey affirmed that each epoch has its *worldview*—that is, an idea that unified the organic and structural totality of its world, a sort of *Gestalt* in which art, religion, mythology, political and philosophical conceptions all held together. This theory of *Weltanschauungen* thought of itself as taking the historicity of meaning seriously. Husserl protests vigorously against the imperialist claims of this theory. Not that he denies the existence of such *Weltanschauungen*, such ideological *Gestalten*, but in his view trying to make the whole of science 197
and philosophy, the idea of science and of philosophy as science, enter into them is to miss the very meaning of truth, and first of all the meaning of the truth claimed by the theory of *Weltanschauung*. The idea of truth, the idea of science, the project of science have as their meaning the claim to escape relativity. Truth is not historical in the Diltheyan sense, insofar as it is truth, precisely, only if it is universally valid, *ad infinitum*, and so forth. During this period, Husserl is above all concerned to mark the independence of truth with regard to history. And the history of truth that he will later make into a theme presupposes this reduction of the empirical historicity of truth.

Consequently, to make of Husserl's philosophy of history a *Weltanschauung* or a *Weltbild* is a particularly heavy and at first blush unsustainable accusation. It looks like a shocking assimilation of Husserlianism and Diltheyism. For it to be something else, a certain path must be followed, a path along which I'll merely point to certain pathmarks. This path is followed in *Sein und Zeit*—one can recognize its trace everywhere—but it is in a 1938 text, *Die Zeit des Weltbildes*, that it is most clearly summed up.

Heidegger wants to show here that the very concept of *world-picture*

belongs to a picture of the world, to an epoch. Not to a world-picture among others but to *the* world-picture. What does this mean? There are not world-pictures in history; there is one epoch that had a world-picture and it is the very one that forged the concept of world-picture and wanted every epoch to have its own. Before the epoch of metaphysics inaugurated by the Cartesian moment, there was no world-picture. The Greeks, the Romans, Medieval Europe did not have a world-picture. That means that for them the world was not a totality of beings organized according to the representation and the production of the subject-man. The fact that modern times look for the possible world-pictures of other epochs signifies first and foremost that
198 the world is determined by modern times in such a way that one can have a world-picture. Before modern times—here before the Cartesian point of reference—the Greek world and the Medieval world were, to the contrary, thought in such a way that the very idea of a world-picture was necessarily and essentially impossible and untenable. What Heidegger says here is perfectly consistent with the theme of the radical historicity of the world. The world, as it worlds itself on the basis of the transcendence of *Da-sein*, is historical through and through. It thus has a different meaning at every epoch. But that it lend itself at a given moment to a concept of world-picture is proper to one epoch, our epoch, in which the world is thought in such a way that it lends itself to this concept.

What is this concept? Let's analyze the expression *Weltbild*. What does *world* signify and what does picture signify? World designates the totality of beings: Cosmos, nature, history and principle of the world. Picture is first of all *representation* of the totality, but it is more than reproductive representation; it is the world itself with which we have dealings and of which we have an idea, as to which we are fixed. Heidegger plays here on a German expression: "*wir sind über etwas im Bilde*" (*Weltbild*) which means we are fixed with respect to something, we know how things stand with it, what to do and how to orient ourselves. We are quite ready, in the picture. To be able to say this of something, the thing must be before us, available and reassuring, in such a way that I orient myself with respect to it.[4] "*Weltbild*," says Heidegger, "the world measured by a conception,"

4. [Translator's note:] Derrida is closely paraphrasing Heidegger here: "What is it—a 'world picture'? Obviously, a picture of the world. But what is a world? What does 'picture' mean here? 'World' serves, here, as a name for beings in their entirety. The term is not confined to the cosmos, to nature. History, too, belongs to world. But even nature and history (. . .) Initially, the word 'picture' makes one think of a copy of something. This would make the world picture, as it were, a painting of beings as a whole. But 'world picture' means more than this. We mean by it the world itself; the totality

> does not mean "picture of the world" but, rather, the world grasped as picture. Beings as a whole are now taken in such a way that a being is first and only in being insofar as it is set in place by representing-producing humanity.
> Whenever we have a *Weltbild*, an essential decision occurs concerning beings 199
> as a whole. The being of beings is sought and found in the representedness of beings. (*Off the Beaten Track*, 67–68)

(We'll be getting back to what we've been saying about representation in Husserl these last two weeks.) Let me specify that this determination of the being of beings as being-represented exhausts in Heidegger's eyes the totality of the world. There is not for him a world that would be sometimes determined this way and sometimes that way without itself being affected by these determinations. The World is entirely, through and through, what it is determined. There is not another world—a lived world—with respect to which the transitory determinations of each epoch would be more or less accurate images. The world *is* entirely in the epoch; it is nothing else.

This modern conception of the world as "representation" was impossible in the medieval world for which a being was primarily an *ens creatum*, belonging to a determinate order of creation and corresponding to the conception of God, to the idea of the understanding of God. God had a conception of the world (i.e., an understanding in which he thought what he created or had created). But the *being* of beings was never thought in its origin, in its essence, as an object for man, available for knowledge and action.

It was even less so for the Greeks. I refer you here to what Heidegger says about this on [German] p. 84 [*Off the Beaten Track*, 68–69]. But I want to hold especially on to the qualification he makes at the end of this analysis: although there could not have been a Greek *Weltbild*, Plato's determination of the beingness of beings as seen *eidos* (aspect) is the distant, historial, summary condition withdrawn in a secret mediation, for the world (*Welt*) to have been able to become an image (*Bild*). Which means that in spite of the differences between the Greek, Medieval and Modern epochs, there is a unity, the unity of one great epoch of the world, ruled by philosophy as destiny of Europe
and that sees the deployment of the world as objectity, from Plato to Hus- 200

---

of beings taken, as it is for us, as standard-giving and obligating. 'Picture' means, here, not a mere imitation, but rather that which sounds in the colloquial expression to be 'in the picture' about something ("*wir sind über etwas im Bilde*"). This means: the matter itself stands in the way it stands to us, before us. To 'put oneself in the picture' about something means: to place the being itself before one just as things are with it, and, as so placed, to keep it permanently before one" (Heidegger, "The Age of the World Picture," in *Off the Beaten Track*, 67).

serl. What was announced with Plato becomes more specific with the God of the philosophy of the Middle Ages, comes to its accomplishment after Descartes, Kant, and Hegel, and modern science and technology. Metaphysics and technology in their radical complicity determine the world as an object and thus as available for an action and a conception. And Heidegger's entire analysis of this mediation, to which I must refer you, has Descartes's search for *Sicherheit* (certainty—security), the primary motif of Cartesianism that itself represents and inaugurates an epoch and that one would have no difficulty also finding in Husserl—Heidegger has the motif of *Sicherheit* communicate with the transformations of science and technology, especially in the twentieth century, with the modification they entail in the structure of science, of the university, of literature, of aesthetics, and so forth. The move to the value of Research (*Forschung*) which takes the place of classical science is an important theme. Why does the concept of *Research* rule the University today when it would have seemed very strange only last century? The idea of *calculability* is also at the center of this analysis. Calculability is the perfection of objectivity (i.e., of beings determined as available, predictable, etc.). And the privilege accorded by Heidegger to journalists in the possibility of historicity could come along to illustrate this theme perfectly.

(Heidegger warns us against any reactionary interpretation of his analysis. The point is especially not to condemn modern times or turn away from them.)

And you can see clearly that to the extent that Husserl's attempt remains Cartesian, that it determines historicity on the basis of the *Telos* of philosophy as science, that it accords the purest historicity to the exact sciences, that it remains a philosophy of the constituting subject, and so on, it indeed does belong to the age of the world-picture. It is enclosed in it. And to the extent that it does not think this closure as such, the historicity it is talking about is not historicity itself but a determination, an epoch of historicity itself, how-
201 ever immense and present this epoch might be. It was during this *Weltbild* that Husserl was able, in a necessary but limited gesture, to criticize Dilthey's thesis of *Weltanschauung*. This was the fifth point of rupture with Husserl's phenomenology of historicity.

The end of the text to which I have just referred and in which, for that matter, Husserl was not named, warns us against the reactionary interpretation. The point is not at all to try to condemn modern times, to turn away from them, to want to escape from them toward another world and another epoch, to deny the progress of science and technology, and so forth. Quite the contrary. Simply, the fact that modern times, our epoch, could think its meaning, appear to itself as what it is, for example through the voice of Martin Heidegger (but also some others), this fact presupposes that it escapes from itself, that it is not simply one with itself and that already a shadow divides it from itself, through which its present meaning appears to it and its future is announced. A certain relation to the incalculable is the shadow that allows the motif of calculability to be thought as what it is. That is where the *question* on the essence of metaphysics and of modern times takes off. This question—a question without a response for the moment, as the response will have to be an epoch—this question as the *in-between* epochs of being opens onto a historicity that is no longer enclosed in one epoch, onto historicity in general, the historicity of being, as the movement and linking of epochs. This question is possible only if the one posing it no longer simply belongs to an epoch (i.e., to the totality of beings), but to the difference between being and the totality of beings. Comment. Historicity of being itself = life [uncertain word].

Before concluding on this necessary break with those two representatives of the metaphysics of history that Hegel and Husserl still are, a break that is necessary to gain access to the question of historicity itself before all epochal determination, before beginning to follow the henceforth unencumbered analysis of the historicity of *Dasein*, I will end by reading these few lines that all but close *Die Zeit des Weltbildes*. 202

Read [French] p. 86:

> *This incalculability becomes the invisible shadow cast over all things when man has become the *subjectum* and world has become picture.
>
> Through this shadow the modern world withdraws into a space beyond representation and so lends to the incalculable its own determinateness and historical uniqueness. This shadow, however, points to something else, knowledge of which, to us moderns, is refused. Yet man will never be able to experience and think this refusal as long as he goes around merely negating the age. The flight into tradition, out of a combination of humility and presumption, achieves, in itself, nothing, is merely a closing the eyes and blindness towards the historical moment.
>
> Man will know the incalculable—that is, safeguard it in its truth—only in creative questioning and forming from out of the power of genuine reflection. Reflection transports the man of the future into that "in-between" in which he belongs to being and yet, amidst beings, remains a stranger.* (*Off the Beaten Track*, 72)

We shall soon come back to this in-between, in a slightly modified sense.

The stage we have just completed was, then, *negative* and *critical*. Now, what are the positive results of Heidegger's move? How will the concrete description of the structures of *Dasein*'s historicity be enriched or at any rate made more rigorous for having gone through these destructions?

As I have already said: although *Dasein* is originarily historical, and his-

torical through and through, the description of its historicity, the theme of its historicity is not primary in *Sein und Zeit*. Because *Dasein*'s originary historicity cannot be thought without the *In-der-Welt-Sein* of *Dasein* and because it is on the other hand rooted in the movement of temporalization, the problem of
203 worldhood and the worlding of the world and of temporalization had to be thematized. In the first two divisions of the first part of *Sein und Zeit* (the only part published), a first part that is entitled, I remind you, "The Interpretation of Dasein in Terms of Temporality and the Explication of Time as the Transcendental Horizon of the Question of Being," in the first divisions of that first part, it is first a question of the world, in the *preparatory fundamental analysis of Dasein*, then of temporality itself (in the second division). It is during these extremely rich and difficult analyses, of the world, of being-in-the-world and of temporality, that a certain number of concepts appear about which there was a lot of talk at a given moment but, it must be said, at the level of public rumor and especially of unscrupulous translations that often did not trouble themselves even with reading. These concepts, those of authenticity and inauthenticity, of care, of fallenness, of being-toward-death, of anxiety, and so forth, will be presupposed by the fifth chapter of the second division on temporality and historicity, which comes then almost at the end of part 1, and in which we shall take a special interest. To do this right, one would have to avoid leaping, as we shall unfortunately have to do, over the explication of these concepts, taking them as though all of you here had read carefully the whole of *Sein und Zeit*. We should especially have to give back their true meaning to the analyses of world and time and wrest them from the mist of romantic pathos in which they have been enveloped. I say "enveloped," as with a rich coat that would hide the skeletal body of a philosophical intention, whereas if pathos there be—and there is—it hangs on an ontological re-understanding of affectivity, which is no longer being understood by way of metaphysics as an accident of sensibility foreign to reason, and so on. So one would need to get back to the rigor of the preparatory analyses. As we shall not have time to do that here, we shall try to limit the damage from the abstraction in which we are going to indulge by picking out the analyses devoted to historicity. We
204 shall limit the damage on occasion by taking a few indispensable glances back.

For example, and it is by this looking back that I will begin, the first chapter had thematized (1) being-toward-death or toward-the-end; (2) the possibility for Dasein to be a whole (*Ganzsein*). By placing in relation the time of essential incompleteness or the essential mode of the *not yet* that is proper to *Dasein*—and which cannot be compared to any other incompleteness of things in the world after the manner of *Vorhandenheit*—placing, then, in relation this essential incompleteness and that strange completion that is always-anticipated death, Heidegger shows in particular that not only does the essential incompleteness not prevent *Dasein* from forming a whole or rather from anticipating its proper totality; not only does it not prevent that, but it is the very form of this anticipation of *Ganzsein*.

Well, it is via this notion of *Ganzsein* that we are going to broach the concrete thematic of the historicity of *Dasein*. Up until now, Heidegger points out at the beginning of §72, the power to anticipate its own totality—a power structurally proper to *Dasein*—has been described only in the ek-stasis of the future, as being-toward-the-end and being-toward-death, as a being for which the possibility of projecting itself toward its own death was an original power that determined the *very being* of *Dasein* as finitude. Determined its being (i.e., not supervening upon it or waiting for it like an external event), as the whole of metaphysics thought one way or another, against a background of infinitude or finitude but always making of mortality the predicate of a being called man (and this is still how Sartre thinks of it, for example), but here indeed as the very being of *Dasein*. I cannot here dwell on that, and I refer you to the corresponding passages. So up until now the anticipation of the totality was precisely described as *anticipation*, a project toward my future in the dimension of a not-yet that determines the very structure of the present. Well, one describes historicity itself when one brings out as no less essential in the structure of this totalization the resumption, as it were, 205
of *birth*. Once again, this presumption and this resumption are not forms of *Bewusstsein* or of *Selbstbewusstsein* but of a transcendence that is not yet determined as intentionality of consciousness.

So we move to the theme of historicity when we consider the totalizing synthesis, or the totalizing transcendence, no longer as we have until now, unilaterally (*einseitig*), as anticipation of *my death*, but as relation to *my* birth and therefore as *Erstreckung*, as ex-tension between my death and my birth. The possessives here do not have an existentiell-empirical meaning but an existential one. *Dasein* is always *mine*, essentially *Dasein* as self-relation, a not necessarily subjective and conscientious self-relation in *Jemeinigkeit*.

This *Erstreckung*, this extension of the ek-sistence of *Dasein* that stretches out from birth to death—how original, they'll say—is what is called *life*, the course of life, the continuity of life, the concatenation of life. *Zusammenhang des Lebens*. Now the fact is that however banal it be and perhaps because that's how it seems, this "continuity of life" has never penetrated as it should have, and in its authentic meaning, the history of philosophy. The historical unity of this *Zusammenhang* has always been missed. Either,

let's say schematically, by empiricism that refused it any pure and essential possibility, the identity of the self having nothing substantial about it, or by a philosophy of the pure identity of the *ego*. Whether it take the form of a Cartesian substantialism of the *res cogitans* or a Kantian or Husserlian-type transcendentalism. In all these latter cases, the possibility of a history of *Dasein*, the possibility of the *Zusammenhang*, is entrusted to a ground that is not itself historical. That's obvious and goes without saying as far as the Cartesian *cogito* is concerned, and the extrinsic and fallen character of memory with regard to the understanding would be merely a sign of that. But it is obvious too in the case of the formal *I think* in *Kant*'s sense, as a principle of unity whose relations with the temporality of experience pose the difficult problems of which you are aware and which are broached by Heidegger in
206 *Kant and the Problem of Metaphysics*. But it is again obvious if one considers the *ego cogito* in the Husserlian sense. One might indeed be tempted to think that, this time, given that the *ego cogito* is a temporal phenomenon, it is not going to organize the unity of temporal lived experience, the totality of the concatenations of life or experience—it is not going to organize them from the outside, as a formal transcendental agency itself stable and ahistorical. And yet we have seen recently—and the right thing would be to study for themselves, here, §58 and §§79–81 of *Ideen I* to which I refer you—we have seen recently, then, that the I think, although temporal, had a permanence that was not affected by the flux of lived experience, by the continuity of the life of *consciousness*, to which it really did have to be transcendent, Husserl would say, if it was to be able to recognize itself in its identity and allow for the synthesis of lived experience. This was the theme of the transcendence of immanence that we encountered several times. How is this transcendence of immanence—which is simply situated and recognized by static phenomenology—genetically constituted? This is something Husserl will often wonder about later, but only in unpublished analyses, most of them after *Sein und Zeit*. Here Heidegger, without contesting Husserl's description, nor the earlier descriptions and their specific aim, takes explicitly and phenomenologically as his theme a region of ek-sistence that is more originary than this constituted permanence of the egological nucleus, as organization and unification of the *Zusammenhang des Lebens* and, above all, the unity of the totalization he is seeking is not a *cogito*, an I think or a consciousness. Bergson too is seeking—for example, in his introduction to *La pensée et le mouvant* (1934)[5]—a unity of the concrete self that refuses humanist empiricism,

5. Henri Bergson, *La pensée et le mouvant* (Paris: Alcan, 1934); trans. Mabelle Andison as *The Creative Mind: An Introduction to Metaphysics* (New York: Philosophical Library, 1946).

without falling into transcendentalism and the stable identity of the formal transcendental subject. This is a seductive attempt that one might compare to Heidegger's if Heidegger did not refuse to speak, unlike Bergson, of the concrete unity of a *self*, and especially of a *psychological* self whose *life*, or pure becoming, would be affected in its purity only by a reflection toward the upsurging of life or spirit as an anonymous being or force. 207

So we encounter again here the necessity of thinking the continuity of life, the *Erstreckung* or the synthesis that makes of the time of *Dasein* a history, the necessity of thinking this synthesis without rushing toward the horizon of a consciousness or a *cogito*—or conversely, of an un-conscious or a force simply borrowed from the model of *Vorhandenheit*.

We are now touching on, we are now brushing up against, the *Root* of the problem. Everything—everything: that is, not only this or that gesture of the destruction of Metaphysics but the totality of the destruction and the meaning that directs it as a whole—everything is played out around the meaning of the *Present* and the privilege accorded by the whole of philosophy to the *present*. Philosophy, what Heidegger wants to transgress, is in its entirety a philosophy of the Present, privileges the Present. First we are going to see, via a narrow access point, how this theme functions at the point we have reached.

Let's begin by reading a few lines from §72 in which Heidegger puts in question the classical philosophical descriptions of the continuity of life, that thing that is so banal and supposedly so trivial.

My translation, [German] p. 373:

> Must we not take back our point of departure of temporality as the meaning of being of the totality of Dasein (*Daseinsganzheit*), even though what we addressed as the *Zusammenhang* [continuity, power of linking] between birth and death is ontologically completely obscure? Or does *temporality*, as we set it forth, first give the *foundation* on which to provide a clear [or univocal, *eindeutig*] direction for the existential and ontological question of that "continuity"? Perhaps it is already a gain in the field of this inquiry if we learn not to take these problems too lightly. (*Being and Time*, 356)

To take them too lightly is just as much to refuse the problem on the pretext that we are dealing with something trivially self-evident—what is better-known than that: the continuity of life, the passage from life to death, and 208
so on? It is thus just as much to refuse the problem as to pose it in empiricist terms—an appeal to what people think they know under the name memory, habit, the social frameworks of memory and all the other notions that govern empirical geneses while presupposing the given self-evidence of the very thing for which they are to account. For what does *memory* or any concate-

nation of experience whatsoever mean so long as the existential-ontological problem of temporality has not been posed as such? But at a more critically elaborated and more vigilant level, the problem is also taken lightly when one speaks of a transcendental, formal or concrete, intemporal or temporal, Kantian or Husserlian permanence supposedly responsible for this continuity of life. It is this superior form of taking lightly that Heidegger especially has in his sights in the text the translation of which I will pursue. You will see appear in it the link between the permanence of the identity of the self (*Selbst*) and the privileging of the *present*.

> What seems "more simple" than the nature of the "continuity of life" between birth and death? *Es besteht aus* [emphasize *stehen*—con-sistency], it consists [implied: or so one thinks] of a succession of experiences (*Erlebnissen*) *"in der Zeit"* "in time" [in quotes]. If we pursue this characterization of the continuity in question and above all of the *ontologischen Vormeinung*: the ontological assumption [if you will, the pre-intention, the ontological pre-interpretation hidden behind this apparently innocent description. Comment.] behind it in a more penetrating way, something remarkable happens. In this succession of experiences only the experience that is present [and note that "present" here is *vorhanden*. Comment: this is not by chance] [open quotes] "each time now," (im *"jeweiligen Jetzt" vorhandene Erlebenis*), is "really" "real," (*"eigentlich" "wirklich"*). (*Being and Time*, 356)

What Heidegger is describing here is not only the point of view of common sense but also that of existentialism or transcendental idealism for which
209 presence (*Vorhandenheit*) and the present, the present lived experience (*vorhandene Erlebnis*), or in Husserlian language the living Present (*lebendige Gegenwart*), are the very form of real, authentic, effective, full experience. It must be clearly understood that this absolute privileging of the Present and the Presence of the Present that Heidegger must destroy or shake up in order to recover the possibility of historicity cannot be destroyed by him the way one criticizes a contingent prejudice. It must be clearly understood that what he is going to *solicit* (I prefer this word to "destroy": comment) in this privilege of the Present is the self-evidence, the assurance, the most total and most irreducible ground of the totality of metaphysics itself; it is philosophy itself. If we had the time we could show this on the basis of any philosopher by following this or that indication of Heidegger's; in particular we could show it of Hegel in whom Western philosophy is summed up and for whom the movement of experience is the movement of presence and of the presence of the *vorhanden* object and of consciousness as consciousness of the presence of the object or presence to self ceaselessly taking itself back up

into itself in a such a way that ultimately absolute knowledge has the form of the absolute self-consciousness of self-presence in *parousia*, and so on. And the text *Hegel's Concept of Experience* shows how, in the *Phenomenology of Spirit*, the theme remains the presence of the present, the presentness (*Anwesenheit*) of the present. The Present is the proximity of *beings* (*ens*), and the presence of the present is therefore the proximity of beings *qua* beings; it is the proximity of beingness, of the being-being of beings (*Seiendheit — ousia*). And Heidegger points out that

> [t]he beingness of beings—which from the beginning of Greek thinking to Nietzsche's theory of the eternal return of the same has happened as the truth of beings—is for us only one mode (. . .) of being which by no means must necessarily appear exclusively as the presentness of what presences.[6]

We shall be returning to this passage. But without getting involved in Hegel again here, and in order to privilege, for reasons I gave last time, the relation to Husserl, it is clear that Husserl, here, is still a metaphysician of the Present 210
(i.e., a metaphysician). This not only for reasons we have already encountered, but for his very thematic of the Living Present. The living Present is, he says, the absolute, absolutely universal and unconditioned form of experience, the ultimate, irreducible and fundamental form of all evidence and of all meaning. And we must first understand the *philosophical invulnerability* of this Husserlian affirmation if we are to grasp the audacity of Heidegger's gesture. Why invulnerable? Well it is evident, it is self-evidence itself that any experience is only ever lived in the *present* and that everything of experience that comes about, everything that appears in it, presents itself in it, as meaning or as self-evidence, is present. We have the absolute certainty that however far back in time we go, in our own time or in that of humanity or in time in general, no experience has been possible that was not had in the present. And we know *a priori*—and if there was only one thing in the world we did not need to learn it is this one—however distantly we anticipate the future, we know *a priori* that in millions of years, if there is an experience, a thought in general (human or not, divine or not, animal or not), it will be in the present, as we are in the present now. My death and the present. Living Present more fundamental than the *I*. Unpublished texts.[7] An assertion that is perhaps trivial but irrecusable: *we never leave the Present*. Life—life in the

6. Heidegger, "Hegel's Concept of Experience," in *Off the Beaten Track*, 116.

7. The three preceding sentences, from "my death" to "unpublished texts," were added in the margin of the manuscript. By "unpublished texts," Derrida might be referring to Husserl's manuscripts.

sense in which life is the opening of the difference that allows appearing—life, animal life or the life of consciousness, life in general (and people have tried to say that Husserlianism is a philosophy of life . . .)—life is living only in the present and the Living Present is a tautological expression in which in any case one cannot tell a subject from a predicate. Ultimate foundation of our being-together. This philosophy of the Living Present does not mean
211 that all temporal differences or modifications are erased in the present.

In particular, all Husserl's analyses of the constitution of time—analyses that are dominated by this concept of the Living Present—all these analyses show the greatest respect for the original experiences which refer us to the past and to the future. But precisely the primary condition of this respect is not to forget that

(1) [t]he past is lived as past only if it refers us to a Present past that the Past comprises in its very signification since it was present.

(2) The future is lived—anticipated—as what it is (i.e., future) only if one knows, only if one experiences *a priori* that what is anticipated is a future Present; there would be no anticipation if the very thing anticipated were not a present to come. What is anticipated in anticipation is a present, the to-come of the future [*l'à-venir de l'à-venir*] is a present just as the past of the past is a present. And what is true of thematic memory and anticipation is also true of immediate retention and protention, incessant modifications of the Living Present, but modifications such that, without them, there would be nothing modif*ied* (i.e., no Living Present). That is the originality of Hegel and Husserl.

(3) It must not be forgotten that not only do the two modifying openings that open onto the past and the future open onto a past present and a future present, but that the opening itself, what opens onto the other presents, is already a *Present*. The Present is thus form, and the form of all experience and all self-evidence. And according to Husserl, to respect the movement of temporalization is to respect this *a priori* unconditionality of the Present. But what is true of temporalization is also true of historicity. For Husserl—as for Hegel for that matter—there is historicity only insofar as the past and the origin can be made present, can be transmitted; insofar as I can for example reactivate—that is, render the past manifestation active and current again—that is, therefore, insofar as a meaning can be transmitted across a chain of Presents in such a way that I can reawaken another presence in my living present. Cf. *Krisis*. Presence would thus be the condition of historicity
212 and its very form. But that means that in itself the form of historicity is not historical and that the condition of historicity is a certain ahistoricity of history, a certain intemporality of time. The present being all at once temporal

and intemporal and omnitemporal. There would be no history according to Husserl without the omnitemporality of ideal objects that can be transmitted as the same. But this transmission of the same would itself be impossible without this fundamental form of the same as the form of manifestation; namely, the Present.

There is something irrecusable about this. In the name of what present self-evidence, in the name of what, then, can one shake the self-evidence of self-evidence? In the name of what fact? One might for example appeal to some psychopathological experiences, some cases, some experiences in which this supposed norm of norms would supposedly be contradicted, *by the fact* of an anomaly: the anomaly of the patient who does not live "in the present," of a fixed experience like a schema of repetition in which a past scene supposedly imposes its meaning on the so-called present experience . . . . You see where this is going.

Well, it goes without saying that presented in such a way, an argument of this type that appeals to *facts* is far from being probative. It will easily be shown that the facts appealed to do not contradict but merely modify—and thereby confirm—the transcendental structure of the Present. It is in the form of the Living Present that the *content* of lived experience can be given the pathological signification of non-presence. It is obvious that the so-called "patient" *lives* in the present, in an unmodifiable transcendental present, the very thing that is apprehended or experienced as a past repeating itself, and so on. And this community of the present of every experience—the fact that *we* always live in the same present and that the ground of this *we* is the *Present*—this community cannot be affected by the separations, the inadequations, be they infinite, between two experiential contents. Absolute non-community, the most radical [illegible word] rupture takes place in the *form* of the common Present that is its very condition of possibility. *213*

Such would be the self-evidence of self-evidence and no science of facts—historical or psychological facts, no science of normal or abnormal facts—can, *qua* science of facts, belie it. And this self-evidence of self-evidence as presence is the form of the rationality in general of meaning in general.

Well, this is what is to be, not criticized or refuted on the basis of an irrationalism or a non-self-evidence that would be the contrary of self-evidence, but brought out as such on the background of a shadowy zone against which it stands out, this—the self-evidence of self-evidence—is what is to be solicited as a determination or as a historical epoch, that is to be subjected *qua* epoch to an epoch, *epokhē* that is to be subjected as epoch of *ratio* to the epoch of *Thinking* (thinking goes beyond *Ratio* for Heidegger), to subject that epoch to this epoch in order to bring out, bring out neither as a present self-evidence nor as another form of evidence, for there are not two forms of evidence—bring out in the sense of giving to think . . . what? *Historicity itself.*

To define the meaning of being as *pre*sence is quite clearly to reduce historicity. At the very moment that one is claiming to make it possible or respect it, as for Hegel and Husserl, by showing the absolute Present to be the condition of historical concatenation and traditionality, one is summing history up [*on résume l'histoire*]. This summation or this reduction of history in the Present is not the gesture of a philosopher, a gesture for which this or that philosophical subjectivity, this or that philosophical system, would be responsible; it is the very form of historialization that is constituted by dissimulating itself in the very *presence* of appearing. In the Present, history is erased or summed up and that dissimulation resounds in philosophical discourse *qua* metaphysics of the Living Present. And in a way, this metaphysics that reduces history, even when it claims to be thematizing it, cannot be overcome, just as the Present and the Presence of the Present cannot be *overcome*.

Nevertheless, one can pose the question of self-evidence and presence and wonder whether the self-evidence of the presence of the present does not
214 refer to a meaning of experience the historicity—that is, the character as past—of which would be the very thing that, while determining meaning in the Presence of the Present, would itself radically and definitively escape the form of the Present. In other words, experience would have a meaning that by its essence would never allow itself to be phenomenalized in the form of the living present. This meaning—which would never phenomenalize itself in the form of the living present—would never phenomenalize itself and would never come to experience as such. Comment.

It is clear that without the possibility of this meaning of being or of experience that would never come forth in the form of presence or would never be exhausted in it, one would never think historicity itself. In particular, one would never think the *origin* and the *end*, birth and death as such; as such: namely, as being unable to appear in the form of presence or appearing as what cannot appear. The certainty of the living Present as absolute form of experience and absolute source of meaning, presupposes as such the neutralization of *my* birth and *my* death. What I grasp when I think the *a priori* necessity of the living Present is the possibility of a temporalization without me, without a me the status of which—empirical or transcendental—is moreover difficult to specify. In any case, holding to the Present as the foundation and the source of meaning is to affirm infinity and eternity as the foundation of meaning and possibly of the historicity of meaning. The Present is essentially what cannot end. It is in itself ahistorical. Even if it is purely temporal, as in Husserl, the present can only open a temporality and

a temporalization that are infinite. That is, non-historical. This is why it will appear to be so indispensible to Heidegger, when he is trying to get back to a buried depth of historicity, to begin by affirming the originarily essential finitude of temporalization. That is, of a movement of temporalization that would not reduce birth and death, and would even be opened on the basis of the anticipation of death and a certain relation to birth. In a passage we shall study later, Heidegger writes (§74), "*Only authentic temporality that is at the same time finite makes something like destiny (Schicksal), that is, authentic* 215
historicity, possible" (*Being and Time*, 366), and later, "*Authentic being-toward-death, that is, the finitude of temporality, is the concealed ground of the historicity of Dasein*" (*Being and Time*, 367).

One sees why the analytic of historicity comes in *Sein und Zeit* after that of temporality and why the being-toward-death structure of *Dasein* was the first chapter of the second division, devoted to *Dasein und Zeitlichkeit*. One cannot gain access to authentic temporalization outside the horizon of death and of freedom-for-death; that is, one can gain access to authentic temporalization only in the horizon of finitude, and one gains access to authentic historicity only on the basis of a finite temporality. There is no history if temporality is not finite. Hegel and Husserl were in a certain way saying the opposite. So one might be tempted to say—and this is the path Heidegger will take—that the philosophy of the Presence of the Present misses *history*. The immense difficulty here is that the philosophies of the Present, philosophy itself, can very well and with very good reasons claim for itself access to historicity.

Here, the pause we are going to make around this formidable and decisive point will allow us to open by anticipation *the* question, the question of being and history, will allow us to perceive the place in which ultimately everything is played out between Heidegger and philosophy, and above all allow us to understand why *Sein und Zeit* is still on the threshold of this question in spite of the immense amount of work done in it.

Let's move forward patiently: philosophy—I shall now say "philosophy" to designate metaphysics, onto-theology or phenomenology, which are all ways of thinking the Present and the presence of the present—philosophy, especially in its Hegelian-Husserlian form, can then legitimately show that it alone lets history be what it is and respects it in its meaning. 216

(1) There would be no history without the present, without the chain of transmissibility ensured by the formal identity of the presence of the present. I will not go over this again. Phenomenology of spirit and Husserlian phenomenology.

(2) In a way that is perhaps less immediate, philosophy could show that

to ground everything on the Presence of the Present is to affirm or recognize finitude, and that there is no historicity without a passage via finitude. Which is, moreover, obvious. How does the affirmation of ground as presence recognize finitude? Because it also consists in affirming the impossibility of getting out of the present—history being born of this impossibility of living, this impossibility for an experience to happen other than in the form of the present, such that it does not reach the past as present but as past. It maintains this, while knowing *a priori* that it is dealing with a past present, but it does not grasp it in itself insofar as it is only ever in the present that one could be in the past. Here the finitude and infinitude of memory [uncertain word] coincide to define the historicity of experience. And this is why theological infinity is on the horizon especially of the Hegelian-Husserlian thinking of history. And this is why Hegel can affirm in his most profound texts the unity of the finite and the infinite. (Abandonment of this notion by Heidegger). [Illegible word.]

And it is incontestable that a certain *historicity* is thus respected and correctly described by philosophy.

But—and this is what Heidegger begins to say in *Sein und Zeit,* although he does not yet articulate it, cannot yet articulate it clearly, for an essential reason—but, then, the historicity described by philosophy is not the historicity of the being of beings; it is the history of beings in their beingness and, more narrowly still, so to speak, of beingness determined as presence and appearing since the Greeks, and still more narrowly since Descartes, as presence in the
217 form of consciousness, in the form of re-presentation. In other words, historicity is described in the closure of beings and even of a determinate form of beings that is the present being, the presentness of the being: experience or experience of consciousness. Outside this closure, the being of beingness and consequently the being of consciousness is not thought in its truth, and still less thought in its historicity. The hidden horizon of being—which allows beings to appear as what they are, in their beingness—this horizon is withdrawn from history. Although the origin of the meaning of experience is historicized by Hegel and by Husserl, the origin of this origin, the origin *qua* being of the beingness of presentness escapes Hegeliano-Husserlian history. It escapes *the history of philosophy*, the history of philosophy (i.e., historicity as it is thought in philosophy—and therefore in the whole history of philosophy). The history spoken of by philosophy, in the final analysis and even when it speaks best about it, is *the limited history of one epoch of being*. An epoch in which being is determined in absolutely general fashion as a being, in more determinate fashion by one epoch in the epoch as presence, and in still more determinate fashion as presence in representation. Epoch of being, which

means both period and suspension, *epokhē*, suspensive withdrawal through which being, in its epoch, withdraws and hides, brackets itself in a historial movement, under its determination, ontic determination in general, and, following that, other more determinate determinations.

In this sense, *Sein und Zeit* announces the end of this epoch but still belongs to it in that the historicity it describes, it doubtless indeed describes in the *now explicit* horizon of being—and that's progress: the question of being is posed as such from the opening pages of *Sein und Zeit*. But—and in this respect it still remains within the epoch of metaphysics—the description of historicity in *Sein und Zeit* still concerns the historicity of one form of beings, beings *qua Dasein*. It is still in a way history as *experience* (in a sense that, in spite of everything, still relates to that of *phenomenology*—that of Hegel or that of Husserl). It is still, as he says himself, a phenomenology. And no doubt, in order to begin to understand Heidegger's path, one must *218*
think together and clarify, one for the other, the abandonment or the incompletion—I do not say renunciation—of *Sein und Zeit*, and a text such as *Hegel's Concept of Experience* in which the idea of phenomenology and the theme of the presentness of the present as determination of the beingness of beings, dissimulating the truth of being, are recognized and repeated, "*destroyed*." And it is not by chance that the word *phenomenology* which, with something of a new inflexion, remained a watchword in *Sein und Zeit*, and the rule of its methodology, is progressively abandoned by Heidegger. The history of being cannot be thought in a phenomenology, which can only think an epoch and I would say *the* epoch itself, the dissimulation and the greatest epoch itself of being.

Having resituated *Sein und Zeit* in this way, let's come back to it. In spite of the limitation I have just indicated, *Sein und Zeit* begins, then, to shake up, to solicit the *epoch* that dissimulates the history of being under the history of beingness determined as presentness. It begins to do this precisely in this §72 from which we started out. You will remember that, in the passage I broke off translating at a given point, the point was to show how the unity of the *Zusammenhang des Lebens* had always been delegated as much by metaphysical idealism as by transcendental idealism to an *ahistorical* agency. And precisely this ahistorical agency is both—not by chance—subjectivity and Present, subjectivity as unalterability of the presence of the present. It is this ahistorical agency that for classical metaphysics ensures the unity of the totalization—that is, of the history, this ahistorical agency that is at bottom without a past because it is the present of the present, the nowness of the now [*la maintenance du maintenant*].

So let me pick up my translation:

> What seems "more simple" than the nature of the "continuity of life" between birth and death? It consists of a succession of experiences (*Erleb-*
> 219 *nissen*) *"in der Zeit"* "in time." If we pursue this characterization of the continuity in question and above all of the ontological assumption behind it in a more penetrating way, something remarkable happens. In this succession of experiences only the experience that is present "each time now," *im "jeweiligen Jetzt" vorhandene Erlebenis*, is "really" "real." (*Being and Time*, 356)

I emphasized a moment ago that present is *vorhanden*. One now sees the same intention of Heidegger as egoical [uncertain word] on the basis of this notion. Philosophy as philosophy of the present—in the sense defined just now—is a philosophy pre-determining being as *Vorhandenheit* (being before me subsisting as an object).

I continue my translation:

> The experiences past and just coming, on the other hand, are no longer or not yet "wirklich," "real." Dasein traverses the time-span allotted to it between the two boundaries in such a way that it is "real" only in each *now*, and *durchhüpft*, hops, so to speak, through the succession (*Jetztfolge*) of nows of its "time." For this reason one says that Dasein is "temporal" (*zeitlich*). The self (*Selbst*) maintains itself in a certain sameness [*Selbigkeit*: le *Selbst* maintains itself in its *Selbigkeit*] throughout this constant change (*Wechsel*) of experiences. Opinions diverge as to how this persistent (*dieses Beharrlichen*) self is to be defined and how one is to determine what relation it may possibly have to the changing (*Wechsel*) experiences. (*Being and Time*, 356)

(In other words, the polemic that animates philosophy in its own field, as to the meaning of this per-sistence, the polemic that opposes empiricism to Kantianism, Kantianism to Cartesianism, and Husserlianism to Kantianism and Cartesianism, etc., etc.) This polemic opposes interpretations
220 of this descriptive schema that is itself according to Heidegger never called into question, is itself the common and intangible axiom of objective rationalism, of empiricism, and of the transcendental idealisms. I think that this affirmation of Heidegger's does not have to be commented on or illustrated: it is entirely self-evident. So the origin of this descriptive schema, and the being-meaning of this structure, are not interrogated: they remain indeterminate. Heidegger continues:

> The being of this *verharrend-wechselnden Zusammenhangs von Erlebnissen*, of this persistently changing continuity remains undetermined. At bottom, however, and whether one admits it or not, *ein "in der Zeit" Vorhandenes, aber selbstverständlich "Undingliches;"* something objectively present [*Vorhandenes*] "in time," but of course "unthinglike," has been posited in this characterization of the continuity of life (*Lebenszusammenhang*). (*Being and Time*, 356)

Comment.

Now, so long as one holds onto this *Vorhandenheit*, not only, as Heidegger will say later, does one have no chance of describing ontologically, of finding an ontological sense to the *Erstreckung*, to the extension of *Dasein* between birth and death, but one even has no chance of posing the *ontological* problem of this extension. This extension is nothing, then; it is merely the empirical and fallen and inessential multiplicity of a presence, of a persistent *Vorhandenheit*. Philosophy, as philosophy of the Presence of the Present (tautology) cannot therefore take seriously the *Erstreckung*, the totalizing extension between birth and death.

I note, no doubt needlessly but as a supplementary precaution, that with the theme of this *Erstreckung* between birth and death we are not in the field of an individual description, of something that would be an individual *Dasein*. First because we never have been. The notion of individuality was 221
never used by Heidegger. Next because by the time we are dealing with historicity, in the fifth chapter of the second division, Heidegger has already described the structure of *Mitsein* as an originary existential structure of *Dasein*. So we are dealing just as much with the birth and death of what we call an individual as of a community or the totality of beings in the form of *Dasein*, the totality of *Dasein* even before its possible determinations as individuals, as more or less broad groups and communities, as humanity, from birth to death, and so forth. The question of knowing whether *Erstreckung* as historicity is the *Erstreckung* of this or that example of *Dasein* is for the moment quite irrelevant; it is a derivative question with regard to the originarity of the analysis. When this analysis is complete, perhaps we will know what an individual is, what an intersubjective community, or humanity is. For the moment we do not know. I close this parenthesis.

The point, then, is to pose the ontological question of the *Erstreckung* on the basis of this destruction of Presence. *Dasein* ek-sists. "But," says Heidegger,

> it does not ek-sist as the sum of *Momentanwirklichkeiten*, the momentary realities of experiences that succeed each other and disappear. Nor does this succession [this *Nacheinander*] gradually fill up a framework. For how should that framework (*Rahmen*) be present (*vorhanden*), when it is always only the experience that one is having "right now" that is "real," and when the boundaries of the framework—birth that is past and death that is yet to come—are lacking reality? At bottom, even the vulgar interpretation of the "continuity of life" does not think of a framework spanned "outside" of Dasein and embracing it, but correctly looks for it in Dasein itself. When, however, one tacitly [silently] regards this being [Dasein] ontologically as *"in der Zeit" Vorhandenen*, something present "in time," an attempt at any

> ontological characterization of the being "between" birth and death gets stranded. (*Being and Time*, 357)

At bottom, as we shall see, it is in the passage, the *in-between*, in that nothing that the present in-between seems to be that the movement of historicity
222 must be recognized. This is what Heidegger does now in the first finally . . . positive gesture of this passage, in order to define what the *Geschehen* is.

> Dasein does not first fill up a *vorhandene* (present) path or stretch "of life" through the phases of its momentary realities, but stretches itself along, *erstreckt sich selbst* [so it does not run over a present expanse], it stretches *itself* along [it is its path] in such a way that its own being is constituted beforehand as this stretching along. The "between" (the *Zwischen*) of birth and death already lies *in the being* [emphasized] of Dasein." (*Being and Time*, 357)

So the in-between is not an empirical transition, a transitory modification of a presence of the First and the Last, such that the first can coincide substantially with the last, the principle with the end once the transition has passed, as is the case in Hegelian speculation; here the in-between belongs to the being of *Dasein*. Which comes down to saying that in this *in-between*, the past and the future are not simply left behind as past present or future present but *more than that*, are *still* or are *already*, but in a still or an already that no longer have the sense of *presence*. *Dasein is* its past and *is* its future, is its birth and its death. But the *is* [*est*] here designates a Being that can *absolutely* not have the form of presence or phenomenality. We are dealing here with an estance of being that does not have the form of consciousness. And really to understand this, and really understand the passage I shall translate in a moment, in which Heidegger shows that *Dasein is* its past and its future without summing them up in presence or in consciousness, to situate clearly the originality of this proposition we must *once again* recall Hegel. Hegel too says that the in-between, the movement of passage, defines historicity—the *dia* and the dialectic as experience of consciousness itself—is the historicity of consciousness. And in commenting on the *Introduction* to the *Phenom-*
223 *enology of Spirit*, Heidegger both brings out the originality of this *dia*, the between-two-consciousnesses—natural consciousness and the philosophical consciousness that knows what the past natural consciousness was—Heidegger brings out both the originality of this *dia*, and the fact that this *dia* is still only the *dia* of the experience of *consciousness*—that is, of a determinate form of Being as presence and more precisely as *presence* in the form of *representation*. I shall simply read a few lines of this commentary without claiming to enter into it systematically.

First passage. Repeating the exchange, the movement of consciousness as the unity of the dialogue between natural consciousness and philosophical consciousness, Heidegger writes,

> In this ambiguity, consciousness betrays the fundamental trait of its essence: at the same time, to be already that which it is not yet. Being in the sense of being-conscious, consciousness (*Bewusstsein*), means: to reside in the not-yet of the already, and to do this in such a way that this Already presences in the Not-yet. This presence is in itself a self-referral into the Already. It sets off on the path to the already. It makes itself a path. The being of consciousness consists in the fact that it moves on a path. The being which Hegel thinks as experience has the fundamental trait of movement. (*Off the Beaten Track*, 138)

A little later:

> Consciousness, as consciousness, is the movement of consciousness, for it is the comparison between ontic/pre-ontological knowledge [let's translate: natural consciousness] and ontological knowledge. The former exerts its claim on the latter. The latter claims that it is the truth of the former. Between (*dia*) the one and the other, is the articulation of these claims, a *legein*. In this dia-logue, consciousness ascribes truth to itself. The *dialegein* is a *dialegesthai*. However, the dialogue does not stand still in *one* shape of consciousness. As the dialogue that it is, it goes through (*dia*) the entire realm of the shapes of consciousness. In this movement of going-through, it gathers itself into the truth of its essence. *Dialegein*, thoroughgoing gathering, is 224
> a self-gathering, *dialegesthai*. (*Off the Beaten Track*, 138)

Never is Heidegger so close to Hegel. Or in any case, *Sein und Zeit* to the *Phenomenology of Spirit*. One could almost literally inscribe what Heidegger is describing here—and is describing without interpreting (the passages I have just read are an unexceptional and uncontroversial paraphrase of Hegel)—one could almost literally, at the point in *Sein und Zeit* where the in-between is mentioned as the already of the not yet and the not yet of the already that are the very structure of the movement, of an *eksistence* that is its own path and does not follow a path assigned in advance, one could *almost* transcribe, I was saying. *Almost*. For the difference appears precisely when Heidegger says Ek-sistence instead of experience (i.e., in the Hegelian sense: experience of consciousness).

No longer saying *experience*, that signifies refusing to make of *consciousness* the form of this progression, and refusing to make consciousness the form of this progression is refusing to see it occur in the form of *presence* and as a prescribed progression, a progression to which is prescribed that it progress toward *absolute presence*, toward the parousia of absolute consciousness, absolute knowledge as absolute self-consciousness and being absolutely with itself—that is, toward a presence in which once again death is gathered up in Presence. If one considers that Presence is merely one determination of being, however privileged it be, well, to replace the notion of experience with that of ek-sistence-to-death is to destroy that determination and begin to shatter the epoch. I'll read one last passage from *Hegel's Concept of Experience* in which Heidegger defines consciousness or experience as *one* way of *being*.

> Experience is what suffices to gain its attainment.[8] Experience is a mode of
> 225 presence, i.e., of being. Through experience, phenomenal consciousness presences as phenomenal into its own presence with itself. Experience gathers consciousness into the gathering of its own essence. (*Off the Beaten Track*, 139)

The difference—apparently subtle but *decisive*—between Heidegger and Hegel being thus approached once again, we can, I hope, better understand the apparently so Hegelian passage in which Heidegger defines the proper field of an analytic of the historicity of *Dasein*.

This is still in §72, [German] pp. 374–75:

> The "between" of birth and death already lies *in the being* of Dasein, [as we were just reading]. On the other hand, it is by no means the case that Dasein "is" [emphasized] real in a point of time, and that, in addition, it is then "surrounded" by the nonreality of its birth and its death. Understood existentially [comment], birth is never something past in the sense of *Nichtmehrvorhanden* [of what is no longer *vorhanden*: present], and death is just as far from having the kind of being of something outstanding that is not yet *vorhanden* but will come. Factical Dasein exists *gebürtig* [as native, as what has a—natural?—birth], and in being born it is also already dying in the sense of being-toward-death. Both "ends" (*Enden*) and their "between" *are* [emphasized] as long as Dasein factically exists, and they are in the sole way possible on the basis of the being of Dasein as *care*. In the unity of *Geworfenheit* [being-thrown] and the fleeting, or else anticipatory, being-toward-death [comment], birth and death *zusammenhängen* [are linked together] in the way appropriate to Dasein (*Daseinsmäßig*). As care, Dasein *is* the "between."
>
> But the constitutional totality of care has the possible *ground* of its unity in temporality. The ontological clarification of the "*Lebenszusammenhang*," that is, of the specific way of stretching along, movedness (*Bewegtheit*), and
> 226 per-sistence of Dasein, must accordingly be approached in the horizon of the

8. [Translator's note:] This is how Young and Haynes translate "Das Erfahren ist das auslangend-erlangende Gelangen" (*Holzwege*, 170); Derrida quotes the French translation, "L'expérience, c'est le parcours qui s'élance," and repeats in brackets "Le parcours qui s'élance!" presumably because of the incongruity of this expression in French.

> temporal constitution of this being. The movedness (*Bewegtheit*) of existence is not the movement (*Bewegung*) of a *Vorhandenen* [of something present]. It is determined from the stretching along of Dasein. The specific movedness of the *erstreckten Sicherstrecken*, *stretched out stretching itself along* [the self-constituting extension, the path that constitutes itself: method . . .], we call the *Geschehen* of Dasein: the historicity of Dasein. The question of the "*Zusammenhang*" of Dasein is the ontological problem of its *Geschehen*. To expose the *structure of Geschehen* and the existential and temporal conditions of its possibility means to gain an *ontological* understanding of *historicity*. (*Being and Time*, 357–58)

Three remarks in conclusion:

We have seen that the condition of this bringing out of *Geschehen* presupposed a solicitation or a destruction of the privileging of the Present in a philosophy or a metaphysics or an onto-theology that had even become the practice of this privileging. We are dealing there, then, with a privileging that is not a contingent, avoidable privilege, corresponding to an error of thought. We are dealing there with an inauthenticity the necessity of which is inscribed in the very structure of Dasein, in particular in the historicity of Dasein and, as we shall see, in the history of being. It belongs to the historicity of Dasein and being that this historicity should hide in philosophy and in its theme: the presence of the present.

My first point will then be the following: never forget what we said at the outset about the concept and operation of destruction. Destruction is neither a refutation nor an annihilation. The destruction of metaphysics, here the destruction of the privilege of the Present, could never erase them. There is an unsurpassable necessity in the dissimulation of the meaning of being in presence and thus in the phenomenality of consciousness. The best proof of this is that one cannot avoid making non-phenomenality appear in order
to speak it and to say of it that phenomenality and presence dissimulate it. 227
At the very moment when Heidegger destroys metaphysics, he must confirm it, destroy it in its language since he is speaking and is making appear in the Present the very thing he is saying cannot be gathered up in presence. And so on.

Second: let me point out the attempt made by Levinas, claiming to go against Heidegger but in many respects still in his wake, to destroy this privilege of phenomenality and the Present. I do not want to get into this here. But let me point out that the latest stage of this enterprise—which otherwise remains caught in a traditional conceptuality that too often weighs it down unbeknownst to it—consists in elaborating a thematic of the Trace, as opposed to the Sign. The Trace being precisely the appearing of what, irreducibly and therefore infinitely, withdraws from phenomenality and presence, and that Levinas most often calls the infinitely other but also the Past, a past to which one has a relation as to an absolute past that can absolutely not be thought as past present, as a modification, in whatever sense, of the Present or of a consciousness.

But ⇒ non-history.

Third: every time one tries today, in the style of Nietzsche, Marx, Freud, and so on (I'm not trying to assimilate them) to solicit the privilege of consciousness, to denounce consciousness as dissimulation and misrecognition, and so forth, it is obvious that, whatever fruitful and concrete results may be reached in empirical practice, the only chance of escaping the legitimate accusation of irresponsible empiricism coming from philosophy, and especially from a rigorous transcendental idealism, the only chance of escaping it is, from the outset, by making a theme of the signification of the Present and the Presence of the Present as the fundamental determination of being by metaphysics, making a theme of this dissimulation of the meaning of being in Pre-sence, making a theme of this dissimulation as history and therefore making a theme of the history of that dissimulation, especially of the move from a Greek form of dissimulation to the post-Cartesian form in which presence becomes consciousness and re-presentational consciousness, and so
228 forth. And therefore in making a theme of the epochs of Metaphysics and of metaphysics as epoch. One of the primordial conditions of this thematization is of course that one meditate especially on the moment when the epoch closes on itself and therefore begins to open, gives a glimpse of its end (i.e., on Hegel's moment). Hegel whom it would be necessary to begin by reading, and reading without precipitation. Failing this thematization, all aggressive gestures aimed at metaphysics and transcendental idealism will remain imprisoned in what they are taking aim at, and will not get beyond the style of impotent and juvenile insult. Failing this patient and "destructive" theoretical thematization, the practical efficacy even of these gestures denouncing consciousness, however real and positive it may sometimes be, will for all that have only the kind of efficacy that characterizes somnambulism. Now we know at least two things about somnambulism:

(1) That its infallibility, however admirable it may sometimes be, is nonetheless at the mercy of an unforeseen breath of air;

(2) That somnambulism is perhaps the very essence of metaphysics. Here I refer you to everything that has already been said.

SESSION SEVEN

22 February 1965[1]

Last time, we applied ourselves to bringing out the most general structure of *Geschehen* and of the Geschichtlichkeit of Dasein. A preliminary stage that could only be passed through after the solicitation of metaphysics, insofar as it is merely the privileged determination of the present and the presence of the present. That is a theme that occupied us during the last two hours and I shall not go back over it. Any more than what preceded that theme itself.

Now we must forge ahead. But can we forge ahead, given where we are? If I ask this question it is because it is tempting to presume, after what has already been said, that, once the place and transcendental structure of historicity have been recognized, and recognized as rooted in temporality, its temporality, there will no longer be much that is very positive and concrete to say about it, from the point of view of the analytic of Dasein.

Before going through this analytic of the historicity of Dasein to the end, I would like to spend some time wondering about this phenomenon of running out of breath that happens in this analytic at the end of *Sein und Zeit*.

This running out of breath shows up in a certain number of signs and it 230
has a certain number of essential reasons. Two signs that can be reduced to one, and two reasons that can be reduced to one.

The first sign is, as we shall verify in a moment, that Heidegger never goes beyond the critical phase of the analysis. He operates a sort of ground-clearing; he clears the space to bring out the proper place for an analysis of the historicity of Dasein. This is moreover very conscious and explicitly recognized by Heidegger who writes, at the end of §72, "In the following reflections [the whole chapter on historicity], we shall content ourselves with indicating, announcing (*anzuzeigen*) the ontological place of the problem of historicity" (*Being and Time*, 360). And this place will be indicated only by

1. Derrida has the following dates in the manuscript: "22.02.65 ⇒ 01.03.65"; it seems likely that the session originally scheduled for February 22 was pushed back to March 1.

exclusion; it will simply be cleared. And, very curiously, even though, as I have already noted, Diltheyanism is profoundly criticized on this or that point, here Heidegger's remarks admit to being Diltheyan or as the extension of an as-yet poorly understood intention of Dilthey's. Immediately after the passage that I have just quoted in which Heidegger proposes merely to announce the ontological place of the problem of historicity, it is written, "Basically, the following analysis is solely concerned with furthering the pioneering investigations of Dilthey. Today's present generation has not as yet made them its own" (*Being and Time*, 360). We shall see a little later what the extension of Diltheyanism signifies.

The second sign of running out of breath is the basically quite remarkable fact that the chapter entitled "Temporality and Historicity" is, with the exception of one chapter, the last chapter of the only part of *Sein und Zeit* to have seen the light of day. It is between the structural determination of the ontological place of historicity and the descriptive, intuitive filling out of this structure that the impossibility of an entirely continuous progress in fact showed up, whatever the signification of this fact may ultimately be. I say "entirely continuous progress": entirely continuous—that is, going beyond
231 the stage of the analytic of Dasein . . . ; "beyond" here meaning toward a problematic of a History of Being liberated from what was still ontic and metaphysical in *Sein und Zeit* and that I pointed out last time; going beyond without a certain discontinuity was in fact impossible . . . .

These two signs come down to one insofar as they both show up as the impossibility of going beyond a limitation at the very moment when that limitation is denounced as a limitation, when the philosophical meaning of the limitation appears as such. This limitation can appear to be double but it is one: it can appear to be double because we are dealing at the same time with an analysis still limited to that type of being—Dasein—however privileged it may be and legitimately so, an analysis that is still metaphysical. But we have seen the necessity of this, and that of a simply destructive analysis that installs itself in metaphysics in order to de-construct it, but which can get beyond destruction only by going positively beyond metaphysics, which is impossible in the simple sense of the word *overcoming*. But this impossibility of a simple overcoming of metaphysics will perhaps have more to tell us, more to let us understand about history.

I'll move on now to the two reasons, in any case the two most immediately apparent reasons, for this running out of breath.

First. What is said about the historicity of Dasein basically prevents one going beyond the destructive moment. The only positive affirmation concerning the historicity of Dasein—namely, the determination of its ontological place—inhibits for reasons of principle a positive and above all an original description of the historicity of Dasein. What I mean here is difficult, difficult to formulate, and we are going to try to get to it slowly and patiently.

Heidegger's fundamental and oft-repeated affirmation about a return to the origin of historicity is that historicity or rather *Geschehen* (historiality) is rooted (Heidegger's term, more than once) in Zeitigung, in the movement of temporality. Among other places, Heidegger says in §72, [German] p. 376: 232

> *The analysis of the Geschichtlichkeit of Dasein attempts to show that this being (Dasein) is not "temporal" ("zeitlich") because it "is in history," ("weil es in der Geschichte steht") but that, on the contrary, it exists and can exist historically only because it is temporal in the ground of its being.* (Being and Time, 359)

And already earlier, Heidegger had declared, as he will often declare again, that the analysis of temporality must orient that of historicity, and in this way provide it with its rootedness, and so forth:

> How history (*Geschichte*) can become a possible *Gegenstand* for historiography (*Historie*) can be gathered only from the kind of being of what is historical (*Geschichtlichen*), from historicity and its rootedness (*Verwurzelung*) in temporality." (*Being and Time*, 358)

One might think that Heidegger's insistence in emphasizing this relation of dependency and the order of dependency, the concern not to invert it, is rather trivial. Being historical because temporal or being temporal because historical—these are quite artificial nuances in which it is quite artificial to become entangled. *Or so some will think*.

And yet what is at stake here is decisive in Heidegger's eyes. Temporalization (*Zeitigung*) is the very movement of ek-sistence, the movement of *Dasein*; one might say the movement of *experience* if this word were not unduly charged with empirical references. Now if historicity were independent of *Zeitigung*, if it were no longer essentially rooted in it, the whole of metaphysics would come back in force. Ultimately, in spite of appearances, it is a metaphysical attitude not to take seriously and not to insist on the rootedness of historicity in temporality. Indeed, that would come down to saying that history happens outside existence and if there is, then, as Hei- 233
degger intends to show, a history of Being, it would come down to saying that the history of Being is independent of the existence of *Dasein*. The *Sein* would be what it is outside the *Da*. Which would come down to making Being into something, a substance, a transcendent being, a god perhaps, and no doubt more specifically a god in the Hegelian manner: that is, an absolute and infinite being happening indeed in history, but in a history that would be

but a modification of his eternity and of which *Da-sein* or ek-sistence would be merely a phenomenon, merely phenomenality.

So, to avoid that, and if one wishes to speak of a history of Being and not of a history of beings or even of the being God, historicity must be rooted in temporality as its condition of possibility.

Having recognized this, one is then threatened by another danger, the very one that Heidegger must confront here. Namely, that if one considers solely or primarily the rootedness of historicity in temporality, one runs the risk—and this is indeed what happens here—of no longer finding anything original about what is rooted, about the rooted with regard to the root. The originality of historicity with respect to temporality suddenly becomes impossible to find; it is now only a modification of temporality. "The analysis of *Geschehen* introduces the problems found in a thematic investigation into temporalization as such" (*Being and Time*, 358).

And we saw last time that the ontological site of historicity and of the problem it poses was sought on the basis of these notions of *Erstreckung* (stretching out), of *Ganzsein* and of Care, which came directly from the phenomenology of temporalization, which explains why in this new stage of the problematic (temporality and historicity) there is no truly new concept. Which also explains this *remarkable architectonic fact* that the chapter on historicity, which I was saying a moment ago is the penultimate chapter, is introduced as a kind of . . . filler between two chapters both devoted to tem-
234 porality. Of the two previous chapters, one was devoted to temporality as the ontological meaning of Care, the other to temporality and everydayness; then comes our chapter "*Temporality* and Historicity," and then the *last* chapter of the volume deals with temporality and *intratemporality* as the origin of the vulgar conception of time that culminates in a critique of Hegel.

The theme of historicity is thus comprehended, enveloped and enclosed in that of temporality. Its originality is still suppressed; it is carried, it is held back in an embryonic and fetal stage and its displacements are bound to those of the thematic of temporality that bears it. Now, finally, what becomes of this thematic of temporality, precisely, in *Sein und Zeit*?

You know, and I have often reminded you of this, that temporality in *Sein und Zeit* has *the meaning of the transcendental horizon of the question of being*. And we must never forget this. We have read Heidegger's explanations about this, and we have seen what that meant. Time is the way into the question of the meaning of being, but it is only a way in because in return the meaning of being ought to reveal to us the meaning and being of time.

The necessity of what one could call, in equivocal and dangerous terms, the impasse of the end of *Sein und Zeit* and the overturning, the *Umkehrung* that it calls for—this necessity, which imposes itself on the subject of the relation between time and being, imposes itself, then, *ipso facto*, for the reasons we have just given, as regards the relations between history and being. The running out of breath whose signs we are pointing out with reference to historicity is the same running out of breath as the one whose signs we could point out on the subject of temporality. And the difficulty in going further into the problematic of historicity is itself a sign, a phenomenon of the difficulty in going further into the problematic of temporality.

To show this, I cannot do better than quote Heidegger from the "Letter on 'Humanism.'" You will see that what I have just pointed out is not interpretation on my part but translates Heidegger's clearest awareness of this signification. 235

So let's see what Heidegger says about this on [French] p. 67 of the "Letter on 'Humanism'." I'll take it from a little earlier than the passage that interests us directly, because it will be clearer. Read [French] pp. 63–67:[2]

> The sentence "The human being ek-sists" is not an answer to the question of whether the human being actually is or not; rather, it responds to the question concerning the "essence" of the human being. We are accustomed to posing this question with equal impropriety whether we ask what the human being is or who he is. For in the *Who?* or the *What?* we are already on the lookout for something like a person or an object. But the personal no less than the objective misses and misconstrues the essential unfolding of ek-sistence in the history of being. That is why the sentence cited from *Being and Time* ([German] p. 42, English p. 41) is careful to enclose the word "essence" in quotation marks. This indicates that "essence" is now being defined neither from *esse essentiae* nor from *esse existentiae* but rather from the ek-static character of Dasein. As ek-sisting, the human being sustains Da-sein in that he takes the *Da*, the clearing of being, into "care." But Dasein itself occurs essentially as "thrown." It unfolds essentially in the throw of being as a destinal sending.
>
> But it would be the ultimate error if one wished to explain the sentence about the human being's eksistent essence as if it were the secularized transference to human beings of a thought that Christian theology expresses about God (*Deus est suum esse*); for ek-sistence is not the realization of an essence, nor does ek-sistence itself even effect and posit what is essential. If we understand what *Being and Time* calls "projection" as a representational positing, we take it to be an achievement of subjectivity and do not think it in the only way the "understanding of being" in the context of the "existential analysis"

2. The beginning and end of the following quotations is uncertain, in the absence of Derrida's copy of the text. See above, p. 18, n. 2.

> of "being-in-the-world" can be thought—namely, as the ecstatic relation to
> 236 the clearing of being. The adequate execution and completion of this other thinking that abandons subjectivity is surely made more difficult by the fact that in the publication of *Being and Time* the third division of the first part, "Time and Being," was held back (cf. *Being and Time*, [German] p. 39; [English p. 37]). Here everything is reversed. The division in question was held back because thinking failed in the adequate saying of this turning [*Kehre*] and did not succeed with the help of the language of metaphysics. The lecture "On the Essence of Truth," thought out and delivered in 1930 but not printed until 1943, provides a certain insight into the thinking of the turning from "Being and Time" to "Time and Being." This turning is not a change of standpoint from *Being and Time*, but in it the thinking that was sought first arrives at the locality of that dimension out of which *Being and Time* is experienced, that is to say, experienced in the fundamental experience of the oblivion of being.
>
> By way of contrast, Sartre expresses the basic tenet of existentialism in this way: Existence precedes essence. In this statement he is taking *existential* and *essentia* according to their metaphysical meaning, which from Plato's time on has said that *essentia* precedes *existentia*. Sartre reverses this statement. But the reversal of a metaphysical statement remains a metaphysical statement. With it he stays with metaphysics in oblivion of the truth of being. For even if philosophy wishes to determine the relation of *essentia* and *existentia* in the sense it had in medieval controversies, in Leibniz's sense, or in some other way, it still remains to ask first of all from what destiny of being this differentiation in being as *esse essentiae* and *esse existentiae* comes to appear to thinking. We have yet to consider why the question about the destiny of being was never asked and why it could never be thought. Or is the fact that this is how it is with the differentiation of *essentia* and *existentia* not a sign of forgetfulness of being? We must presume that this destiny does not rest upon a mere failure of human thinking, let alone upon a lesser capacity of early Western thinking. Concealed in its essential provenance, the differentiation of *essentia* (essentiality) and *existentia* (actuality) completely dominates the destiny of Western history and of all history determined by Europe.
> 237 (*Pathmarks*, 249–50)

Comment.

Three remarks: you see that the interruption in the drafting of *Sein und Zeit* does not intervene between the first and a second part, but within the first part and before a last division that was to be entitled, according to the very plan and the very letter of what Heidegger indicates on [German] page 39 of *Sein und Zeit* [*Being and Time*, 37], "Time and Being."[3]

3. [Translator's note:] Derrida's manuscript in fact mistakenly has "Being and Time."

Second <remark>: this is not the sign of an impasse or a renunciation. Read [French] pp. 107–9.

> It is everywhere supposed that the attempt in *Being and Time* ended in a blind alley. Let us not comment any further upon that opinion. The thinking that hazards a few steps in *Being and Time* has even today not advanced beyond that publication. But perhaps in the meantime it has in one respect come further into its own matter. However, as long as philosophy merely busies itself with continually obstructing the possibility of admittance into the matter for thinking, i.e., into the truth of being, it stands safely beyond any danger of shattering against the hardness of that matter. Thus to "philosophize" about being shattered is separated by a chasm from a thinking that is shattered. If such thinking were to go fortunately for someone, no misfortune would befall him. He would receive the only gift that can come to thinking from being.
>
> But it is also the case that the matter of thinking is not achieved in the fact that idle talk about the "truth of being" and the "history of being" is set in motion. Everything depends upon this alone, that the truth of being come to language and that thinking attain to this language. Perhaps, then, language requires much less precipitate expression than proper silence. But who of us today would want to imagine that his attempts to think are at home on the path of silence? At best, thinking could perhaps point toward the truth of being, and indeed toward it as what is to be thought. (*Pathmarks*, 261–62) 238

Third remark, which immediately links to this allusion to silence and which touches on the second reason I announced. As Heidegger says in the second passage from the *Letter* that I read just now, if one cannot go further, this is because in the language of metaphysics what is now announced cannot be said. The categorial, the categorial system of metaphysics can no longer serve us to speak that on the threshold of which we have arrived.

Which is to recognize, of course, that up until now, up until the end of *Sein und Zeit*, we could make do with this categorial after a fashion, customizing it, using it for its own destruction, borrowing from it the stones that were thrown against its own edifice, or more peaceably by recognizing, in deconstruction, the structure of its stones and its contours and its capstone. So *Sein und Zeit* in this sense is still a metaphysical gesture, however self-destructive it be. And we have also seen why this whole language of civilization in which we have begun to speak is metaphysical, is metaphysics itself, and that language itself is metaphysics and that to that extent one should not expect by speaking to *overcome* metaphysics, in the simple sense of the word *overcome*.

But more profoundly, the suddenly *obsolete* and *useless* aspect of metaphysical conceptuality must not be thought as a sort of imperfection or incompletion of metaphysics; as if metaphysics had not reached the end of its resources and had not left us enough instruments for what still remains to be said or read in metaphysics. It is not some particular metaphysical tools, a few conceptual instruments that are lacking and remain to be found; it is metaphysical conceptuality itself that was wanting, and therefore its very meaning, in its very origin, with regard to what is announced.

One can understand this, when reading *Sein und Zeit*, only if at every moment one transposes the proper—that is properly metaphysical, therefore metaphorical—meaning of the word toward what is announced beyond it. This is why, since this transgressive intention is at work on the part of the
239 writer of *Sein und Zeit*, it had to be at work on the part of the reader who must simultaneously understand the beyond of metaphysics, the beyond of the conceptuality of *Sein und Zeit* and the necessity—for which Heidegger accounts—of continuing to dwell in or to pass *through* metaphysical inauthenticity. This schema explains why sometimes, in a style I find here a little disappointing because it is a bit ethico-psycho-sociological, Heidegger explains the unfinished nature of *Sein und Zeit* partly by his disappointment faced with the lack of understanding and the passivity of the reader who understands the words in their habitual signification—the words of *Sein und Zeit*.

Read *Letter on Humanism*, [French] pp. 145–47:

> But as long as the truth of being is not thought all ontology remains without its foundation. Therefore the thinking that in *Being and Time* tries to advance thought in a preliminary way into the truth of being characterizes itself as "fundamental ontology." It strives to reach back into the essential ground from which thought concerning the truth of being emerges. By initiating another inquiry this thinking is already removed from the "ontology" of metaphysics (even that of Kant). "Ontology" itself, however, whether transcendental or precritical, is subject to critique, not because it thinks the being of beings and in so doing reduces being to a concept, but because it does not think the truth of being and so fails to recognize that there is a thinking more rigorous than conceptual thinking. In the poverty of its first breakthrough, the thinking that tries to advance thought into the truth of being brings only a small part of that wholly other dimension to language. This language even falsifies itself, for it does not yet succeed in retaining the essential help of phenomenological seeing while dispensing with the inappropriate concern with "science" and "research." But in order to make the attempt at thinking recognizable and at the same time understandable for existing philosophy, it could at first be expressed only within the horizon of that existing philosophy and the use of its current terms.

> In the meantime I have learned to see that these very terms were bound to
> lead immediately and inevitably into error. For the terms and the conceptual 240
> language corresponding to them were not rethought by readers from the matter particularly to be thought; rather, the matter was conceived according to the established terminology in its customary meaning. The thinking that inquires into the truth of being and so defines the human being's essential abode from being and toward being is neither ethics nor ontology. Thus the question about the relation of each to the other no longer has any basis in this sphere. (*Pathmarks*, 271)

I have, then, just distinguished two reasons for the *running out of breath*: the rootedness of historicity in temporality, and the absence of new categories appropriate for thinking what is still to be thought. But you can see clearly that, as I had said, these two reasons are one and the same. It is because one sets off from time as the transcendental horizon of being in order to talk about history and about being that categories are lacking, that non-metaphysical categories are lacking. Which comes down to saying very broadly that determining time as the transcendental horizon of the question of being, a title that summarizes the whole enterprise of this first part of *Sein und Zeit*, remains a metaphysical gesture. And, as Heidegger himself says, the overturning that became both necessary and in a way impracticable, this overturning happens very curiously at the moment when the question of history is posed and when the question of being is finally going be posed again beyond the analytic of *Dasein*. And thus also the question of the history of being, about which one comes to wonder if it can be posed otherwise than on condition of this overturning that will interrupt the continuity of the analytic of *Dasein*.

The fact that the two reasons I distinguished are essentially united in this turning is something that Heidegger himself recognizes in a way when he writes, still in this famous §72,

> After this first characterization of the course of the ontological exposition of
> historicity in terms of temporality, do we still need explicit assurance that the 241
> following inquiry does not believe that the problem of history can be solved by a sleight of hand (*durch einen Handstreich*)? The paucity (*Dürftigkeit*) of the available "categorial" means and the uncertainty of the primary ontological horizons become all the more obtrusive, the more the problem of history is traced to its *primordial rootedness* [emphasized: . . . seiner *ursprünglichen Verwurzelung* zugeführt ist]. (*Being and Time*, 360)

The two reasons unite, then, in that the more the problem of historicity is brought back to its root (i.e., to the problem of temporality), the more the categorial means and the security of the horizon become elusive. But the fact that this eluding is denounced as such suffices to make *Sein und Zeit,* this book that is still metaphysical, take a step beyond metaphysics.

And especially—here is the preliminary point I wanted to get to this morning—and especially one has a clearer sense of the scope and the meaning of what will happen after *Sein und Zeit* in the relations between time, history and Being.

(1) *On the one hand* the theme of temporality will slowly disappear from Heidegger's discourse. Which does not mean that it will be canceled out or contradicted. Simply, it will no longer be the privileged transcendental horizon of the question of being. A remarkable phenomenon, this kind of neutralization of temporality—in the strict sense—that happened after *Sein und Zeit*, and which a statistical analysis at least could already show to be [illegible word]. This means then that the analytic of the structure of Dasein as Care and Temporality will no longer be privileged as a way into the question of being. Not that *Dasein* will now be considered superfluous and accidental as to the truth of being—on the contrary. But a new inflection is placed on the *Da* of *Dasein* that spares us, in a way, from the thematic of temporality.

(2) On the other hand, the second phenomenon worthy of note from our point of view here is the following. One might have expected, given that
242 the theme of historicity in *Sein und Zeit* is rooted in that of temporality and comprehended in it or on the basis of it, that it would follow temporality in its effacement and even that it would be effaced *a fortiori*.

But it is precisely the opposite that happens. The theme of historicity is going to be liberated from that of temporality by the overturning we are talking about: of course, it is no longer just a matter of the historicity of *Dasein* but of that of being. Besides, the history of being would not happen without the *Da* of *sein*.

Simply, something remarkable nonetheless happens in the fact that now the historicity of *Sein*, even given that it presupposes the *Da* of *Sein*, is no longer described as the temporality of being. This—I will not say substitution—but this slippage in thematic insistence, which moves us from the temporality of *Dasein* to the historicity of being, is a move that might seem surprising if one thinks of the insistence of *Sein und Zeit* in rooting and enveloping the theme of historicity in that of temporality. This liberation of historicity might seem surprising, unless one is attentive, precisely, to the difficulty, the awkwardness and the properly *aporetical* style of these last chapters of *Sein und Zeit* on historicity and temporality.

All these remarks are designed to situate clearly these last pages of *Sein und Zeit* on the historicity of *Dasein*, on which we have not yet commented, on which we are going to comment, but now with a better sense of what sort of overturning is brewing more or less silently.

Before broaching this commentary, I would like to specify clearly or recall two points. Namely, that (1) *on the one hand*, in Heidegger's eyes, nothing has really begun before this famous *turning*. Nothing essential has begun; we are on the eve of, and amidst the preparations for the great question.

But (2) *on the other hand*, what has happened up until now—that is, *Sein und Zeit*, including the last chapters on temporality and historicity—what has happened is nonetheless decisive and untimely. The decisive question, the *Decision* has not yet appeared but the gesture preparing it has been decisive. *243*

And these two propositions are not contradictory. And we must understand how they are not contradictory if we wish to understand anything of Heidegger's intention. They would be contradictory if being were a being and if its manifestation or its history could do without the *Da* of the existence of *Dasein*. In this case one could make a theme of the history of Being without going via the historicity of *Da-sein*. *But* Being itself is not a being and there is no history of being without the history of its manifestation. That is, the *Da*. *On the other hand*, there would be a contradiction if there were some possibility of speaking about the historicity of *Dasein* outside the horizon of *Sein* and without any relation of ek-sistence to being. *But* we saw that without this relation there was no history, and that what constituted *Da-sein* was first of all its relation [illegible word] of precomprehension—to the meaning of being. One must then think at one and the same time that the history of being depends on the historicity of *Dasein* and conversely. One must not think here in alternatives. It would be easy to show how the alternative schema corresponds here to a metaphysical thesis opposing subject to object, *ego* to world, thought and Being, and so forth. From the point of view of this metaphysical logic, these two gestures of Heidegger's would be contradictory. In fact, it is this logic that is put into question by the necessity of this gesture. In any case, to confirm these two points we are going to read two passages from the "Letter on 'Humanism'" that show that, twenty years after *Sein und Zeit,* this is indeed the reading Heidegger gives of this first gesture: both pre-liminary to the decision and already decisive ([French] pp. 89, 111).

See first [French] p. 110, the eve of the decision:

Whether the realm of the truth of being is a blind alley [a cul-de-sac: *Sackgasse*] or whether it is the free space (*das Freie*) in which freedom conserves

> its essence (*ihr Wesen spart*) [comment] is something each one may judge after he himself has tried to go the designated way, or even better, after he has gone a better way, that is, a way befitting the question. On the penultimate page of *Being and Time* ([German] p. 437) [in fact it's the last] stand the sentences: "The *conflict* (*der Streit*) with respect to the interpretation of
> 244 being [introduction to the gigantomachia of the *Sophist*, but it has not yet happened] (that is, therefore, not the interpretation of beings or of the being of the human being) cannot be settled, *because it has not yet been kindled (entfacht)*. And in the end it is not a question of 'picking a quarrel,' [*lässt er sich nicht "vom Zaun brechen"*; Zaun is a hedge. It's an adverbial locution that means "provoke a quarrel for no reason"] since the kindling of the conflict does demand some preparation. To this end alone the foregoing investigation is under way. (*Pathmarks*, 262)

And Heidegger adds, after this quotation, "Today after two decades these sentences still hold."

Therefore the affirmation is still valid that the conflict has not yet been kindled in *Sein und Zeit* when, for example, it raises the question of the historicity of the ek-sistence of *Dasein*.

But, second affirmation: the necessity of these preparations also remains valid. Cf. pp. 89 and 95 [*Pathmarks*, 251, 258].

Let's go further. After this anticipation which has allowed us better to situate these analyses at the end of *Sein und Zeit*, we can now broach them in their content.

The order of considerations in the fifth chapter is rather surprising at first blush.

And when one has recovered from one's surprise—that is, when one has understood what the meaning of the linkages was, what their order was, in this chapter on historicity and temporality—well, one notices quite simply that *it is never a question of historicity in the proper sense in Sein und Zeit*.

It is never a question of historicity *in the proper sense* in *Sein und Zeit*: what does that mean? It means at least two things:

(1) That it is not even a question of the historicity of *Dasein*. It is not only a matter, as we were pointing out a moment ago, of the history of being of
245 which it is not yet a question in *Sein und Zeit*. What is deferred, against all expectation, is the problem of the historicity of *Dasein*.

(2) That means, secondly, that there is no question of the historicity of *Dasein* in the proper sense (*eigentlich*). *Eigentlich* is what is translated as *authentically*. Well, it is the problem of the *authentic historicity* of *Dasein* that is deferred and deferred *sine die* such that what will be in question after *Sein und Zeit* under the name of the history of being will come to fill out the hol-

low left by an expectation that in truth led one to hope for the theme of an authentic historicity of *Dasein*.

That puts a different light, then, on the problem of the turning that has been occupying us today. We must now understand what all that means.

Historicity is rooted in temporality.

> The existential project for the historicity of Dasein only reveals [development: *Enthüllung*] what already lies shrouded (*eingehüllt*) in the temporalizing of temporality. (*Being and Time*, 359)
>
> Thus the interpretation of the historicity of Dasein turns out to be basically just a more concrete elaboration of temporality (*eine konkretere Ausarbeitung der Zeitlichkeit*). (*Being and Time*, 364)

Rooted in temporality, historicity will, then, be structured like temporality. As a first consequence, there will be an authentic historicity and an inauthentic historicity just as there is an authentic temporality and an inauthentic temporality. The difference between authentic and inauthentic temporality has been described previously around the themes of anxiety, care, freedom of being-toward-death, and so on. And from the opening of the chapter on historicity, Heidegger announces that he will have to distinguish between an authentic historicity and an inauthentic historicity. And the authentic 246
historicity must be elucidated on the basis of authentic temporality, [German] p. 375.

> If historicity itself is to be illuminated in terms of temporality, and primordially in terms of *authentic* temporality (*aus der* eigentlichen *Zeitlichkeit*), then it is essential to this task that it can only be carried out by structuring it phenomenologically. (*Being and Time*, 358)

And later:

> Corresponding to the rootedness of historicity in care, Dasein always exists as authentically or inauthentically historical. (*Being and Time*, 359)

This authentic historicity—just like authentic temporality—is veiled, covered over, concealed (*erobert*)[4] by the vulgar conception of history, a vulgar conception that is moreover the very conception held by classical philosophy, and it is against this vulgar conception that proper historicity must be discovered.

4. [Translator's note]: Derrida probably intended to give instead the German "verdeckend," used by Heidegger at the very beginning of German page 376. "Erobert," also used on that same line, means "conquered," "captured," and so on; "verdeckend" translates as "veiled," "covered over," "concealed."

And then, in a very odd gesture, instead of beginning with what he defines as the originary (*ursprünglich*) Heidegger begins with the inauthentic and the derived. From which, moreover, he will not really emerge in *Sein und Zeit*.

How does Heidegger justify this order of description? He does not justify it solely or in the first place by the methodological and commonsense necessity of beginning with a ground-clearing critique. For that is not the point. Inauthentic historicity and the vulgar conception of historicity lodged in it are not errors that must be corrected or of which one must rid oneself. They are necessities of ek-sistence that have their status and their signification, and they must be described as such.

In a sense—and this is why the point here is not simply to criticize it—
247 the vulgar or standard or philosophical understanding of historicity has its legitimacy, and it conforms to a certain structure or structural composition of the ek-sistence of *Dasein*.

Inauthentic historicity and the vulgar concept of historicity consist essentially in experiencing and thinking that the subject, man, existence, whatever you like, is *in history*, the *in history* able to signify as much the empirical immersion of a thing in a milieu as the station around a subject in history, the *in history* being the structural concept common to empirical historicisms and to substantialist and subjectivist a-historicisms. Now, this structure of *being in history* reflects the structure of *being in time* (*Innerzeitigkeit*) that is the inauthentic form of temporal ek-sistence.

So that in the chapter that concerns us at the moment (the one before the last), Heidegger will proceed as follows: he will describe the vulgar concept of historicity and inauthentic historicity, showing that they are rooted in *Innerzeitigkeit*. And in the last chapter, he will be exclusively and expressly dealing with this intra-temporality—the last chapter will be entitled "Temporality and Intra-temporality as the Origin of the Vulgar Concept of Time." This chapter will culminate, as I have said, in a critique of the Hegelian concept of time.

You see that basically this chapter on the historicity of *Dasein* is architectonically a sort of hors-d'oeuvre or appendix that comes to add itself on to an analysis of temporality, as a consequence of inauthentic temporality as intra-temporality. The only section that will attempt to speak of authentic historicity will be §74. We shall see a little later that it says nothing other than what is said elsewhere about authentic temporality.

We can now translate more clearly a few lines from the end of §72 that will pin down what I have just suggested.

> Nevertheless, Dasein must also be called "temporal" [in quotes] in the sense of its being "in time" [*in der Zeit* in quotes]. Factical Dasein needs and uses

> the calendar and the clock even without a developed historiography. What occurs "with it" (*was "mit ihm" geschieht*), it experiences as *occurring* "in time" (*als in der Zeit geschehend*). In the same way, the processes of nature, whether living or lifeless, are encountered "in time." They are within-time (*innerzeitig*). So while our analysis of how the "time" of intratemporality has its source in temporality will be deferred until the next chapter, it would be easy to put this before the discussion of the connection between historicity and temporality. [Comment.] What is historical is ordinarily characterized with the aid of the time of intratemporality. But if this vulgar characterization is to be stripped of its seeming self-evidence and exclusiveness, historicity is to be "deduced" [in quotes] *beforehand* purely (*rein*) from the *primordial* temporality of Dasein. [Comment.] This is required by the way these are "objectively" (*sachlich*) connected [the order of things]. But since time as intratemporality also "stems" (*stammt aus*) from the temporality of Dasein, historicity and intratemporality turn out to be equiprimordial (*gleichursprünglich*). The vulgar interpretation of the temporal character of history is thus justified within its limits. (*Being and Time*, 359–60) 248

So you follow Heidegger's strange procedure here.

(1) By rights one should begin from originary temporality to gain access to authentic historicity and from derived or inauthentic temporality (intratemporality) to gain access to the vulgar interpretation of historicity. So everything demands that we defer totally the analysis of historicity and [illegible word] in order to [illegible word] that of temporality.

But

(2) As historicity in the vulgar sense is understood on the basis of intratemporality or else is co-originary with it, one can start from this historicity in the vulgar sense, in order then to return to its true motif: intra-temporality. So that the theme of historicity is not only broached here from its inauthentic side but even on that side it is broached *obliquely*: this is a detour to get back 249
to temporality as inauthentic, as intra-temporality. If you will, considered in *itself*, this analysis is only a detour; considered from the point of view of *that to which* it is referred, it is a guiding thread.

But (3) as inauthenticity is not an accident, as it has its structural necessity, the vulgar conception of historicity has its legitimacy since inauthentic historicity exists, as intra-temporality exists.

And either *a priori* or by anticipation, it is noteworthy that everything that makes possible these methodological subtleties, these turns and turns about, this whole labyrinth that leaves you out of breath, is a distinction between *Eigentlichkeit* and *Uneigentlichkeit*—authenticity in the sense of the proper and inauthenticity in the sense of the improper—which, if not simply *ethical* in the classical sense of the word, since it does not depend on a moral deliberation and since, in a sense, inauthenticity is never avoidable like an accident, is a distinction that is nevertheless not foreign to all ethical preoccupation. Let's think of *Entschlossenheit* (resoluteness, resolute decision) that continues to draw on a metaphysics of *proper* (*eigentlich*) subjectivity. Now it is not by chance if among all the movements of transgression of *Sein und Zeit* that I mentioned a moment ago, we must also include an erasure of the reference to the authenticity or inauthenticity of ek-sistence.

To move from the historicity of *Dasein* to the history of being will be in particular, in one and the same gesture, on the one hand to repress the ethico-metaphysical reference to *Eigentlichkeit* and *Uneigentlichkeit* and to *Entschlossenheit*, and on the other, in what corresponds to it under the guise of the revelation and the dissimulation of being, no longer to establish the privilege, ontological or otherwise, nor even, at the limit, the distinction between the two terms, revelation being dissimulation and vice versa. This impossibility, on the basis of this first fundamental couple—*dissimulation, revelation*—of preventing significations from signifying the opposite of what they signify, sums up the sense of Heidegger's itinerary, from *Sein und Zeit* to the last writings. If dissimulation of being means revelation of being, and
250 reciprocally, it follows that all concepts derived from those two (i.e., no doubt almost all discursive significations) mean the same thing and its opposite. From that point on, one will no longer be able either to say or to live any *simple* signification, and *Entschlossenheit*, the condition of authenticity, will be just as much precipitation toward inauthenticity. Whence the move from the initial *Entschlossenheit* to the *Gelassenheit* of the texts at the end.

These two notions are each as difficult to translate as the other. *Entschlossenheit* is the decided project, the resolute decision as it is usually translated. But we would have to show how, insofar as *Entschlossenheit* is also the resolute decision against the return of classical metaphysical ethics, one cannot simply translate it by significations that denote or connote ethico-metaphysical values. Nevertheless, one cannot simply erase these connotations or denotations and that is not a random accident. In the same way, *Gelassenheit*—which has never yet been translated[5]—could be translated

5. [Translator's note:] Not translated into French at the time. The English translator, Bret Davids, comments: "I have followed the established consensus in translating this term [*Gelassenheit*] as 'releasement.' However, it should be kept in mind that the traditional and still commonly used German word conveys a sense of 'calm composure,' especially and originally that which accompanies an existential or religious experience of letting-go, being-let, and letting-be" (*Country Path Conversations* [Indianapolis: Indiana University Press, 2010], xi).

by "serenity," "peaceful waiting," "letting-be," and so forth, but all of these translations would be going in the wrong direction insofar as they are, when not taking into account the Heideggerian contexts of this notion, loaded with resonances that are still ethico-metaphysical, which are not simply absent from them, but whose presence consists in being annulled, present in order to be destroyed.

A last word before returning to *Sein und Zeit*: one can consider that so long as the *ethico-metaphysical* horizon remains dominant, so long as truth—in the renewed or rediscovered sense of this word—depends on an *Entschlossenheit*, then history, the historicity of history will remain concealed from us. If there is an *a priori* signification that cannot be erased from history—and that Heidegger is moreover the last to want to erase—it is a certain irreducible passivity of ek-sistence and *Da-sein*. Passivity, nucleus of passivity, which must not be understood on the model of thingly intra-worldliness or as sensibility, but at the very least as auto-affection of time by itself. Now it is this originary passivity that *Entschlossenheit* runs the risk of dissimulating and, having recognized at the outset the signification of this passivity of being in history (comprehended in history) or of being in the world, Heidegger was bound to seek further than *Eigentlichkeit* and *Entschlossenheit*. It is dif- 251
ficult, in spite of Heidegger's express intention, to reduce all reference to a *free subject* both in the notion of *Entschlossenheit* and in that of *Eigentlichkeit* (proper, i.e., close to oneself).

Now precisely the common feature of all the vulgar conceptions of *Geschehen* is the presupposition of a *subject* to whom events happen (*geschehen*).

So let's go into this §73 devoted to *Das vulgäre Verständnis der Geschichte und das Geschehen des Daseins*—(why "*vulgäre*"?)—Heidegger's procedure in this section is simple: he untangles from the current concept of history four entangled significations, and then he makes manifest the hidden unity that is diffracting in these four directions.

Here I shall go quite quickly. The four significations concern not history as "the science of history nor history as an object, but rather this being itself which has not necessarily been objectified." (*Being and Time*, 360)

The four significations through which this not necessarily objective historical being is aimed at are, then, supposed to be the following:[6]

(1) *Vergangenheit*, "being past," "pastness." In common discourse, one calls historical what belongs to the *past*. <">Here 'past' means on the one hand

6. The four points that follow are quasi-quotations of *Being and Time*, 361. [Translator's note: When dealing with an exact quotation, I give Stambaugh's translation with Derrida's comments as insertions.]

no longer present (*nicht mehr vorhanden*: present or available), or else indeed still present, but without effect (*Wirkung*) on the present. However [but still in the same direction], what is historical as what is past also has the opposite significance when we say that *one cannot evade history* [its determinism: meaning that the effects of the past do not let up, are still present]<"> (*Being and Time*, 361). So that, in any case, here, in both cases, be it in a positive or negative sense, it is always in terms of influence or of relation to the present that history is, vulgarly, represented; relation to the present that alone, as we have seen, is actual. What gathers exemplarily this determination of the word *historical*, is the fragment of the past, that in the form of the monument or the ruin of a Greek temple, for example, belongs to the past without
252 ceasing to be in the present.

(2) The second signification, which goes hand in hand with the first, determines *Vergangenheit* not simply as a relation to *Vorhandenheit*, but as *origin*, provenance (*Herkunft*). <">Whatever 'has a history' is in the *Zusammenhang* [nexus] of a becoming. In such becoming the 'development' is sometimes a rise, sometimes a fall. Whatever 'has a history' in this way can at the same time 'make' history (*epochemachend*). 'Epoch making,' it 'presently' defines a 'future.' Here history means 'an event nexus (*Zusammenhang*), or a tissue that is a 'productive nexus' that moves through the 'past,' the 'present,' and the 'future.' Here the past has no special priority<">(*Being and Time*, 361).

(3) Third signification: history signifies beyond this the totality of beings that change "in time" (*in der Zeit*). Here, history does not embrace what we call nature, but only culture, the *Geschehen* of that region of beings that distinguish themselves from nature by existence and "spirit" (quote-marks).

(4) Finally, fourth signification. One calls *historical* in everyday language what is *transmitted*, tradition as such, whether it be recognized as such by historical science or remain hidden in its provenance.

The four significations have in common, says Heidegger, "that they are related to human being as the 'subject' of events" (*Being and Time*, 361). It is this affirmation, more or less implicit depending on the discourse, that animates every common conception of history, and that Heidegger properly wants to "destroy." Destroy (i.e., not refute) because it is true that man is flux in a certain sense, subject, and that history gets related to a subject. But the point is to destroy this affirmation for the question that it *encloses* (implies and hides) and that Heidegger formulates thus at the end of §73.

> *To what extent, and on the basis of what ontological conditions, does historicity belong to the subjectivity of the "historical" subject (zur Subjektivität des*

Le titre de ce cours est: **Heidegger**: la question de l'Être et l'Histoire (1.)
16.XI.64.

—

Je dois d'abord m'expliquer sur le titre de ce cours, sur sa lettre même, à laquelle je tiens.

Si je dis la question de l'être et non l'ontologie c'est parce que le mot d'ontologie doit se révéler de plus en plus inadéquat, à mesure que nous nous enfoncerons dans le lieu de Heidegger, pour désigner ce qui est en question chez lui sous le titre de question de l'Être. Non seulement l'ontologie en question ici, [de Heidegger] n'est pas la fondation d'une ontologie, ni même d'une ontologie en un sens radicalement nouveau, ni même nouvelle, [illegible] d'une ontologie [illegible] jaillir la fondation la plus propre [illegible] de l'ontologie — la [illegible] dont il s'agit ici c'est plutôt d'une destruction de l'ontologie — la Destruktion [illegible] comme une tâche préliminaire. Si la destruction est destruction (Destruktion) de l'histoire de l'ontologie, telle qu'elle a été [illegible] de l'histoire de l'ontologie, cette histoire étant déjà, pensée et pratiquée au cours de toute son histoire, [illegible] décrite par H. comme un recouvrement non ontologique mais ontique de l'ontologique, comme une dissimulation [illegible] « Cette tâche, dit Heidegger, nous la comprenons, comme [illegible] question de l'Être.

From Session One; see p. 1.   1

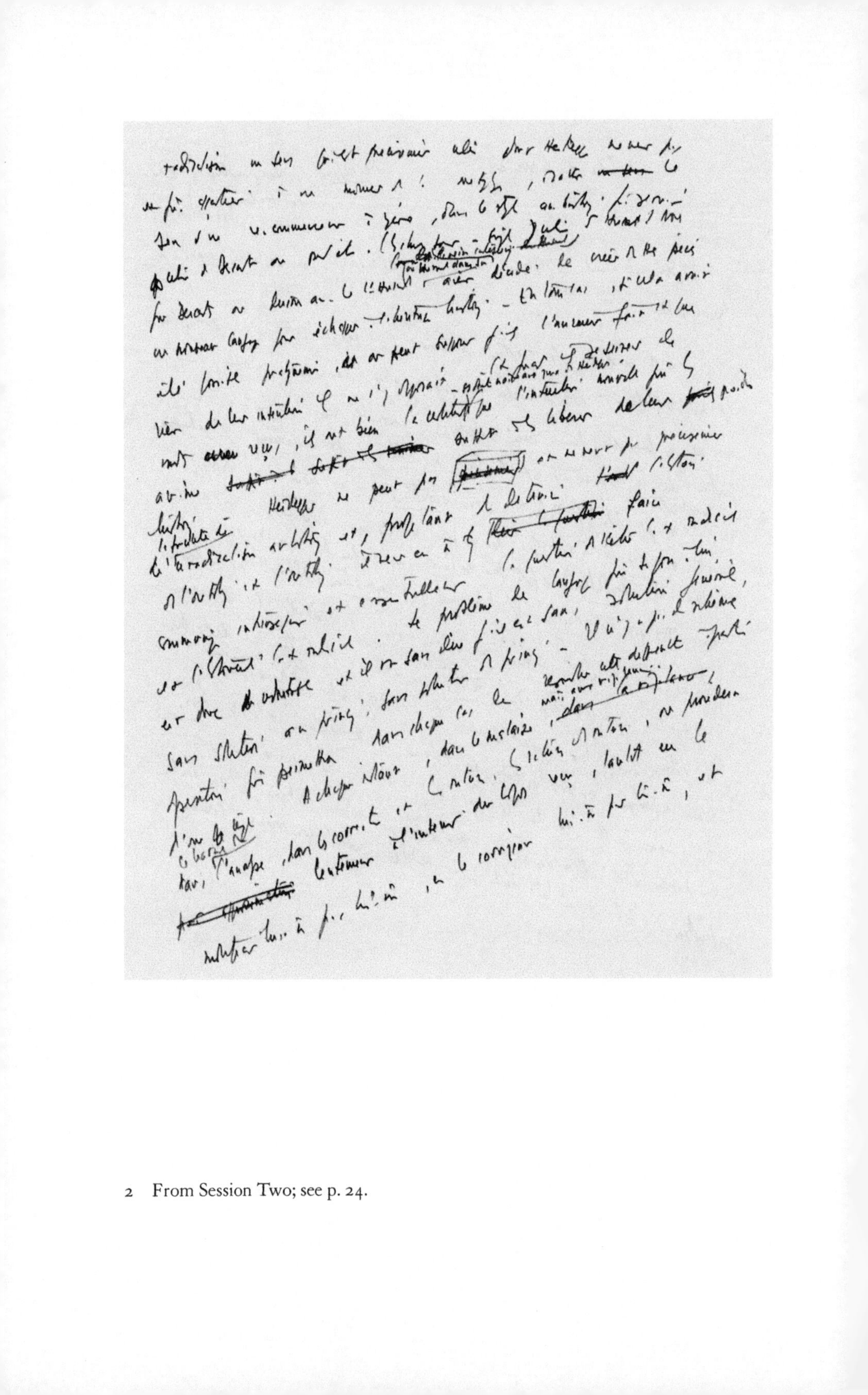

2 From Session Two; see p. 24.

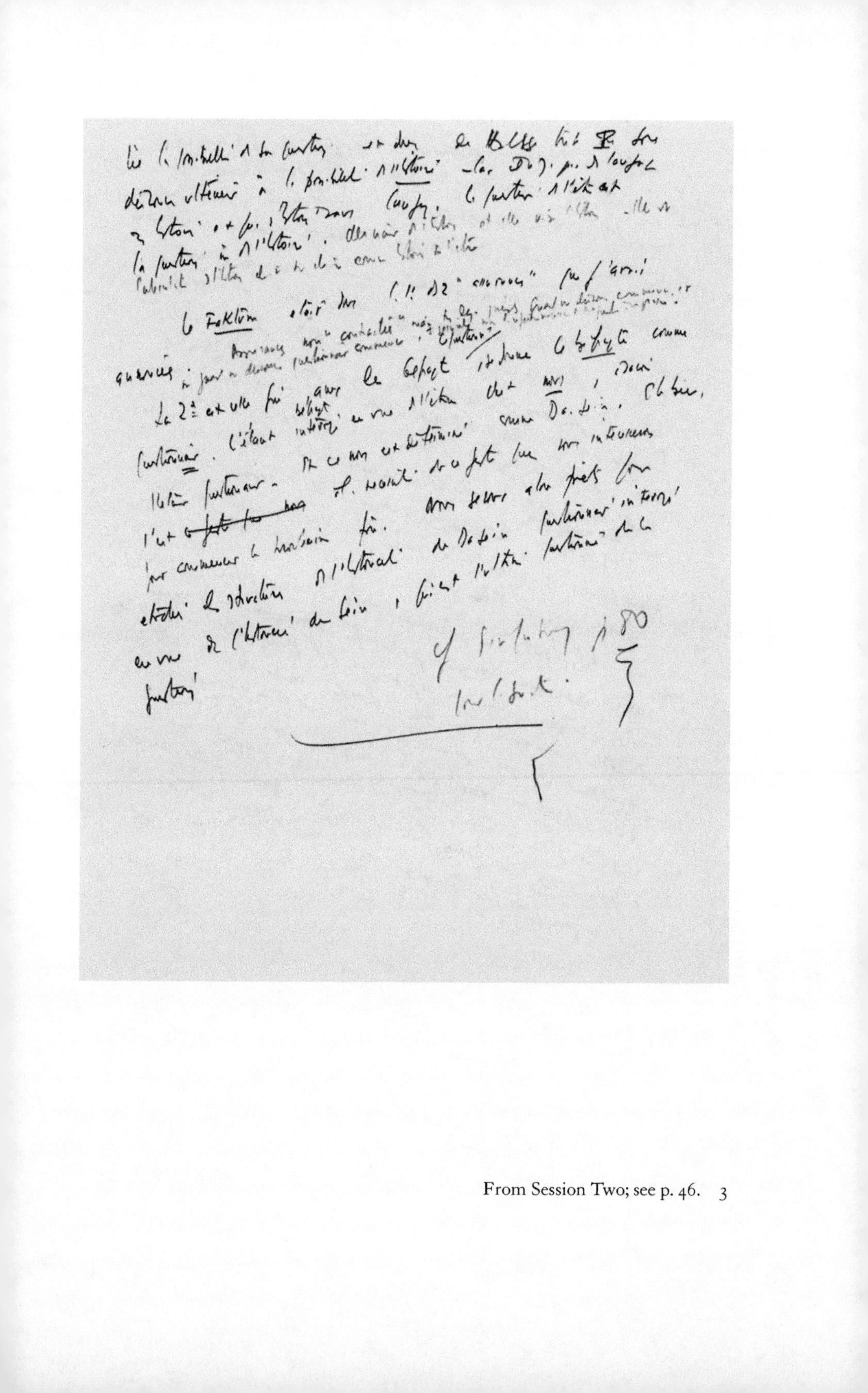

From Session Two; see p. 46.

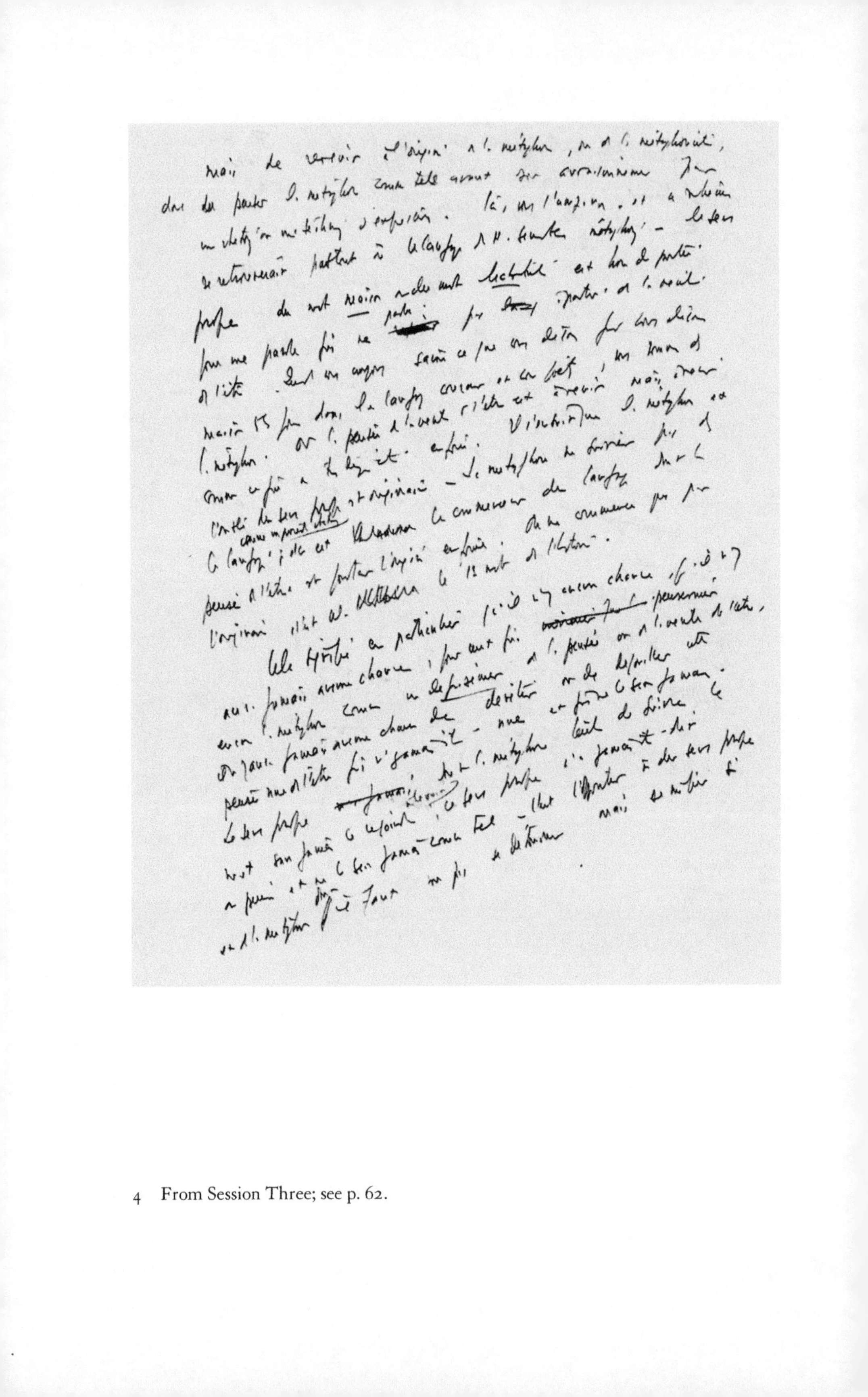

4 From Session Three; see p. 62.

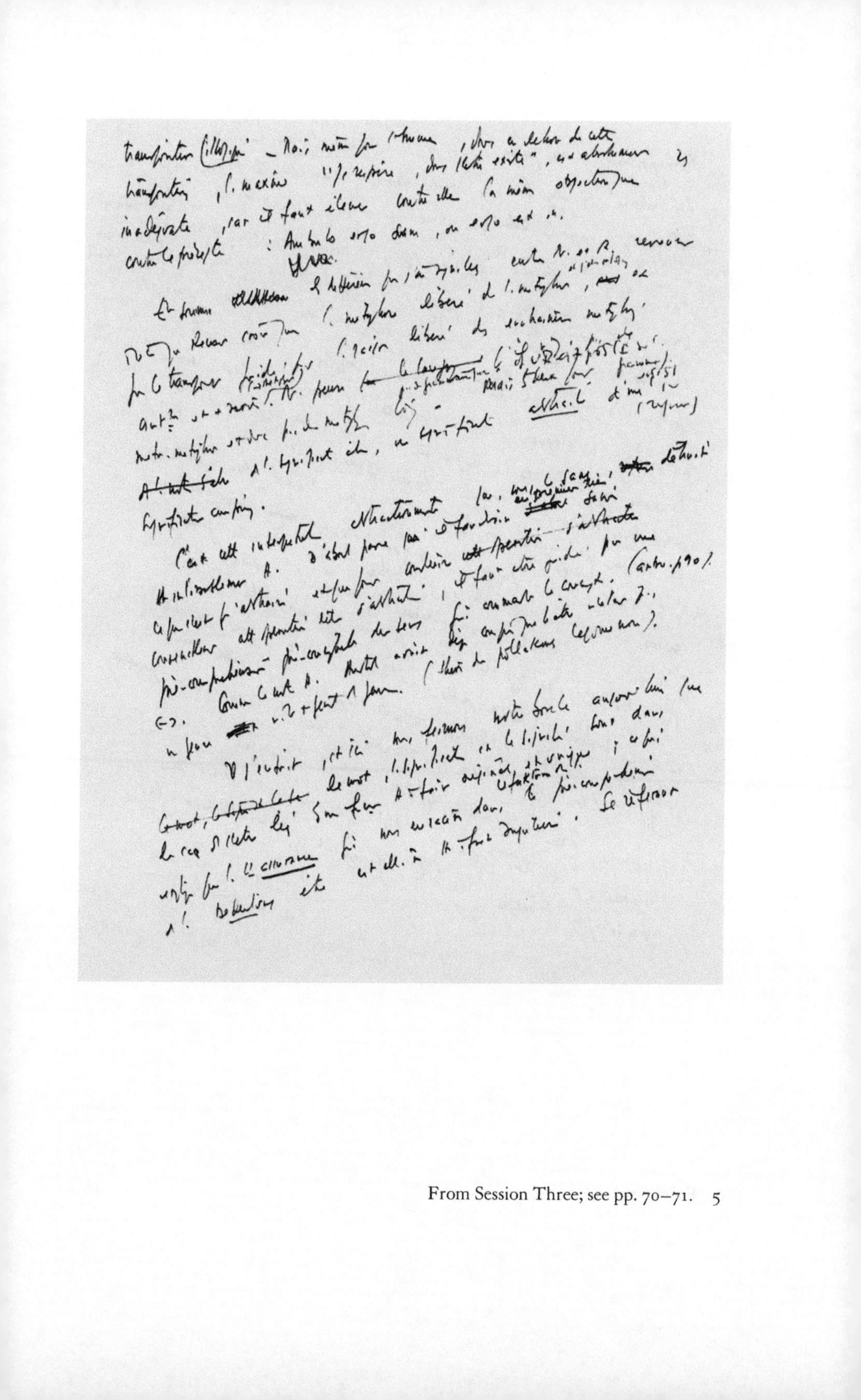

From Session Three; see pp. 70–71.

6 From Session Four; see pp. 77–78.

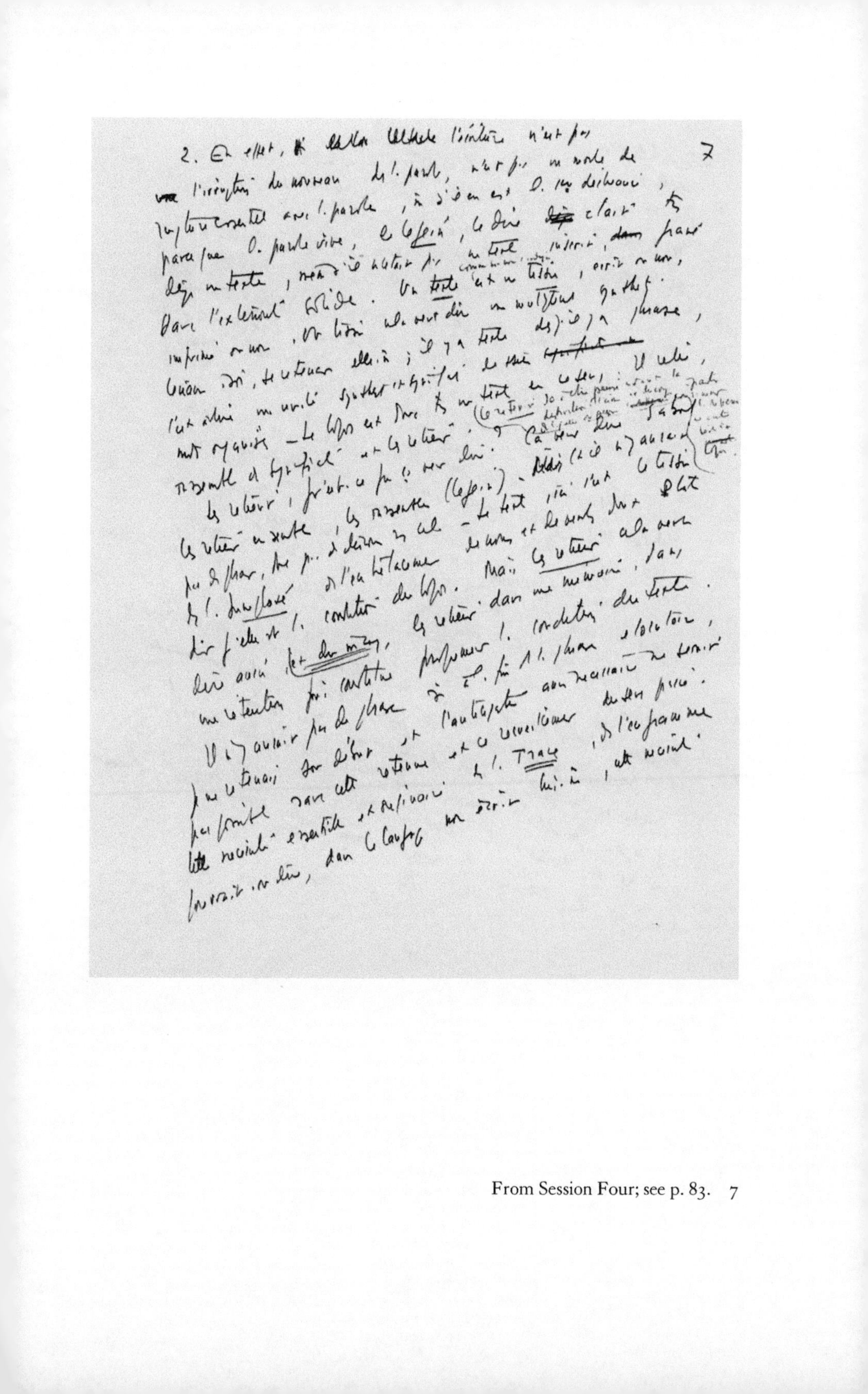

From Session Four; see p. 83.

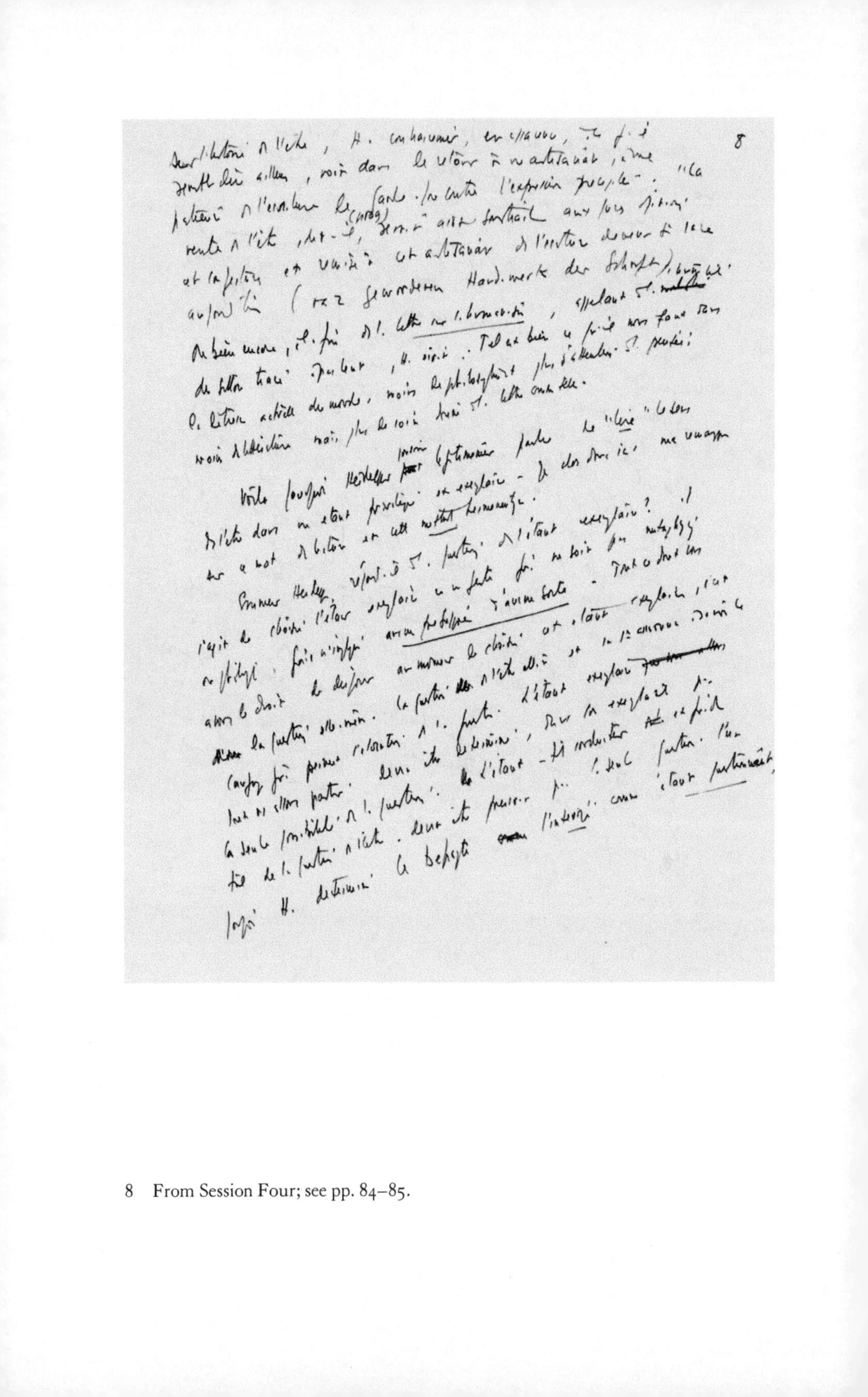

8 From Session Four; see pp. 84–85.

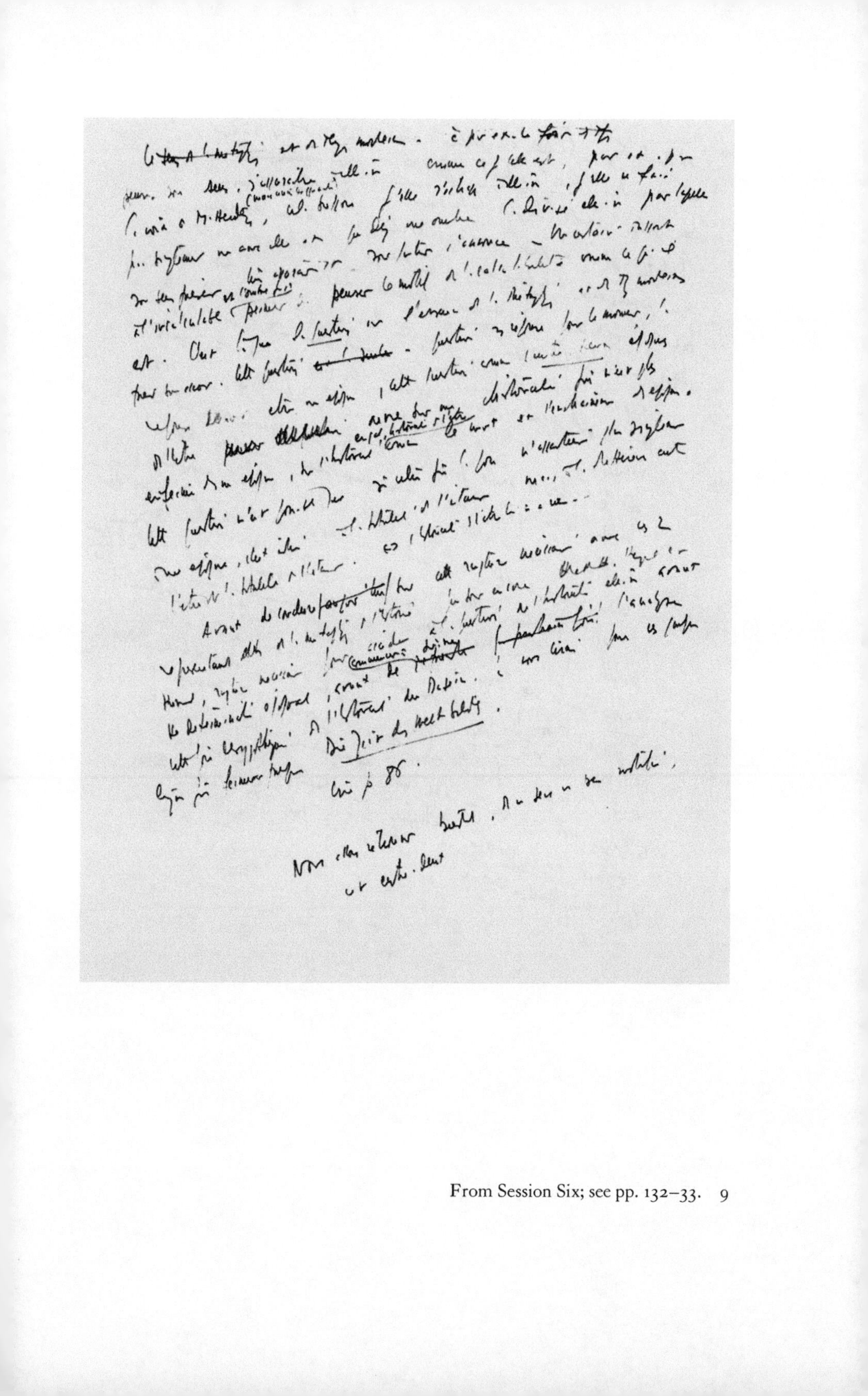

From Session Six; see pp. 132–33.

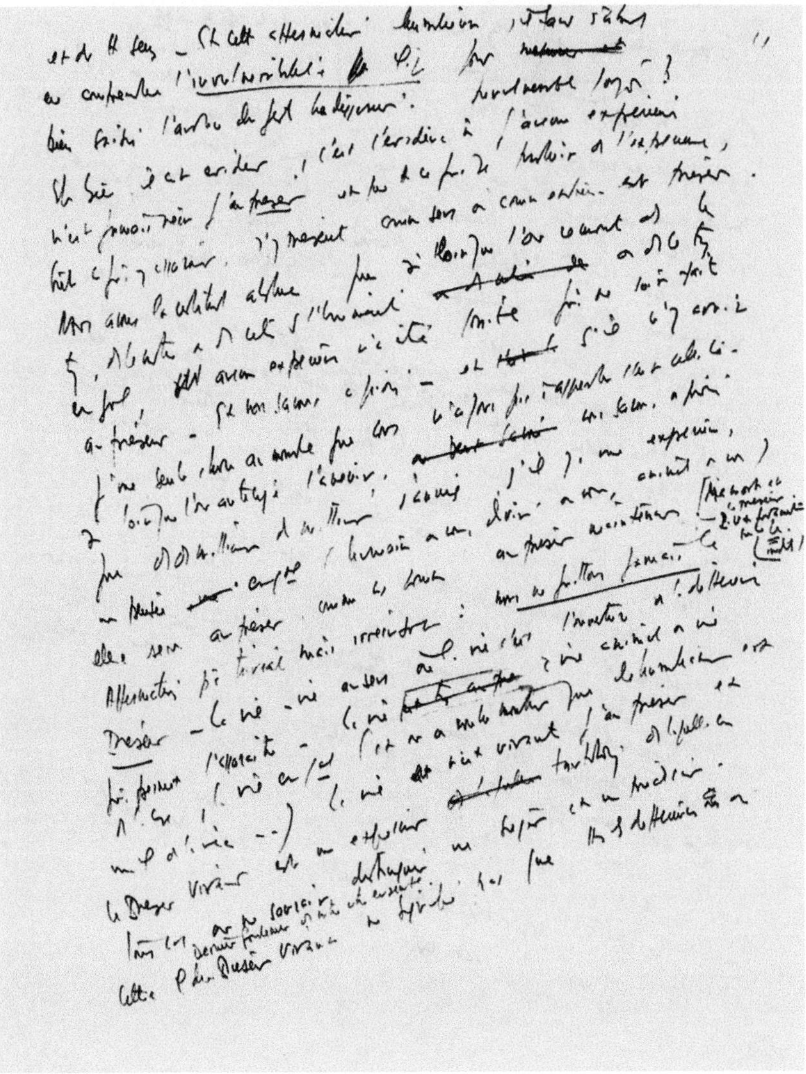

10 From Session Six; see pp. 139–40.

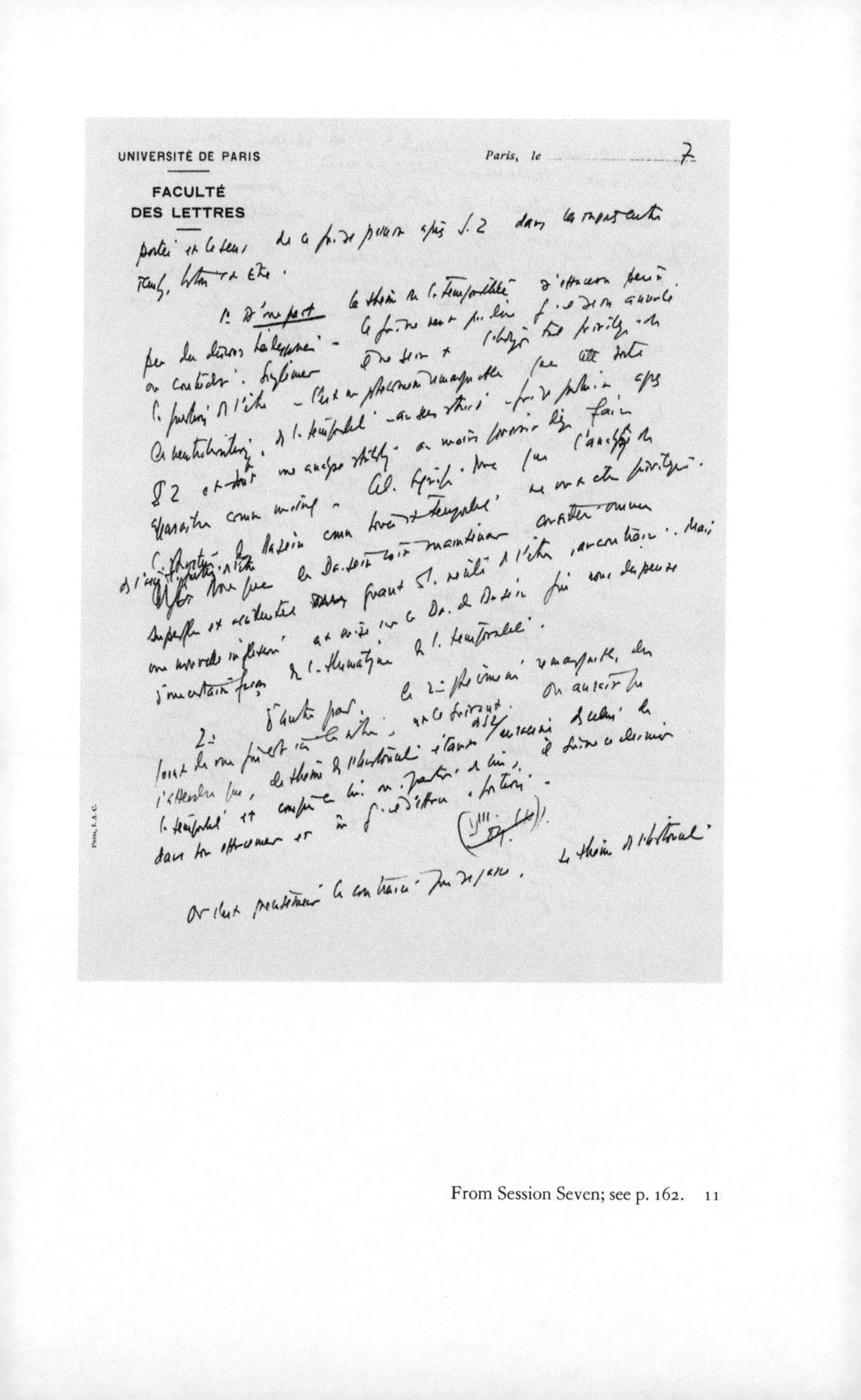

UNIVERSITÉ DE PARIS

FACULTÉ DES LETTRES

Paris, le 7

[illegible]

From Session Seven; see p. 162.

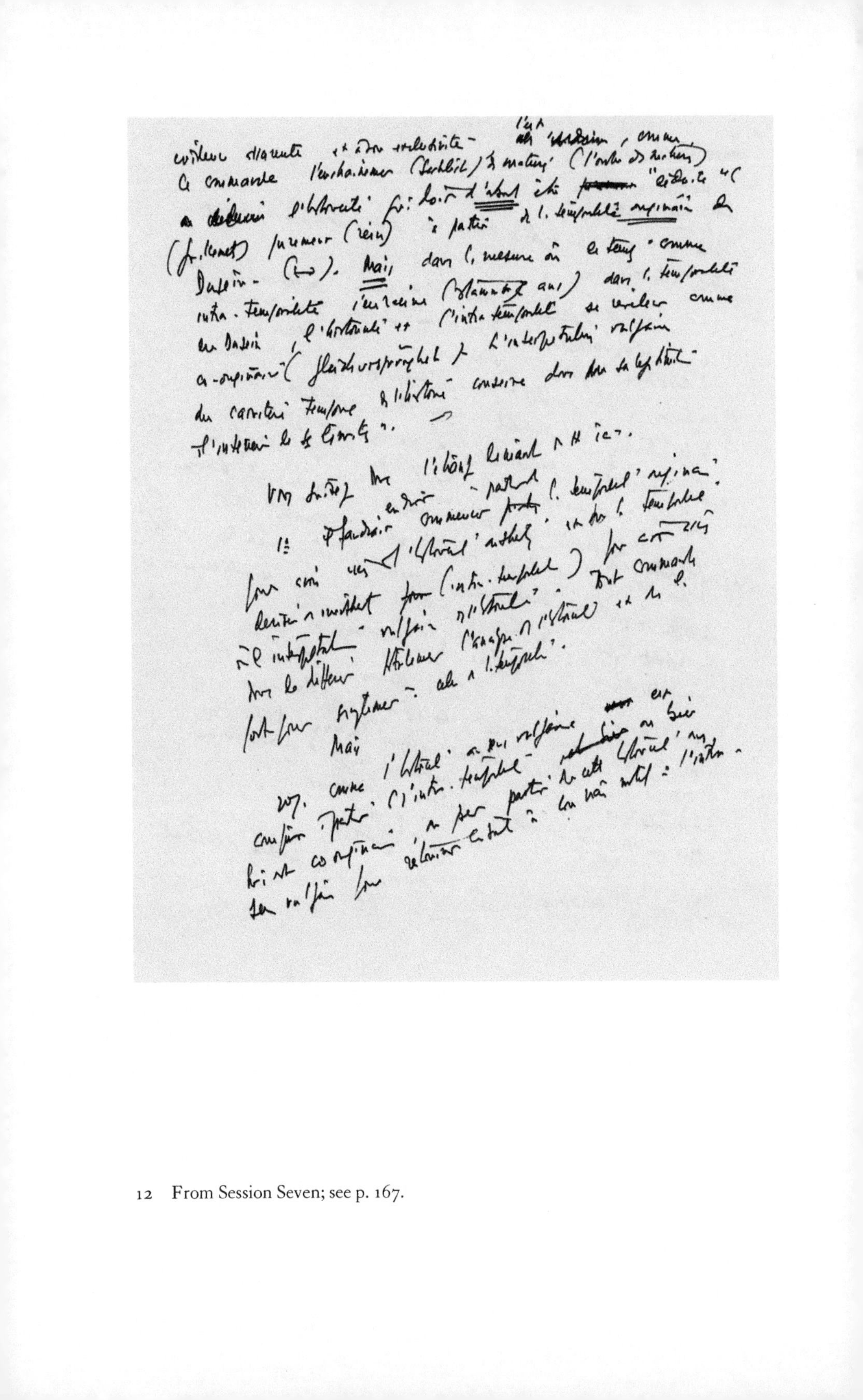

12 From Session Seven; see p. 167.

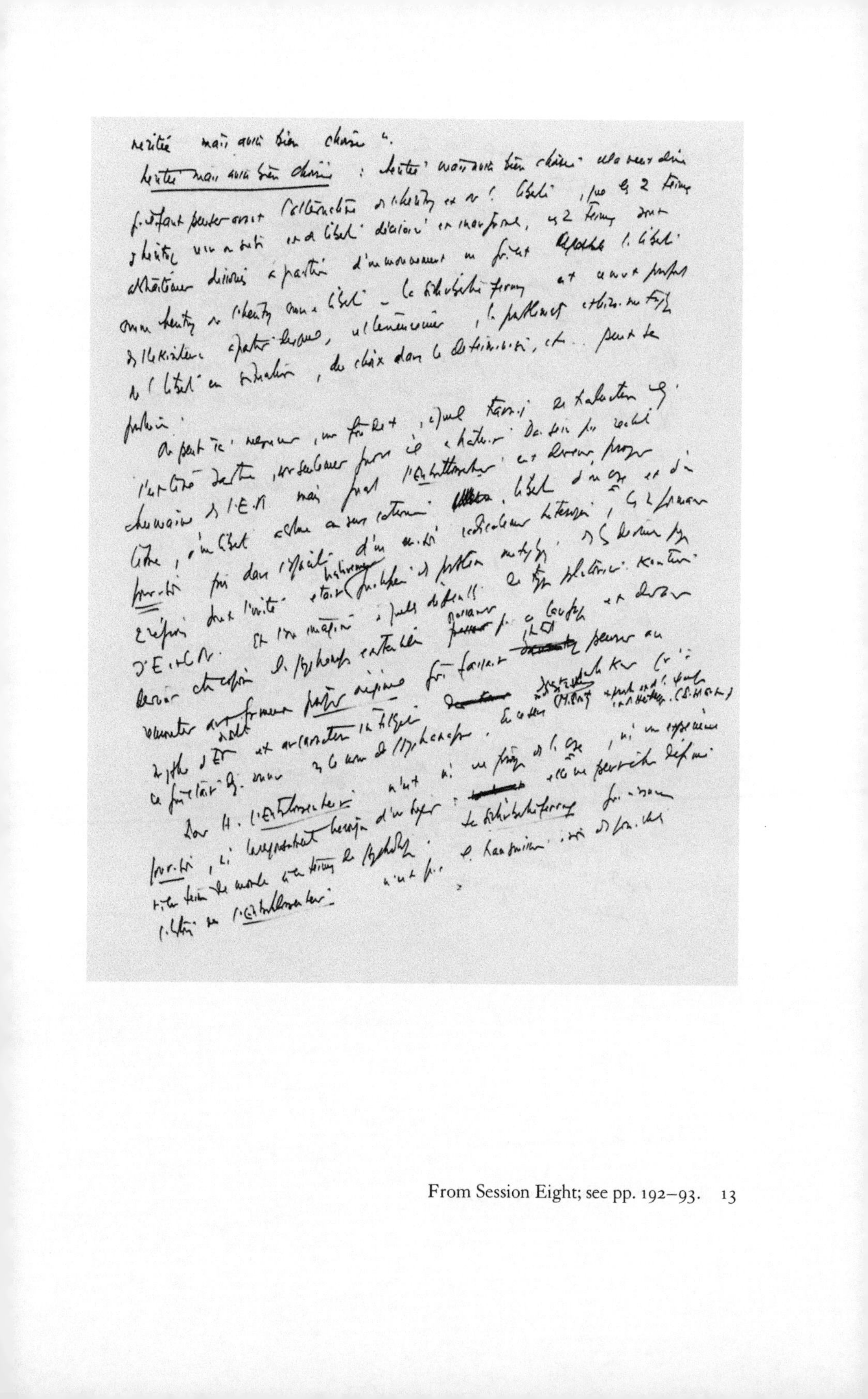

From Session Eight; see pp. 192–93.

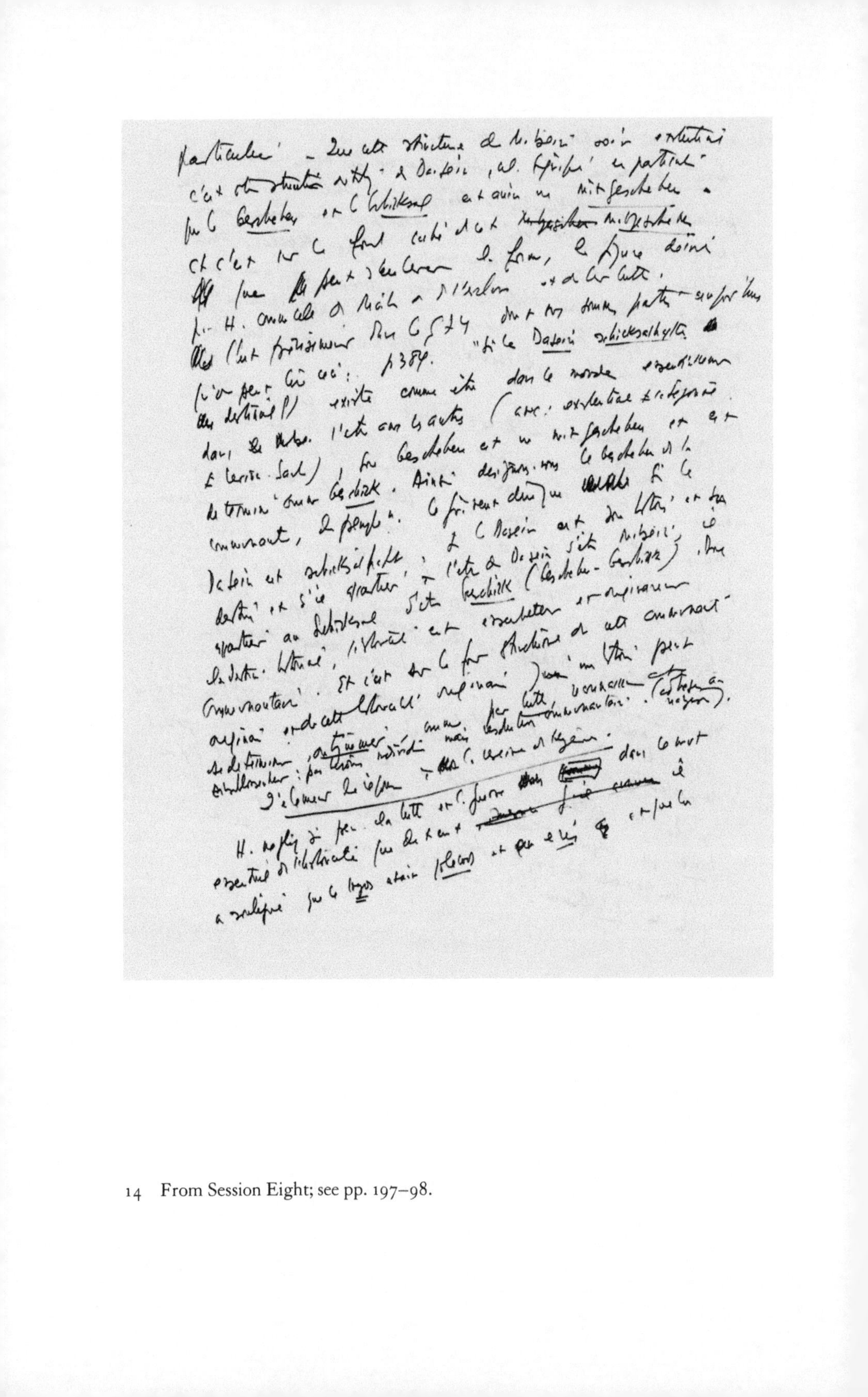

14 From Session Eight; see pp. 197–98.

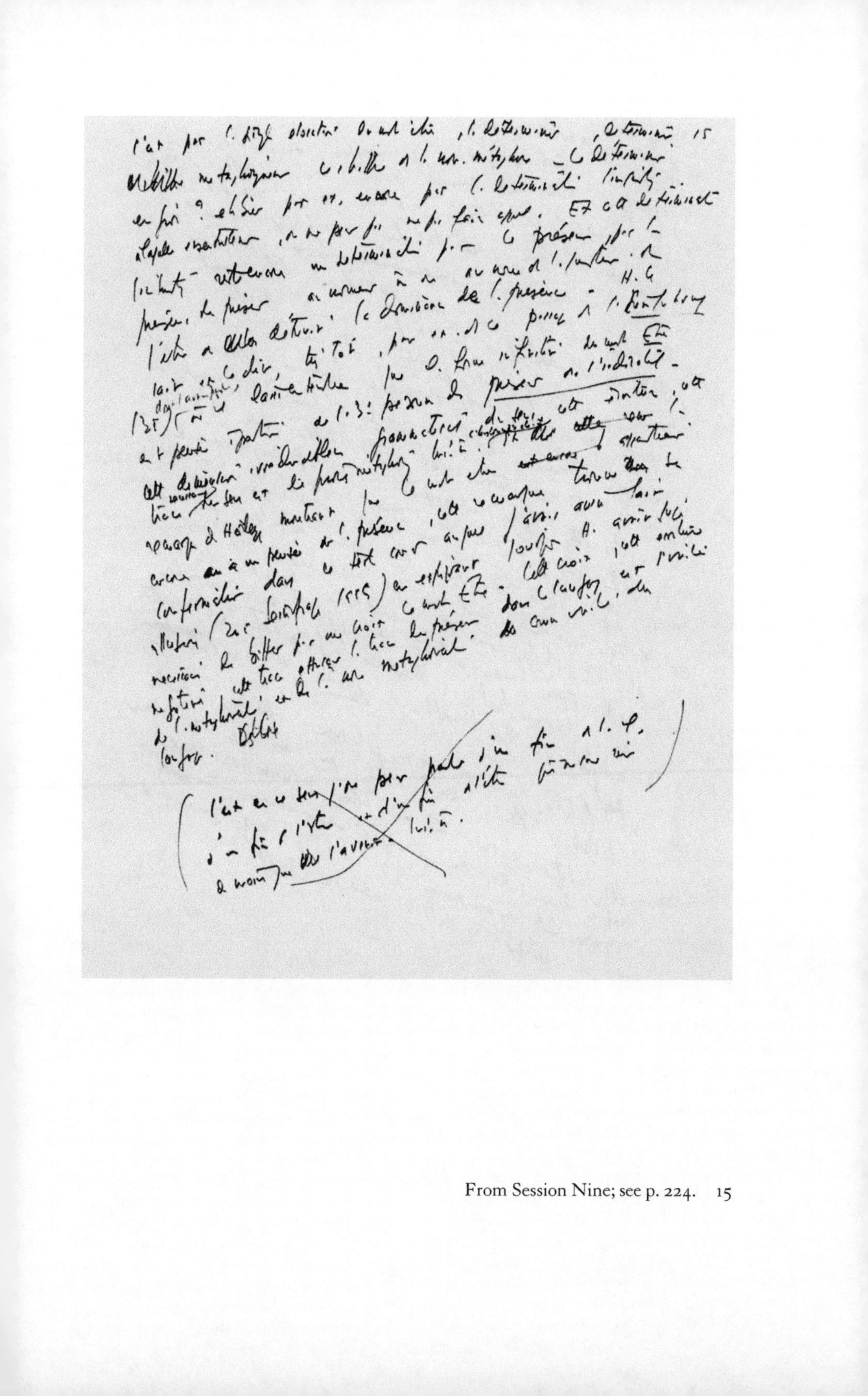

From Session Nine; see p. 224.

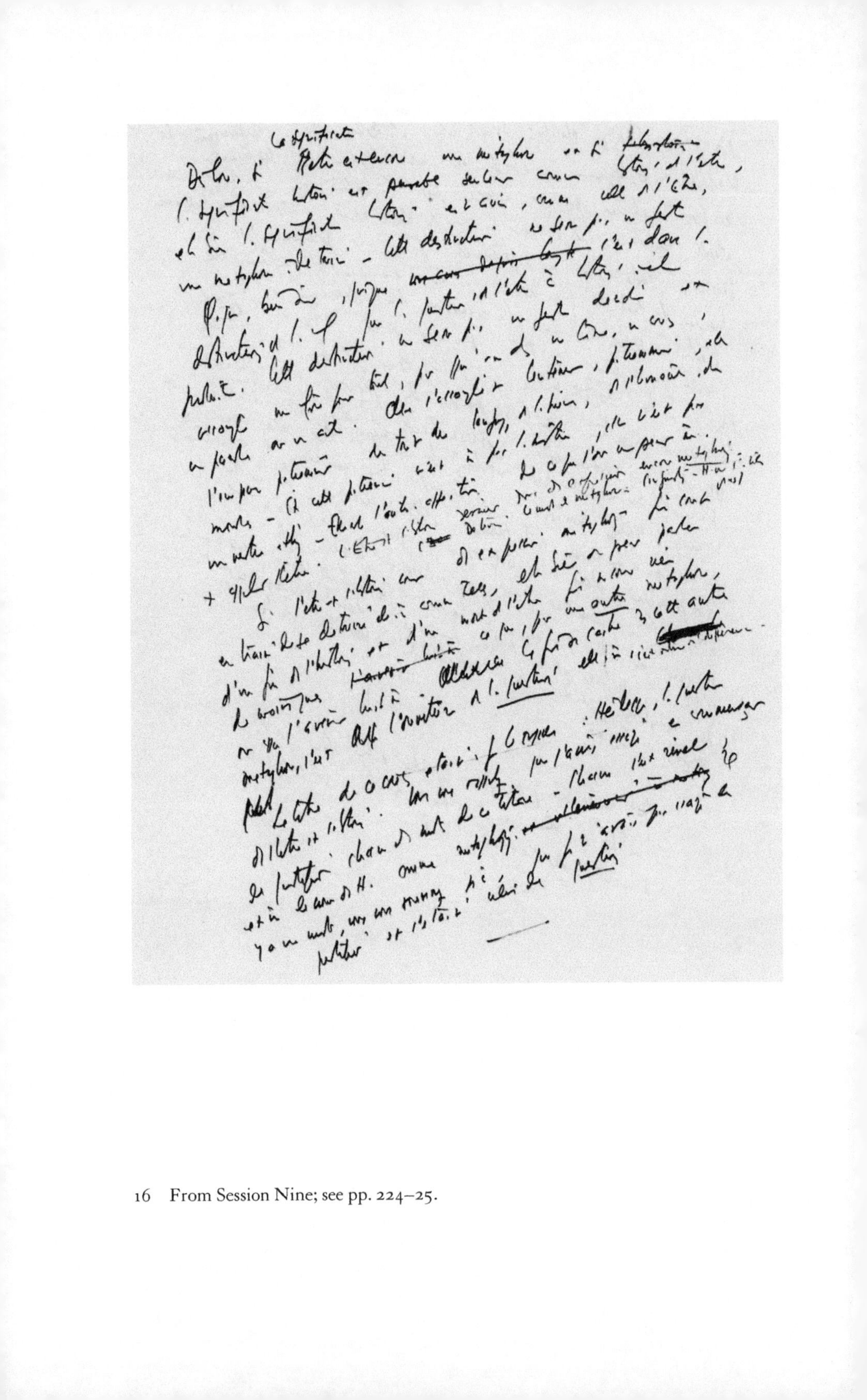

16 From Session Nine; see pp. 224–25.

"geschichtlichen" Subjekts) as its essential constitution (als Wesensverfassung)? (Being and Time, 364)

The path that leads from the discovery of the signification *subject* implied in the four common significations of the concept of history to the question soliciting the subjectivity of the historical subject—this path of destruction passes though a number of stages.

First of all, we must begin by *inverting* the naïve order of the classical vulgar or metaphysical discourse. The Subject is subject to events; it is historical in the sense of being subject to events only because it is *itself* historical. In other words, the *Geschehen* is not a sequence of events, an appearing and disappearing flux of givens. What is designated by the name *subject* is not a *Vorhandenes*, a present or a presence factually given to which occasionally and, in addition, accidentally, a history would supervene. The *Da-sein* that is designated by the name subject does not *become* historical by getting entangled in sequences of givens, in "circumstances" (*Umstände*), that would come to surround it, press in around the subject who would on this view be the present, the upright presence, the status and subject of history. On the contrary—but here Heidegger says it in interrogative form to shake up naïve certainty—is it not because, in a sense to be elucidated, *Dasein* is already historical in its very being that circumstances, *Umstände*, givens, a destiny can . . . concern it? [Cf. *Being and Time*, 361–62]

Which would mean, once again, that the present, and the presence of the present, is not the origin of the historical meaning of *Dasein* but what is called, always so enigmatically, the past, and a past that could never, in principle, if *Dasein* is historical in its being—and not in its accident and its circumstance—be summed up in the form of a past present or another present—"other" becoming the accident and the epithet of "present." In this sense, at least, the *Da* of *Dasein* no more lets itself have its meaning determined on the basis of the *now* than earlier it let it be determined on the basis of the *here*.

Now if one persists in considering *Dasein* according to the vulgar conception as *in der Zeit*, one will have to wonder where this *betonte Funktion* of *Vergangenheit*, this privileged function of pastness, of the being-past of the past, comes from. What must "past" signify in order no longer to be able to be recuperated in the form of consciousness (i.e., a phenomenon of the present, 254
as past present or present past)? Here too only the analysis of temporality can help us understand historialization. It is by understanding this strange privilege of the *past* that we will prepare our access to the meaning of historicity.

What does *past* mean when we say, to use a very modest example, that the

antiquities in a *Museum* belong to time past?[7] Let's suppose we are dealing with a piece of equipment, a piece of furniture, for example. It subsists, it is present, what in it is trace is *in the present.* It is not only because it does not function that it is historical and proper to past time. It can just as well function and still serve as an instrument of navigation, or a weapon or a piece of furniture. It will still for all that be a historical object. No more is it historical because it is the object of a historical science—archeology, for example. On the contrary, it can become the object of a historical science, it can be *historisch* only because it is already historical (*geschichtlich*). If one pursues the reductive analysis and puts aside everything through which the object is not essentially historical, one sees that nothing in its proper and present [illegible word], appearing, is historical: it is not historical in itself, nor in its present being, nor in anything I can recognize in it or attribute to it now. It is historical because it belongs to a *world* that is no longer. This proposition is trivial, so long as one does not think the *world* as Heidegger has invited us to re-think it in the preceding chapters. To understand what signifies for a world "no longer to be," one must understand the world—but here I cannot redo the analysis—in the sense it has in the expression *In-der-Welt-sein des Daseins*, in the sense of the ek-sistence and the transcendence of *Dasein*. So one must gain access to the signification of the past of *Dasein* to get to the no-longer-being of the world. What does the being-past of Dasein signify? It does not signify that *Dasein* is now only past, in the sense of no longer being present. *Vergangenheit* is not the non-*Vorhandenheit*, the *nicht mehr Vorhandenes*, the no longer being present. It is not the negative modification of the *present*, or the erasure of a present in the *having been present.* The question that Heideg-
255 ger poses here—a question we can better understand on the basis of what was said last time about the present—this question implies the response in its very syntax. Here it is.

> *Is Dasein something that has-been only (nur gewesenes)* [is only having been: obviously the translation gets difficult because of the fact that what is translated is the past participle of the verb *be,* the past participle being derived, being the modification of a fundamental form of the verb. Privilege of the *is* grasped on the basis of the perfect tense] *in the sense of da-gewesenen, of having-been-present* [So is Dasein having been in the form or meaning of having been present], *or has it been (ist es gewesen) as gegenwärtigendes-zukünftiges, as something making present and futural, that is, in the temporalizing of its temporality (das heißt in der Zeitigung seiner Zeitlichkeit)?"* (*Being and Time*, 363)

7. [Translator's note:] The following paragraph is a close paraphrase of *Being and Time*, 362.

What do these Jesuitical formulas even mean? It goes without saying that for Heidegger the second formula is the correct one and the only one that has a chance of describing the originary historicity of *Dasein*. If the past of *Dasein* signifies a having-been-present, that would mean that the present is the fundamental form that is modified, that temporalization is a modification, a modalization of a fundamental and absolute present. That is the absolutely fundamental proposition of Western metaphysics from Plato to Husserl via Hegel, as we saw last time. And for those among the representatives of all this metaphysics, such as Hegel and Husserl, who tried to think and respect temporality and history, there is a movement of historialization and temporalization only in the absolutely absolute and absolutely a-historical form of the Present. We have seen why, and for what reasons, reasons in a sense irrecusable for a philosophy in general. At the same time, we saw last time 256
that for Heidegger the privileging of the present, an irrecusable ontic privileging, closed us off from originary historicity itself, relegated it to the rank of a modification even if one granted it as such many rights. The Present (i.e., phenomenality, manifestation) is the dissimulation of originary historicity itself, which must therefore not be thought of as another present, but as a past origin in a sense that is not that of a past present. And if one wishes to use this signification of the Present as dissimulation, and of manifestation as the withdrawal of an origin that was never a present phenomenality, if one wishes to use this proposition, in any discourse whatsoever, in any discursive field whatsoever, in any determinate circumscription of discourse whatsoever, it must first be understood in itself, which one can do only in an explicit and responsible dialogue with the thinkers of the metaphysical tradition.

To the sense of the past of *Dasein* as *having been* present, Heidegger opposes, then, *Gegenwärtigendes-Zukünftiges*, the future presentifying itself as temporalization of temporality. Which means of course that the present never is as such (Present = past of the future), but above all that temporalization is not primarily a movement of the presence of presence, an exiting out of itself in itself of the present (a formula that is Hegelian as well as Husserlian), but an absolute exiting, an ek-stasis that is radical, originary and without return. It is ek-stasis and not presence that is the fundamental origin of temporality. Ek-stasis: that is, that movement of the temporality of *Dasein* projected toward the to-come [*à-venir*] that Heidegger calls Care. If Care is fundamental and originary, the form of presence is not. The unity of temporalization is an ek-static and not a static unity. Saying that it is not static does not mean that it is movement in the sense in which movement is opposed to rest, *kinēsis* to *stasis*. There is an ekstatic unity of the ekstases of temporality (present, past, future) that constitutes the past as a future having been, as a future having presentified itself.

257 So, of course, getting back to the questions posed earlier, one will wonder whether, in order to dethrone the present, Heidegger is not illegitimately privileging here the ekstasis of the future—and this is consistent with the privileging of *Entschlossenheit* and the finite horizon of death, (Death ≠ history)—and whether in so doing he is not dissimulating historicity for the reasons I gave earlier. Does he not end up making of the past a secondary ekstasis with regard to that of the future and the presentification of the future? This is why Heidegger cannot get out of the enigma of the origin of historicity, so long as he substitutes—as he always does in *Sein und Zeit*—the privileging of the future for that of the present. He cannot escape the enigma he formulates himself when he writes, for example, [German] p. 381:

> But saying this only makes the enigma more acute: why is it that precisely the "*Vergangenheit*," pastness, or, more appropriately, the *Gewesenheit* [being having been] *vorwiegend* [in a privileged manner] determines what is historical when, after all, *Gewesenheit* temporalizes itself equiprimordially with present and future? (*Being and Time*, 363)

Enigmatic, then, is the discourse—and the enigma is always, as its name indicates in Greek, *ainos*, a discourse and even a story—enigmatic, then, is the discourse on history at the moment that it really must speak about the *past*. Enigmatic is the discourse on the past, enigmatic is the past as origin of discourse, enigmatic is historicity as discursivity. The time of the past in discourse and the past of time in ek-sistence are the enigma itself. They are not enigmas among others but the enigma of enigma, the enigmatic source of the enigma in general, enigmaticity. [One or two illegible words.]

This enigma has thus returned to its own obscurity the common concept of historicity as the concept of what supervenes, what advenes, what happens *to a subject in general*. By asking what is the subjectivity of this subject claimed to be a present, the station, the stance of a present to which history
258 or stories happen, one is not far from saying that subjectivity is not that to which history happens but what happens to history.

Subjectivity as what happens to historicity is a formula that one must not rush to think or determine in the precipitation of overturning or inversion. Failing which one would be saying the same thing as what one no longer means. One would say for example that the subject is merely an event arriving at, landing on, the essential and implacable shore of history, which is, first of all, absurd and comes back, curiously enough, to the vulgar thesis.

The subject, on this account, *would not be historical*, but *qua* event it would be in history or derived with respect to history, and so forth, which for its part would not budge.

Subjectivity having happened to historicity: that needs to be thought otherwise without making of historicity a sort of substance of things existing in itself without [any existing originary relation]. This must mean that the dimension of subjectivity supervenes on a historicity of ek-sistence, of *Dasein*. The historicity of *Dasein* is originary but it is not originarily determined as subjectivity. Which means that it does not originarily appear to itself as subjectivity and that it is not originarily subjectivity. *Dasein* (ek-sistence) is originarily history, and it happens in the course of its history that it constitutes itself and appears to itself as subjectivity, for essential and necessary reasons. In the course of its history, that means here—as we are dealing here with *essential structures of Dasein in general*—that, *for example*, in the course of an individual, human, history or, *for example*, in the course of the history of what is known by the name *humanity*, or for example in that remarkable form of the history of humanity that is the *European form*, or for example that remarkable form of European, ideological, political, economic, aesthetic, history, and so on. [Comment: history of philosophy].

Once again, in spite of appearances, we are not here speaking a Hegelian language. The point is not to say that substance becomes subject, that there is a becoming-subject of a substance that for Hegel is absolute substance—the absolute, absolute being, God—which from being a substance becomes a free subject. And it is ultimately a *Present with* itself that announces itself, separates itself from itself in order to find itself again with itself; it is upon an 259
absolute as Presence that every becoming supervenes—this whole history, and in particular this moment, the event of becoming-subject, the advent of the subject. It is upon a non-history that history advenes. Such at least is literal and conventional Hegelianism. If now we were to hear in Hegel something else that would cancel the difference with Heidegger, that would mean that something has been thought—perhaps by those who heard it, and among them, at least, Heidegger—something has been heard and thought as such in the destruction, that was only murmured by Hegel, the difference between what is implied [*sous-entendu*] and what is heard [*entendu*] being perhaps the whole difference in their thought. But I do not want to get into that here.

The fact remains that for Heidegger subjectivity does not supervene upon a non-historical absolute that awakens to it (Substance, Present). It supervenes upon an experience or an ek-sistence that is already historical. It is an adventure that happens to history [*une histoire qui arrive à l'histoire*]. Now, this does not mean that it is one history among others, one event among others that happens to history. This is almost the whole of metaphysics. The advent of subjectivity or of the epoch of subjectivity is not a *secondary* encounter. It modifies *primary* historicity; it is an epoch of *primary* historicity.

You know that at the end of §73 Heidegger makes a distinction between what he calls *primary historicity*, the historicity of the ek-sistence of *Dasein* as *being-in-the-world*, and *secondary historicity*, what is encountered in the world and that does not have the form of being of *Da-sein* but of the *Zuhandenes*, and even of what is called nature as the ground of historical culture. In other words, primary is the historicity of *In-der-Welt-sein* in the form of *Dasein* with the precise sense we have recognized in the *in* of *in-der-Welt*. Secondary would be the historicity of beings that are in the world in the banal sense of the word *in*.

Heidegger's only effort at describing concretely this *primary* historicity of *Dasein* in *Sein und Zeit* is to be found, then, as I said, in §74, entitled *Die*
260 *Grundverfassung der Geschichtlichkeit*—the fundamental constitution of historicity. I have already said that this effort to grasp authentic historicity here brought nothing new, no new concept with respect to the ones from the analysis of authentic temporality: those of care, the anxiety of being-toward-death and *Entschlossenheit*.

The only new concept that properly belongs to a historicity that does not simply merge with temporality is the concept of inheritance and tradition or transmission, of *Erbe* and *Überlieferung*, the more important, structuring concept of *Sichüberlieferung*, of the self-tradition of an auto-transmission: that is, originary historical synthesis of ek-sistence in its ekstases. [Comment]

But this *Sichüberlieferung*, this passage from self to self that constitutes the nuclear synthesis of historicity and is, properly speaking, the first tissue, the first text, that text that I was saying a few sessions back we would see appear, or reappear at the point where it would ground in return the hermeneutic intention; this first tissue, this first text is authentically historical only if it is constituted, I would almost say written on the basis of an *Entschlossenheit*, a resolute anticipation and a freedom for death. I have already given a glimpse of what the consequences of this proposition should be. In conclusion, I will translate a passage from §74 that sums up this movement. We'll comment on it next time.

> *Nur Seiendes, das wesenhaft in seinem Sein z u k ü n f t i g ist,* only a being that is essentially futural in its being, *so daß es frei für seinen Tod an ihm zerschellend auf sein faktisches Da sich zurückwerfen lassen kann,* so that it can let itself be thrown back upon its factical there, free for its death and shattering itself on

it, *das heißt nur Seiendes, das als zukünftiges gleichursprünglich gewesend ist,* that is, only a being that, as futural, is equiprimordially **having-been** [comment (Present = past of a future)], *kann, sich selbst die ererbte Möglichkeit überliefernd,* can hand down to itself its inherited possibility, *die eigene Geworfenheit übernehmen und augenblicklich sein für "seine Zeit,"* can [therefore] take over its own [its authentic] throwness and be **in the Moment** for "its time." *Nur eigentliche Zeitlichkeit, die zugleich endlich ist, macht so etwas wie Schicksal, das heißt eigentliche Geschichtlichkeit möglich.* Only authentic temporality that is at the same time finite makes something like fate, that is, authentic historicity, possible. (*Sein und Zeit*, 385; *Being and Time*, 366)

SESSION EIGHT

15 March 1965

For two sessions now, we have been lingering on these last chapters of *Sein und Zeit*, without denying ourselves anticipations and references to much later texts. But always to attempt to situate—and it isn't easy—the intention of this penultimate chapter devoted to temporality and historicity. Two sessions ago we tried, following Heidegger, to bring out the most general structure of the *Geschehen* and the *Geschichtlichkeit* of *Dasein*. And this preliminary stage could only be passed after the *solicitation* (what I shall now call solicitation rather than destruction) of metaphysics and onto-theology insofar as they are but the determination of being as Present and Presence of the Present. Thinking the always on the basis of the now. Historicity cannot be thought so long as Presence is the absolute form of meaning. And we have seen what that means, and that it is precisely the metaphysically and philosophically irreversible and profoundly invulnerable character of this metaphysical proposition determining being as presence that had to be destroyed, solicited. I will not go back over this. In this vein, we wondered last time about what I called the phenomenon of running out of breath that happens at the end of *Sein und Zeit*. I tried to analyze the signs of this—two signs coming down to only one, and the *reasons*—two reasons coming down to only one. I cannot take them up again, any more than I can take up
264 everything we said about the strange architectonic procedure that gives the last three chapters of *Sein und Zeit* their rhythm. We drew some anticipatory conclusions from this concerning the meaning of the abandonment of *Sein und Zeit* and the future treatment of the theme of the history of being, the erasure of the theme of *Entschlossenheit* and even of temporality in the texts to come. And above all we recognized this noteworthy phenomenon: that at bottom it is never really a question of historicity in the proper sense in *Sein und Zeit*. Not only is it not a question of the historicity of being (but there was no question in Heidegger's intention of it being a question of this). But it is also not even a question of the historicity of *Dasein* in the *proper sense*. And I showed this by explaining what I meant here by proper sense.

Because basically, as we saw, Heidegger almost without exception deals only with inauthentic (non-proper, *uneigentlich*) historicity and only insofar as it is rooted in inauthentic temporality, in intratemporality (*Innerzeitigkeit*). As to all that, I firmly insisted, referring to later texts, on the necessity of what is more a decisive *turning* than an *impasse*. And we commented on this chapter devoted to the common—inauthentic—conception of historicity, to the enigma of a *Vergangenheit* or a *Gewesenheit* that no longer had the sense of past present as present past or past present of a subject. (The four meanings of the common concept.) And once again, venturing the formula according to which history did not happen to a subject in general but the subject happened to history, we had to take many precautions to understand this formula appropriately and first of all to understand it neither in an empiricist sense nor in a Hegelian sense.

Finally, in conclusion, I began to look at this §74 that presents itself as a descriptive sketch of the authentic historicity of *Dasein* and that I proposed to show, precisely, (1) comprises no new concept allowing us to distinguish the root from the rooted (i.e., temporality from historicity); (2) depended on the *Entschlossenheit* that I had earlier shown runs the risk, in privileging the ekstasis of the *future*, of *death*, and a *freedom* still not fully released from ethico-metaphysics and which will subsequently be abandoned for good rea- 265
son by Heidegger, ran the risk, then, of barring our access to historicity.

The only *apparently* new concepts, as we saw, were those that designated the first tissue, the nuclear tissue, the first text, I said for specific reasons, the first phrase of historicity, or at least the first phrase as first historicity; these were the concepts of heritage (*Erbe*), of *transmission* (*Überlieferung*) and, especially and first of all, of auto-transmission, auto-tradition (*Sichüberlieferung*):[1] a tradition of self that, for the moment, obviously, has no intra-worldly or intra-temporal meaning. No intra-worldly or intra-temporal meaning since we are dealing with the originary synthesis, with traditionality and the originary tra-jectory that allows temporalization and thus worldization in general to happen. So one must not understand these words *heritage* and *tradition* in the everyday sense. On the contrary, there is heritage and tradition in the common sense only if this originary synthesis is possible and if it is possible first of all as *self-tradition of experience or rather of ek-sistence*, this being no longer the experience of a subject.

This *Sichüberlieferung*—auto-transmission—is analogous to the syn-

1. [Translator's note:] Stambaugh translates *Sichüberlieferen*, when it appears as a verb or as an infinitive noun in *Sein und Zeit* (where it never in fact appears in the nominal form *Sichüberlieferung*), as "handing oneself down" or slight variations thereof. I translate Derrida's term literally as "auto-transmission."

thetic movement of protentions and retentions described by Husserl, only with these two decisive differences: (1) that here it is no longer a matter of the movement of a *consciousness*, but of an ek-sistence that is not determined at the outset as consciousness; (2) that the absolute form of transmission is ekstasis, going outside oneself and not Present, self-presence (present going outside itself in itself), a present only modified and originarily and ceaselessly modified by protentions and retentions. *Sichüberlieferung* is therefore, if you will, a complementary *concept* or, if you prefer, the other side of the concept of the concept[2] of *pure auto-affection* that describes time in *Kant and the Problem of Metaphysics*. And if we could do so, this is the book we would need to delve into here. Auto-affection and auto-tradition—such is the movement of the
266 temporalization of time. Setting off, for example, from the theme of Kantian affectivity and receptivity (*intuitus derivativus*), Heidegger shows how Kant does not limit himself to saying that time like space is the universal form of sensibility (i.e., affectivity, affection), but that time itself affects, must always affect, says Kant, "the concept of the representation of objects."[3] Comment. Now every affection is a manifestation through which an already given being announces itself. A rigorously Kantian proposition. Being-affected, spirit, is the form of appearing, the phenomenalization of a being that appears to me, that touches me, that affects me precisely because I have not created it. *Intuitus derivativus*. Now, how is one to maintain this definition of affection as an affection already given to me? How to maintain it when it is a matter of time? What does being affected by time mean, given that time is nothing, is not an already-given being, is nothing external to us? [Illegible word][4] Idea. Comment. To clarify what he calls Kant's "obscure assertion" that "time affects a concept, in particular, the concept of the representations of objects" (*Kant and the Problem of Metaphysics*, 133), Heidegger shows what time as pure intuition must signify: originarily, it can in no way signify affection of something by something, affection of a being by another being, affection of an existing subject by something outside it: because time is nothing, as such it cannot affect anything. It is *affection of self by self*. Auto-affection, a concept that is as incomprehensible as is, in truth, the movement of temporalization. This auto-affection as temporality is not a characteristic affecting transcen-
267 dental subjectivity, one of its attributes; it is, on the contrary, that starting

2. Thus in the manuscript.

3. Quoted in Heidegger, *Kant und das Problem der Metaphysik* (1929; Frankfurt am Main: Vittorio Klostermann GmbH , 1991), 189; trans. Richard Taft (Bloomington: Indiana University Press, 1990), 132.

4. [Translator's note:] Perhaps "Esthetic."

from which the self, the *Selbst*, the I think constitutes itself and announces itself to itself. Heidegger writes, [French] p. 244:

> As pure self-affection, time is not an acting affection that strikes a self which is at hand (*vorhandenes Selbst*). Instead, as pure it forms the essence (*Wesen*) of something like self-activating (*Sich-selbst-angehen* as self-relating, to relate to self, *angegangen werden zu können*). However, if it belongs to the essence of the finite subject to be able to be activated as a self, then time as pure self-affection forms the essential structure of subjectivity. Only on the grounds of this self-hood can the finite creature be what it must be: dependent upon taking things in stride (*angewiesen auf Hinnahme*). (*Kant and the Problem of Metaphysics*, 132)

It follows that it is only by referring to inauthentic temporality, to intra-temporality, that Kant would have been so determined to separate the I think from temporality, to make it into an intemporal subject. The I think is intemporal only with regard to intra-worldly intra-temporality, but, if one gets back to originary and authentic temporality, the I think is temporal. The separation of the I think from temporality is in the end nothing other than the difference that separates originary temporality from constituted and intra-worldly temporality.

You know that this theme of pure auto-affection is merely the opening in Heidegger's thought to the theme of the transcendence of *Dasein* and to the question of being, beyond the metaphysics of subjectivity. The notion of affection or of affectivity is at bottom—as is time, precisely, of which auto-affection is the name—the notion of affectivity is at bottom merely the name of the transcendence of *Dasein* toward the being of beings, and as time, the meaning of the transcendental horizon of the question of being. Affectivity is in this sense transcendence. Well, let it be said in passing and elliptically, it *268*
is in this proposition that—according to M. Henry, the author of *The Essence of Manifestation*,[5] that book of rare power and depth in its movement but, it seems to me, totally *pointless* in its result—it is this proposition—affectivity as transcendence or transcendence as essence of manifestation—that would sum up today the history of Western philosophy, whether it be summed up in Hegel, Husserl or Heidegger. It is this proposition that M. Henry wishes in turn to try to destroy in order to restore a concept of affectivity that has supposedly been dissimulated, affectivity as pure subjectivity, without transcendence outside itself, auto-affection of being for itself, as spirit. So that at

5. Michel Henry, *L'essence de la manifestation* (Paris: Presses Universitaires de France, 1963); [trans. Girard Etzkornas as *The Essence of Manifestation* (The Hague: Martinus Nijhoff, 1973)].

the end of a very strong, very meticulous and very profound critique of Hegel in particular, strictly Hegelian or even infra-Hegelian conclusions are formulated. This is not the first and no doubt is not the last time this will happen.

This detour—which I cannot extend here, via Kant and the problem of metaphysics—was supposed to bring us back to this notion of *Sichüberlieferung*, of self-transmission, that Heidegger makes, as it were, the originary synthesis and the nucleus of historicity, and that I would say is basically the other side of what will be called auto-affection in *Kant and the Problem of Metaphysics*. This reference and this detour were already necessary for two reasons.

(1) By reason of the fact that *Kant and the Problem of Metaphysics* occupies with respect to *Sein und Zeit* a situation that is not without interest from the point of view that is ours here. For, *on the one hand*, the essential content of this book was presented in lectures in 1925–26[6]—and so not long before the writing of *Sein und Zeit* and before its publication. On the other hand, Heidegger tells us in the foreword to the first edition of this book that the explication of the *Critique of Pure Reason* that is proposed in it has its origin in a first working out of the second division of *Sein und Zeit*, the very one that was never definitively worked out and published. *Kant and the Problem*
269 *of Metaphysics* thus gives us an idea of the path into which Heidegger ventured and gave up finding his footing after *Sein und Zeit*, and this becomes very illuminating if one thinks of what we said about the impossibility of a *continuous* progress from *Sein und Zeit*. [Interlinear: ______..... dotted line. . . . renunciation.] A risky path, full of pitfalls, as Heidegger recognizes himself, since he writes in the foreword to the first edition,[7]

> The instances in which I have gone astray and the shortcomings of the present endeavor have become so clear to me on the path of thinking during the period referred to above that I therefore refuse to make this work into a patchwork by compensating with supplements, appendices and postscripts.
>
> Thinkers learn from their shortcomings to be more persevering. (*Kant and the Problem of Metaphysics*, xx)

That *Kant and the Problem of Metaphysics* was thought of as a *stone* supposed to be added to the edifice of *Sein und Zeit*, then having to be abandoned on the building site, like a discarded and unusable piece of material, some distance

6. [Translator's note:] In fact, Heidegger refers his *Kantbuch* to the 1927–28 lecture course *Phänomenologische Interpretation von Kants Kritik der reinen Vernunft* (GA 25), trans. Parvis Emad and Kenneth Maly as *Phenomenological Interpretation of Kant's "Critique of Pure Reason"* (Bloomington: Indiana University Press, 1997).

7. In fact, this is the foreword to the second edition.

from the unfinished edifice itself, is confirmed when one reads, for example on [German] pp. 23–24 of *Sein und Zeit*, the plan for this explication of the Kantian design. I'll read rapidly in the translation (here because we are not looking at it closely) this passage from *Sein und Zeit* in which an essential clarification of the unpublished second division is, programmatically, announced:

Read French translation, pp. 39–41:

> *In accord with the positive tendency of this destruction, the question must first be asked whether and to what extent in the course of the history of ontology in general the interpretation of being has been thematically connected with the phenomenon of time. We must also ask whether the problematic of temporality, which necessarily belongs here, was fundamentally worked out or could have been. Kant is the first and only one who traversed a stretch of the path toward investigating the dimension of temporality—or 270
> allowed himself to be driven there by the compelling force of the phenomena themselves. Only when the problem of temporality is pinned down can we succeed in casting light on the obscurity of his doctrine of schematism. Furthermore, in this way we can also show *why* this area had to remain closed to Kant in its real dimensions and in its central ontological function. Kant himself knew that he was venturing forth into an obscure area: "This schematism of our understanding as regards appearances and their mere form is an art hidden in the depths of the human soul, the true devices of which are hardly ever to be divined from Nature and laid uncovered before our eyes."[8] What it is that Kant shrinks back from here, as it were, must be brought to light thematically and in principle if the expression "being" is to have a demonstrable meaning. Ultimately the phenomena to be explicated in the following analysis under the rubric of "temporality" are precisely those that determine the *most covert* judgments of "common reason," the analysis of which Kant calls the "business of philosophers."
>
> In pursuing the task of destruction along the guideline of the problem of temporality the following treatise will attempt to interpret the chapter on the schematism and the Kantian doctrine of time developed there. At the same time we must show why Kant could never gain insight into the problem of temporality. Two things prevented this insight: first, the neglect of the question of being in general, and second, in conjunction with this, the lack of a thematic ontology of Dasein or, in Kantian terms, the lack of a preliminary ontological analytic of the subjectivity of the subject. Instead, despite all his essential advances, Kant dogmatically adopted Descartes' position. Furthermore, although Kant takes this phenomenon back into the subject his analysis of time remains oriented toward the traditional, vulgar understanding of it. It is this that finally prevented Kant from working out the phenom-

8. *Critique of Pure Reason*, A141/B180–81.

> enon of a "transcendental determination of time" in its own structure and function. As a consequence of this double effect of the tradition, the decisive connection between *time* and the "*I think*" remains shrouded in complete
> 271 obscurity. It did not even become a problem. By taking over Descartes' ontological position Kant neglects something essential: an ontology of Dasein. In terms of Descartes' innermost tendency this omission is a decisive one. With the "*cogito sum*" Descartes claims to prepare a new and secure foundation for philosophy. But what he leaves undetermined in this "radical" beginning is the manner of being of the *res cogitans*, more precisely *the meaning of being of the* "*sum*." Working out the tacit ontological foundations of the "*cogito sum*" will constitute the second stage of the destruction of, and the path back into, the history of ontology. The interpretation will demonstrate not only that Descartes had to neglect the question of being altogether, but also why he held the opinion that the absolute "being-certain" of the cogito exempted him from the question of the meaning of the being of this being.* (*Being and Time*, 22–23)

Such then was the first reason for this detour via *Kant and the Problem of Metaphysics.* The *second reason* is, then, more immediately, this notion of auto-affection as the other side of the *Sichüberlieferung* that interests us here directly. Thus, for example, on [French] page 244 of *Kant* . . . , describing time as pure auto-affection, Heidegger writes,

> According to its essence, time is pure affection of itself. Furthermore it is precisely what in general forms [aiming: intuition, the way] seeing which, setting off from itself, heads for . . . [which translates *so etwas wie das, "Von-sich-aus-hin-auf-zu"*] something like the "from-out-itself-toward-there . . . ," so that the upon-which looks back and into the previously named toward-there. (*Kant and the Problem of Metaphysics*, 132)

Read the German, pp. 180 and 181[9]:

> **Die Zeit ist ihrem Wesen nach reine Affektion ihrer selbst. Ja, noch mehr, sie ist gerade das, was überhaupt so etwas wie das, 'Von-sich-aus-hin-zu-auf . . .' bildet, dergestalt, dass das so sich bildende Worauf-zu zurückblickt und herein in das*
> 272 *vorgenannte Hin-zu . . .*[10]*

Well, this exiting from self that rebounds onto self and holds itself in the exit from self, gives itself and transmits itself so as to keep it, its own ekstatic movement, in itself, and that is auto-transmission, taking rigorously into

9. The page is in fact 189.

10. Heidegger, *Kant und das Problem der Metaphysik* (Frankfurt am Main: Vittorio Klostermann GmbH, 1929), 189.

account the fact that the absolute form of this movement, of this self-keeping, is not the present or the now . . . for the reasons we know.

I think we can now broach the commentary announced last time on the sentence I translated at the very end of the session. Let me read it again. (Open the German text to p. 385.)

> Only a being that is essentially **futural** in its being, so that it can let itself be thrown back upon its factical there, free for its death and shattering itself on it, that is, only a being that, as futural, is equiprimordially **having-been** [Present = past of a future], can hand down to itself (*sich selbst überliefernd*) its inherited possibility [inheriting from itself the inherited possibility], can [therefore] take over its own [its authentic] thrownness and be **augenblicklich** for "its time." Only authentic temporality that is at the same time finite makes something like fate, that is, authentic historicity, possible. *(Being and Time*, 366)

In recognizing the *Sichüberlieferung* as another name for the auto-affection of pure time, we clearly recognize that we are dealing here with an auto-tradition that is pure, *a priori*, non-empirical, non-ontic and the condition of possibility for any ontic history. We are dealing with an ontological structure of traditionality in general.

You see that here authentic historicity is described in the same terms as authentic temporality and that its authenticity depends on the authenticity of what is translated as decision or resolute anticipation: *Entschlossenheit*. What does this mean? 273

First, let's recall the premises of this analysis.

1. *Dasein* has its history not because history befalls it but because it is historical in its very being.

2. The being of *Dasein* has been recognized as *Care*, in the rigorous sense of this term, which can be thought only on the basis of its grounding in the movement of temporality.

3. "Thus, the interpretation of the historicity of *Dasein* is," says Heidegger, "basically just a *more concrete elaboration* of the interpretation of temporality" (*Being and Time*, 364). Clearly, as I noted, it is only this admittedly vague notion of a *more concrete elaboration* (*konkretere Ausarbeitung*) that distinguishes the theme of temporality from that of historicity, and this is rather disappointing.

In any case, since the analysis of historicity is rooted in that of temporality and of care, authentic historicity will have to depend, as does authentic temporal existence, on *Entschlossenheit*.

We will have, then, to retain from the analyses of *Entschlossenheit*, which we obviously would need to reread patiently here—something we cannot do—only what pertains directly to this problematic of historicity.

The translation of the notion of *Entschlossenheit* is difficult and heavy with philosophical decision. We will keep the translation "resolute decision," making quite clear that this is not the decision of a consciousness that deliberates, initiates absolutely, decrees, is decisive, all these significations designating precisely the interruption of historicity, the progress of a voluntarist radicalism, a philosophy of consciousness deciding and tearing the tissue and the text of [illegible word] history with its verdicts and its absolute beginnings. If that is what resolute decision means, then we should not translate *Entschlossenheit* as resolute decision.

Entschlossenheit, as Heidegger reminds us here, has been determined as "*verschwiegene angstbereite Sichentwerfen auf das eigene Schuldigsein*,"[11] as secret (hidden, reserved, discreet) and anxiety-laden self-projection, self-projection toward one's own *Schuldigsein*: *schuldig* here means neither simply guilty, nor simply responsible (in the abstract and formal sense of freedom
274 and moral responsibility); here it is a matter of a non-empirical debt of which I am the debtor as if I were always already bound by a contract—and that's historicity—a contract that I did not sign, that I did not have to sign but that obliges me ontologically. This means both that I never had to sign *in the present* and in consciousness this contract (for example, here the one that binds me to the tradition that reads me and binds [*qui me lit et lie*] my responsibility to the received heritage, to all the heritages, on the basis of which the meaning of my ek-sistence finds a horizon already there). So I never had in the *present* and in *consciousness* to sign this contract, but its terms and content obligate me anyway—that is, do not affect me empirically, do not fall upon me like falling roof-tiles, but to the contrary constitute my own freedom, like the possibility of death and the anxiety that constitute my own freedom. [The historicity that is awakened in *Schuldigsein* ≠ accident and event.] So the proper debt—this *Schuldigsein* with respect to the very thing to which I have not simply chosen to obligate and bind myself—this *Schuldigsein* is that toward which the self projects itself. That the self projects itself does not mean that this self exists first and then projects itself or not, but that the self constitutes itself in projecting itself. The self is this projection. Authenticity is this projection when it is taken up and *vorlaufend*: anticipation. "In this *Entschlossenheit*," says Heidegger,

11. [Translator's note:] "Resoluteness as self-projection upon one's own being guilty that is reticent and ready for anxiety" (*Being and Time*, 364, 284).

> Dasein understands itself with regard to its potentiality-of-being in a way that confronts death [literally *unter die Augen,* under its eyes] in order to take over completely the being that it itself is in the *Geworfenheit* of its throwness. Resolutely taking over one's own factical "*Da*" "implies" at the same time decision (*Entschluss*) in the situation. (*Being and Time*, 364)

In other words, the taking up of the factical *Da*, the taking charge of facticity and the factical conditions of my ek-sistence—that is, of the *Da*, of my historial relation to Being—and we know, and Heidegger in any case will say so later on, it is Being that destines the *Da*, and the history of being that destines the *Da*. Which means that human ek-sistence does not purely and simply produce, does not at every moment invent, the conditions of its existence. [Three illegible interlinear words] not empirically. So, the taking up of the factical *Da*, the resolute taking charge of the factical conditions of the *Da* and of ek-sistence, will be simultaneously the decision of the situation, 275
which means that the taking up will be neither conformist acceptance nor fatalistic resignation but *decision in the situation*. The freedom of the decision and the taking up of the facticity of ek-sistence will be one and the same thing, and they *constitute* and *unite with* each other through this double limitation that they seem to oppose to each other. In fact, they do not each exist authentically before their mutual opposition. There is not, strictly speaking, a mutual opposition—for that would suppose the prior existence of separated terms—but the freedom and the taking up of the situation constitute each other in and by the other, before having to oppose each other or come to an agreement in the form of paradox, as in the degraded form that these themes took in the heroic voluntarism which, in the early Sartre, was externally associated with a kind of mechanism of contingency. Cartesian regression of Heideggerian themes.

Naturally, here, Heidegger does not provide, and does not have to provide, an ethics or a politics. Insofar as he is analyzing the essence of the decision in the situation—the decisionality and being of the structure in general—he does not have to tell stories and say what must be done, in fact, here or there, in this or that situation. He does not have to propose a morality as he has often been asked to do. That the constitution of a morality or a politics on the basis of these originary structural analyses might be simply derivative or simply impossible is a matter of consequences that should not inflect the ontological analysis.

Nonetheless, not to have to decide here about what ought to be decided in *Entschlossenheit* does not totally eliminate the question of knowing *in general*,

in an absolutely general way, at the level of principles, the place from which the possibilities that are projected in the decision are to be drawn. Whence to draw them? That is, on what basis to *create* them, since possibilities cannot be drawn like water from the spring, but rather open up, are invented. It is obvious that one must respond to this general question of the resource of possibilities and that one cannot respond by simple resolute anticipation of death or anxiety before death. Heidegger is the first to know and say this, and it is in knowing and saying it that he is, precisely, led to pose the problem
276 of traditionality. In particular, he writes this, German p. 383: "Wozu sich das Dasein je *faktisch* entschliesst, vermag die existentiale Analyse grundsätzlich nicht zu erörtern."

> Anticipatory self-projection [pre-cursory: *vorlaufende Sichentwerfen*] upon the insuperable possibility of existence—death—guarantees only the totality (*Ganzheit*) and authenticity of *Entschlossenheit*. But the factically disclosed possibilities of existence are not to be learned from death. All the less so since anticipation [the *Vorlaufen*] of that possibility is not a speculation about it [i.e., about death], but rather precisely means coming back, a recourse (*Zurückkommen*) to *das faktische Da*, the factical *Da*. (*Being and Time*, 365)

≠ Contemplation of the possibility of death.

Among many others, such a declaration would confirm, if it were still necessary, that what Heidegger is calling us to in *Sein und Zeit* is not a philosophy of death, a piercing of the self by rending anxiety that paralyzes us in a kind of fright and romantic seizure. As he says elsewhere,[12] the point is not to speculate on death or on what is beyond death, nothingness or survival; the point is not to resign oneself to one's mortality as though to a castration that is a relief for the master or the disciple, but to constitute the present as the past of a future: that is, to live the present not as the origin and absolute form of lived experience (of ek-sistence), but as the product, as what is constituted, derived, constituted in return on the basis of the horizon of the future and the ek-stasis of the future, this latter being able to be authentically anticipated as such only as finite to-come, that is, on the basis of the insuperability of possible death, death not being simply *at the end* like a contingent event befalling at the far end of a line of life, but determining at every—let's say moment—the opening of the future in which is constituted as past what we call the present and which never appears as such. The "*Da*" emerges and is
277 taken up in the horizon of death. Horizon and anticipation of death which are, then, I recall, neither a consciousness of my mortality nor a vigilance to

12. [Translator's note:] *Being and Time*, 238.

save me at every moment from what threatens me with death nor a desire for death or a death-instinct, and so on. So many notions that, by making the signification of death enter into the configuration consciousness of . . . , instinct or desire of . . . , presuppose as self-evident the meaning of death, and this on the basis of an unelucidated relation to death which is not yet a consciousness or an instinct, and so on. The notions of consciousness and instinct or desire being precisely borrowed from discourses, philosophies or zoologies that have as principal common feature their neutralization of the relation to death as originarily constituting or constitutive of ek-sistence, reducing it in countless ways, even when they were talking about it. Finite temporality.

Now here, the expression "anticipation of death" does not at all predetermine the relation to death by any appeal, any pre-recourse to a determinate signification such as "consciousness of," instinct or drive. It is on the basis of an absolutely in-determinate, non-predetermined relation to death, a relation precisely to indeterminacy itself (anxiety of death), relation to the indeterminate as opening of the horizon of the future, that what designates the *relation* itself is, in return, determined. Whence the effaced neutrality of the expression "being-toward-death," the "toward" here designating only the opening to that indeterminate possibility that, in return, determines, on the basis of the pure future, my present as the past of that future. The *toward*, to the extent that it still has a determinate meaning (preposition requiring the *dative* and implying that existence is given to death, dedicated to death, devoted to death), this *toward* insofar as it is determinate has a metaphorical value that must be crossed out in discourse. Philosophical discourse or rather the discourse of thought destroying the grammatico-metaphysical metaphorics has as its function this destruction of metaphor, a destruction carried out with the certainty that one will only ever destroy metaphors with the help of other metaphors. But that does not suffice to strike down as pointless the gesture of destruction, once the meaning of this gesture and of this [illegible word] destruction appears as such. It will be said that in an expression
such as "consciousness of mortality" or "certainty of mortality," or in a quite 278
different register, the expression "death-instinct" and all the significations that determine it and that are connotations (force, aim, source, animate-inanimate, conservation, etc., etc.)—it will be said, then, that these expressions are also held to be metaphorical by their authors. But, supposing that that is the case, it is clear that so long as the metaphorical dimension is not destroyed as such expressly or systematically, even gestures that are the most scientific in intention and the most faithful in their description cannot fail to import a whole latent metaphysics at the very moment when one believes oneself and plans to be placing the whole of metaphysics into parentheses.

I do not need to insist here to show what this presence of metaphysics, this adherence of metaphysics to the skin of language, can in fact import in the way of metaphysical thesis or presupposition when one pronounces the words *consciousness*, *certainty*, *drive*, and so on, in Heidegger too, for that matter. The work of philosophy in general, or rather, let's say, of thinking, far from simply consisting in crowning scientific work from the outside, in reflecting on it or criticizing it from the outside, in working on it; the work of thinking is basically nothing other, in what is called science or elsewhere, than this operation of destruction of metaphor, of determined and motivated reduction of metaphor, whenever and wherever it happens. Which does not mean that one leaves the metaphorical element of language behind, but that in a new metaphor the previous metaphor appears as such, is denounced in its origin and in its metaphorical functioning and in its necessity. It appears as such. One can perhaps call thinking and the thinking of being (the thinking of being as the horizon and the appeal of an impossible non-metaphorical thought) what calls for such a gesture of de-metaphorization. Given that, it could happen that there is more thinking in the gesture of a scientist or a poet or a non-philosopher in general when he gives himself up to this, than there is in the philosophical-type gesture that moves around in metaphorical slumber, in non-vigilance faced with the metaphorical character of language.
279 If, then, using another metaphor, one calls vigilance this thinking destroying metaphor while knowing what it is doing (knowing what it is doing, for it is not only a matter of substituting one metaphor for another without knowing it: that is what has always happened throughout history, that universal history that Borges says is perhaps only the history of a few metaphors or of various inflections of a few metaphors).[13] So it is not a matter of substituting one metaphor for another, which is the very movement of language and history, but of thinking this movement as such, thinking metaphor in metaphorizing it as such, thinking the essence of metaphor (this is all Heidegger wants to do). So I return to my proposition: If by another metaphor one calls thinking this vigilance destroying metaphor while knowing what it's doing, there is no need to wonder where there is more thinking, in science, metaphysics, poetry, and so on. There is thinking every time that this gesture occurs, in what is called science, poetry, metaphysics or elsewhere.

I return now to that being-toward-death and that possibility in general as a general structure of ek-sistence of which Heidegger says that one cannot

13. [Translator's note:] Jorge Luis Borges, "The Fearful Sphere of Pascal," trans. Anthony Kerrigan, in *Labyrinths*, ed. Donald A. Yates and James E. Irwin (New York: New Directions, 1964), 189.

expect from it determinate possibilities in fact. In the movement in which the authentic anticipation of my death sends me back to my *da* and to my *thrownness*, I discover myself as being already in the world, assigned to a world, and originarily to a being with others. Being in the world with others: I have not constituted this structure, and I can moreover always *inauthentically* dissimulate the phenomenon of originary finding oneself, and of being assigned to a world with others, but I can also, *Da-sein* can also, returning to itself, take on this thrownness and this being in the world with others, and so forth.

And here Heidegger's way of proceeding can be surprising. One might think that this is indeed the moment to broach the problem of heritage and the taking up of the heritage: that is, of our relation to the historical situation and the historical past to which we are appointed, which is assigned to us. And in fact, Heidegger does here pronounce the words *taking up*, *heritage*, and so on. And one might think that his question is: How is it with our relation to history as past, as set of traditions, and so on? In fact, via a 280
sort of new regression or reduction, Heidegger is going to fold his question back toward a form that in principle comes before that one, and that would basically be the following: Whatever possibilities of ek-sistence we find in the world to which we are in fact assigned, whatever our decision with regard to our heritage, because this decision should be authentic (i.e., governed by *Entschlossenheit*, etc.), one must first be sure of the conditions of a historicity of *Entschlossenheit* itself. The transcendental condition of all the determinate projections through which I shall determine myself with regard to history and the situation is, for these projections to be authentic, that they transmit themselves authentically, that the fidelity to the projection be authentic, be itself a history and a destiny. So one must pose the problem of the traditionality of *Entschlossenheit* before that of the relation of *Entschlossenheit* to traditionality in the world. The authenticity of historicity requires the historicity of authenticity. It is to this that the notion of *Sichüberlieferung* responds—auto-tradition, a concept describing, well before what is called the psychological movement of memory or forgetting, the ethical movement of fidelity or infidelity, and so forth—we are dealing with a concept describing this tradition of a projection that is itself defined neither in terms of consciousness nor of moral will and without which all of these concepts would themselves be meaningless. Even before remembering anything or forgetting anything, before being faithful or unfaithful to anything, my tradition of myself must be secured and, if I am to secure it authentically, this cannot be decided by *fiat* once and for all, but my authentic projection must ceaselessly transmit itself to itself. That is the ontological condition of a proper or authentic historicity and of what Heidegger also calls a *destiny*. *Schicksal* (≠ inevitability,

history as destiny, ≠ freedom, decision or inevitability). It is on condition that the authenticity of *Entschlossenheit* be constituted as destiny and inherit from itself that heritage in general—the heritage of goods, of values, of culture—
281 the tradition of meaning in general, will be possible and authentic. Without the authentic auto-tradition of *Entschlossenheit*, every relation to history will be inauthentic, whether, for that matter, it takes the form of a conservative traditionalism or of a revolutionary demolition. *Entschlossenheit* is not sufficient, then, to constitute historicity; only the authentic auto-tradition of *Entschlossenheit* can do that.

Concluding an important sub-paragraph of §74, Heidegger writes thus:

> The finitude of existence thus seized upon tears one back out of endless multiplicity of closest possibilities offering themselves—those of comfort, shirking and taking things easy—and brings Dasein to the simplicity of its destiny. This is how we designate the primordial *Geschehen* of Dasein that lies in authentic *Entschlossenheit*, [originary *Geschehen*] in which it transmits itself to itself, free for death, in a possibility that it inherited and yet has chosen. (*Being and Time*, 365–66)

"Inherited and yet has chosen." "Inherited and yet has chosen" means that one must think, before the alternative between heritage and freedom, that the two terms of a heritage received or undergone and of a decisive or inaugural freedom are abstractly dissociated on the basis of a movement that is freedom as heritage or heritage as freedom. *Sichüberlieferung* is this profound movement of ek-sistence on the basis of which, later, the ethico-metaphysical problematic of freedom in situation, of choice in determinism, and so forth, can come about.

Here again we can measure the labor of philosophical translation that Sartre indulged in, not only when he translated *Da-sein* as "human reality" in *Being and Nothingness*, but when *Entschlossenheit* became free projection, with an absolute freedom in the Cartesian sense, the freedom of a *consciousness* and a *for-itself* caught in the opacity of a radically heterogeneous in-itself,
282 the two forming two regions the unity of which was hastily qualified as a metaphysical problem in the final pages of *Being and Nothingness*. And one imagines to what Platonico-Kantian-type difficulties must be exposed the existential psychoanalyses that use this language and supposedly get back to the famous *original project* that made one think of Plato's myth of *Er* and of the intelligible character that Kant talks about rather than what was already known by the name of psychoanalysis. In this sense [two illegible words] and these two themes Merleau-Ponty closer both to psychoanalysis and to Heidegger [four illegible words in parentheses].

For Heidegger, *Entschlossenheit* is neither a projection of *consciousness*, nor an experience *for-itself*, nor the heroic responsibility of a subject: it can be defined neither in terms of morality nor in terms of psychology. The *Sichüberlieferung* that ensures the history of *Entschlossenheit* is not the transmission to the self of the possibilities of an already-constituted subject; it is the very movement on the basis of which something like a subject will be able to emerge, and might be for-itself, and so on. The traditionality of *Sichüberlieferung* does not befall a subject but constitutes it, and the *Sich* of *Sichüberlieferung* is not primary with regard to the *Überlieferung* but is constituted by and in the *Überlieferung*.

One might once more be tempted to say that, basically, this is still Hegel. Indeed, *to say first* that the for-itself and consciousness are constituted on the basis of the traditionality of experiences and as the appearing of the movement of transmissibility, the passage from one shape of consciousness to another being the condition of coming to consciousness and becoming for-itself what it was in-itself, and so forth; *to say secondly* that consciousness is secondary and depends, for its constitution and its recognition and its being-for-itself, on the courageous affirmation of its mastery as freedom for death; *to say finally* that the primary movement, prior to the constitution of a conscious subject, is elevation above life, the risking of one's life, the courage to lose one's life, the preference of freedom over life, and so forth. Is this not, as in Hegel, to place at the origin of subjectivity and consciousness or the *Da* the taking up of the anxiety of death and freedom for death—that is, mastery (since the slave who feels anxiety, as Hegel says, not about
this or that thing, not during this or that moment, but with regard to the 283
whole of his essence, for he has experienced the fear of death, the absolute master, the slave who has felt this anxiety has preferred—this is at least one of the abstract moments of the dialectic—to preserve (*servare*) his life and has constituted himself as preserved in life, kept, *servus*), the repressed servile consciousness (*zurückgedrängtes Bewusstsein*) having to turn around (*sich umkehren*) into true independence?[14] And indeed one might think that Heidegger also makes of freedom for death, of anxiety, of the resolute taking up of death, and so forth, the condition of that return to the *Da* as such that one might be tempted to call consciousness. And no doubt one could push this analogy very far, showing for example that at bottom it is indeed a *mastery*, a *lordship* that is described by Heidegger by the name *authentic freedom* and

14. [Translator's note:] G. W. F. Hegel. *Phänomenologie des Geistes* (Frankfurt am Main: Suhrkamp, 1970), 152. Translated by A. V. Miller (Oxford: Oxford University Press, 1977), 117.

resolution for death. And when a little later in §74, a little later than the passages I commented on just now, he speaks of *destiny* or history no longer in terms of *Dasein* in general but of a *people*, you see where you could easily be led, basically without leaving Hegel.

I am not saying that this analogy has no value or truth. Besides, you know that this analogy has been pursued, precisely around this theme of freedom and death (and not in general, as is often done), by Kojève, so far as I know, in at least two notes added to his lectures on Hegel ([French], pages 566–75).[15] These two notes are noteworthy in that,

(1) *on the one hand*, Kojève here extends to Heidegger the anthropological reading he had already—*or so it seems to me*—unwisely performed on the *Phenomenology of Spirit*. And in Heidegger's case this misreading is unforgivable, for Heidegger's declarations on this matter are explicit.

(2) *On the other hand*, these notes make of Heidegger and Marx the two best examples of Hegelian filiations (still around death and the master-slave
284 dialectic) and at the same time of regression with regard to Hegel. For different reasons, both Marx and Heidegger supposedly dropped an essential element of the master-slave dialectic. Let me read these notes. [French] p. 566:

> Heidegger will say, following Hegel, that human existence (*Dasein* [comment]) is "life in view of death" (*Leben zum Tode*). The Christian also used to say it, a long time before Hegel. But for the Christian death is but a passage into the beyond: He does not accept death properly speaking. The Christian man does not place himself face-to-face with Nothingness. He relates himself in his existence to an "other world," which is essentially *given*. There is not therefore in him any "transcendence" [= freedom] in the Hegelian, and Heideggerian, sense of the term. (*Hegel and Contemporary Continental Philosophy*, 73, n. 6)

Nothing more to say about this passage. French p. 575.

> Heidegger has taken up again the Hegelian themes concerning death; but he neglects the complementary themes concerning Struggle and Labor; thus his philosophy does not succeed in rendering an account of History.—Marx

15. Alexandre Kojève, *Introduction à la lecture de Hegel* (Paris: Gallimard, 1947). [Translator's note: These are two footnotes to Kojève's essay "The Idea of Death in the Philosophy of Hegel," an essay omitted from the partial English translation *Introduction to the Reading of Hegel*, ed. Allan Bloom, trans. James H. Nichols (Ithaca, NY: Cornell University Press, 1980). The essay was subsequently translated in Dennis King Keenan, ed., *Hegel and Contemporary Continental Philosophy* (Albany: State University of New York Press, 2004), 27–74 (nn. 6 and 9, pp. 73–74).]

> retains the themes of Struggle and Labor, and his philosophy is thus essentially "historicist"; but he neglects the theme of death (even while admitting that man is mortal); that is why he does not see (and even less do certain "Marxists") that the Revolution is not only in fact but also essentially and necessarily—bloody (the Hegelian theme of the Terror). (*Hegel and Contemporary Continental Philosophy*, 74, n. 9)

Let's not pursue the remark about Marx here. As regards the themes of Labor and Struggle that Heidegger supposedly neglected, and of death that he supposedly picked up from Hegel, a certain number of remarks are necessary. Common sense and the most immediate appearances indeed make it seem that Kojève is right, and in a way, in these cases, common sense is never absolutely nor simply wrong. But it is rarely as right as it thinks it is. 285
Labor, Struggle, and Death.

Labor. Of course, Heidegger says little about labor, by this name. And he explains this, with reference to Marxism, in a note from the "Letter on 'Humanism'" I read at the beginning of this course.[16] But really, and here a remark such as Kojève's is really not serious, the whole of *Sein und Zeit* and many later works can be read as works about labor. Of course, Heidegger does not tell us stories about this; his analysis is ontological and thus is in a certain sense formal, but Hegel's is no less so, and also no doubt, at bottom, Marx's. What Heidegger is trying to do, for example in chapter 3 of the first division of *Sein und Zeit,* is to provide the concrete description of the essence of labor and technology, of the structure of equipmentality and the enormous structure of *Zuhandenheit* in general, of putting to work, of such practical precision on this theme, and so forth. This whole analysis, which I cannot get into here, being an existential analysis of the structure of *Dasein* (i.e., of a behavior that does not befall *Dasein* accessorily and arbitrarily, but which belongs to the very essence of its being-in-the-world) and of care (i.e., of finite temporality as a structure of that being-in-the-world, etc.). One might perhaps say that it is on the condition and on the ground of this existential structure that *subsequent* and essential determinations of the meaning of *labor*—in Hegelian, for example, Marxist or Christian terms—can make an entrance, and that one can once more tell *stories*, be they those of original sin and of what follows, or those of the phenomenology of spirit. Even supposing that Kojève is right when he says that the phenomenology of spirit describes an *anthropogenesis* and that labor and the negativity of labor are indispensible to it, Heidegger, for his part, is describing an ontological structure that precedes anthropogenesis . . . (relation of *Dasein* to *Vorhan-*

16. See above, session 2, pp. 21–23.

denheit and to *Zuhandenheit* in Care, etc.) that alone can make possible and
286 intelligible the movement of *phenomenology* . . . , which presupposes at least at a given moment being-in-the-world conditioning the relation of the self to the this, and all that follows, up to the point where it finds itself face to face, consciousnesses at war, and so on. However ontological in their intention these Hegelian analyses may be with respect to other empirical descriptions, they would thus remain ontic and derived with regard to Heidegger's. In particular and above all in what concerns *labor*, Hegel has its moment appear only after the emergence of self-consciousness in itself and of the self that has had the experience of the independence of its object; on the other hand, he has to *give* himself, beyond consciousness and life, beyond the two "individuals" as he says who are going to become master-slave and who will be persons only after they have risked their lives, beyond that, beyond consciousness and life, Hegel gives himself *thingliness*, without however distinguishing *thingliness* from what, in its essential structure, can make of it a piece of equipment or material for labor, or what, in thingliness and as a function of the relation between what he himself calls *Da-sein* and thingliness, can be determined as nature or material for labor [on the one hand], and on the other hand as equipmentality or object of value. One might consider that it is all these ontological preliminaries that Heidegger is trying to satisfy (before consciousness, the individual, etc.).

On this theme of labor, and still very schematically, I shall add three remarks.

(1) Even if the content of the two analyses, the Hegelian and the Heideggerian, were, at a pinch, the same, and in particular as regards labor, well, the fact that Hegel's consists in *telling a story* in the language of *metaphysics*, which for the very general reasons that we went over at the beginning, prevents him from transgressing the onto-theological closure and posing the question of labor within the horizon of the question of being.[17]

(2) And consequently, even if Hegel links labor to freedom for death, this latter is thought against the infinitist backdrop of Hegelian thought. And against an infinitist background, the essence of labor is always the essence of
287 an accident. Here of course I am going quickly and I am referring to a literal reading of a rather conventional Hegel. But it could be shown that the very direction/movement by which one wrests Hegel from conventionality is a Heideggerian gesture.

(3) It is difficult to reproach Heidegger with neglecting labor if one remembers that Heidegger's entire thinking, and well beyond *Sein und Zeit*, is in the

17. This sentence is left incomplete in the manuscript.

end but a meditation on the essence of technology in its non-accidental relations with thought and notably with philosophy and metaphysics as interrogation about the beingness of beings. And so forth. Impossible to go into that here.

It will perhaps be said that technology is not labor, labor insofar as it implies . . . sociality. To which one might reply:

(1) Technology is the very movement that transforms activity in general into *labor*.

(2) The description of technology and of the relation of equipmentality and of putting to work is inseparable, in *Sein und Zeit*, from the structure of *Mitsein* that is *co-originary* with it.

The problem of *Mitsein* leads us to the second of Kojève's objections: the supposed neglect by Heidegger of the theme of *struggle*. One can here give two types of response. (1) The first of these, the principle of which would resemble the principle that inspired the previous one. In describing *Mitsein*, Heidegger is trying to get at a stratum of ek-sistence that is absolutely originary with regard to any modification of relations with the other—for example, in the form of war and peace, domination and slavery, the recognition of consciousnesses especially—because *Mitsein* and in a general way all the structures of *Dasein*'s ek-sistence are prior and lower, so to speak, deeper than the strata of *knowledge* and of *consciousness*, of *Wissen*, of *erkennen*, of *anerkennen*, of *Bewusstsein*, and of *Selbstbewusstsein*. It is on the ontological basis of the existential structure of *Mitsein* that all the *phenomena* described, for example, by Hegel by the name of "struggle for recognition" can possibly come about, come about in a history, or produce a history that will thus be the modification of a deeper historicity. 288

There is no doubt that, for Heidegger, *Mitsein* is a co-originary structure of *Dasein*. Being unable to expand upon this point, I refer you to §26 of *Sein und Zeit*, [German] pp. 119–21 [*Being and Time*, 116–17] in particular. The fact that this structure of the *Mitsein* is existential (i.e., an ontological structure of *Da-sein*) means in particular that the *Geschehen* and the *Schicksal* is also a *Mitgeschehen*. And it is against the hidden background of this *Mitgeschehen* that the form or figure described by Hegel as that of the master and the slave and their struggle can appear. It is precisely in §74 from which we began today that one can read the following, [German] p. 384:

> But if *schicksalhafte* [fateful] Dasein essentially exists as being-in-the-world in being-with others [with: existential ≠ categorial ≠ [illegible word]. Sartre], then its *Geschehen* is a *Mitgeschehen* and is determined as *Geschick*. With this term, we designate the *Geschehen* of the community, of a people. (*Being and Time*, 366)

Which means that if *Dasein* is *schicksalhaft*, if *Dasein* is its history and its destiny, and if it belongs to the being of *Dasein* to be *Mitsein*, it belongs to the *Schicksal* to be *Geschick* (*Geschehen — Geschick*). And so the historial destiny, historicity, is essentially and originally communitarian. And it is against the structural background of this originary community and this originary historicity that a history can be determined *ontically*, as by *struggle*, recognition, and so forth. *Entschlossenheit*: not heroic individuals but communitarian resolution (support of Nazism).

Second element of a response to Kojève's reservation.

Heidegger neglects struggle and warfare so little in the essential movement of historicity that he increasingly emphasized that *logos* was *polemos* and *eris* and that the revelation of being was *violence*. One of the clearest passages on this subject, but there are many others, could be found in the *Einführung* . . . , where Heidegger, commenting on Sophocles's *Antigone*, puts into relation Parmenides and Heraclitus, the revelation of being, *deinon*, and
289 *tekhnē*, and where, in particular, he writes this, among other passages (p. 181 of the [French] translation). Read.

> *So now we must show the sobriety of thinking in its true light. We will do so through the detailed interpretation of the saying. We say in advance: if we should show that apprehension, in its belonging-together with Being (*dikē*), is such that it uses violence, and as doing violence is an urgency, and as an urgency is undergone only in the necessity of a struggle [in the sense of *polemos* and *eris* (confrontation and strife)], and if in addition we should demonstrate that apprehension stands explicitly in connection with *logos*, and this *logos* proves to be the ground of human Being, then our assertion that there is an inner affinity between the thoughtful saying and the poetic saying will have been grounded.
>
> We will show three things:
>
> 1. Apprehension is not a mere process, but a de-cision.
> 2. Apprehension stands in an inner essential community with *logos*. *Logos* is an urgency.
> 3. *Logos* grounds the essence of language. As such, *logos* is a struggle and it is the grounding ground of historical human Dasein in the midst of beings as a whole.* (*Introduction to Metaphysics*, 178–79)

Combat, conflict, is not first determined as an authentic structure but as the *essence* (*Wesen*) of being. Estance of being: on the basis of which one can think, in the light of being, an authentic combat that will no longer simply be a raw *collision* of two beings of the form of thingliness (which no one could ever call warfare) but a phenomenon that implies language and transcendence. Without the pre-comprehension of being that opens language, there would

be no war. War is therefore the history of being itself, and the phenomenon of the meaning of being . . . . *Phainesthai* is *polemos*. And it is *polemos* primarily because in the meaning of being, in the manifestation of being, is dissimulation of being. We have seen why the history of Being was this truth of the dissimulation and the unveiling of being. If there were simply unveiling of pure being, outside the being, or dissimulation of being in beings, there 290
would be no history of being. *Polemos*, then, means this unity of unveiling and dissimulation as movement of history. This is why, for example, in the "Letter on 'Humanism,'" Heidegger says that "being itself is the polemical, the conflictual" (*Pathmarks*, 272), not, as Munier translates it, the place of combat but combat, the combative itself. "[. . .] *das Sein selber das Strittige ist*" (*Wegmarken*, 357). And if war were not the history of Being itself, well, that's when one would have to say that war is an accident and an ontic modification, something that befalls non-historical and therefore peaceful being, one without disquiet. Taking struggle seriously is thus to take it seriously not merely at the level of the ontic, or even at the level of the ontological (in the sense in which Heidegger is trying to destroy [illegible word] the ontological), but at the level of the thinking of being or of the truth of being.

Naturally, when he speaks of war, Heidegger does not tell stories, he speaks neither of the struggle between individuals or consciousnesses, like Hegel (and we know why), nor of groups, states or classes. But he indicates the conditions on which one might possibly talk about them on this level of ontic determination without making them into accidents and by thinking them at the level of the originary and in the horizon of the question of being.

Such would be the elements—highly schematic and preliminary—of a dialogue on the points emphasized by Kojève (struggle and labor) between Hegel and Heidegger. But it is on the basis of the theme of *death* that we got to this point. Perhaps we can see more clearly now how, in spite of the apparent and real proximity, freedom for death has a radically different sense in Heidegger and Hegel.

First, freedom for death, as it appears as a moment in the phenomenology of spirit, is precisely only a necessary moment and *mediation*. Death is not the unsurpassable horizon of a finite ek-sistence or a finite temporality. The anxiety of death, which the slave flees or the master takes on, thereby constituting themselves through this gesture the one as slave, the other as 291
master—the anxiety of death with these two possibilities that are, in truth, the very essence of phenomenality and the becoming of consciousness—this anxiety of death has the sense of a *passage*. A passage from life to life, first of all. A passage from life in the sense of natural being-there, the life above which the point is to raise oneself through consciousness; then after the pas-

sage through struggle and anxiety, the primary inessentiality of life, as it appears to the master, shifts into essentiality (self-certainty). For in fact, at a certain moment, the truth of consciousness that was supposed to be pronounced by death and the risk of death runs the risk of being compromised by death itself. By raising myself above life, I become certain of myself as free consciousness, but I lose my life and *therefore also* the certainty of myself and consciousness . . . . "This trial by death, however, does away with the truth which was supposed to issue from it, and so, too, with the certainty of self generally" (*Phenomenology of Spirit*, 114). Just as life is the *natural positing* of consciousness, independence without absolute negativity, so is death the *natural* negation of that same consciousness . . . .

Whence the discovery that mediates freedom for death: the discovery that life is *essential* and that it must be *preserved by living it*, preserved by living it in the *Aufhebung*: i.e., in a negation that is not abstract like the first one.

In the first moment, consciousness, which has only the alternative choice of raising itself above or else saving its life, is placed before an *abstract* negation: in both cases one loses, either as slave or as master, who in dying, also loses what he has won. So the master would have to keep what he loses (life), just as the slave, through labor, will also keep what he loses: freedom. To do so, he must pass from abstract negation to the *Aufhebung*: up to this point, says Hegel,

> Their act is an abstract negation, not the negation coming from consciousness, which supersedes (*aufhebt*) [sublimates . . . [illegible word]] in such a way as to preserve and maintain what is *Aufgehobene* [suppressed subli-
> 292 mated], and consequently survives its own *Aufgehobenwerden* [becoming suppressed]. In this experience, self-consciousness learns that life is as essential (*wesenhaft*) to it as pure self-consciousness. (*Phenomenology of Spirit*, 114–15.)

From then on, it's the game with which you are very familiar: mastery as the slavery of the slave, slavery as mastery of mastery, mediation through labor, and so forth. It is the work [*l'oeuvre*] that in the end *sublimates* death. Labor itself, mediation of the economy without loss of meaning. This mediation of death comes down, in spite of this great Hegelian revolution, to thinking death within the horizon of the infinite and the parousia of absolute knowledge, which is pure *life*, life with itself of consciousness, just as, generally, consciousness—the movement of the experience of phenomenology—is only a mediation of Spirit and of God reflecting on himself, and so on.

There is none of that left in Heidegger. And without even being concerned with theology or teleology as the final horizon of this thinking in which it would suffice to notice right on the level of experience that freedom for death is not for Heidegger a movement of *consciousness*, no more than it is one of unconditional life, consciousness and the unconscious being, as we have seen, concepts marked by an epoch of metaphysics. Such concepts would oblige us to think as representation or non-representation, clear or blind representation, a movement that no longer has anything to do with representation or with the *Idea* (in the Cartesian sense, and you know that, for Heidegger, Hegel still remains a metaphysician thinking in the epoch inaugurated or signified by Descartes).

Entschlossenheit and freedom for death must be thought outside of the metaphysics that is subjected to the present and to representation, and so can no longer be described in terms of consciousness, self-consciousness, cognition and recognition, nor above all in terms of teleology, death being the negation, the very impossibility of teleology in the Hegelian sense. At the
bottom of all this, of this whole dialogue, there is the problem of temporality 293
and the theme of finite temporality that we have seen to be so fundamental in Heidegger. Now the decisive reproach that Heidegger addresses to Hegel in *Sein und Zeit* would ultimately be the following: he missed the movement of temporality in the finitude of its horizon. And this would depend, on the deepest level, on Hegel's concept of time, which Heidegger shows, in the last published chapter of *Sein und Zeit*, to be the most radical and the most systematic concept of the vulgar interpretation of time as *Innerzeitigkeit* (being in time . . .): that is, the concept inherited from the Aristotelian tradition that thinks time on the basis of an ontology of *nature* and as essentially linked to *place* and to movement (§44 of *Kant and the Problem of Metaphysics*).

So that's where we have been led by this theme, so non-classical in spite of appearances, of *Sichüberlieferung*. What I would like to suggest here is that once we have thought this concept correctly with all its connotations: *Geschehen* or *Geschick* (determined not individually but at the level of *Mitsein*), as a movement that lets itself be determined only *secondarily* as a movement of consciousness, of theoretical cognition of truth in the classical sense, of human existence, of ethics, and so on, one notices that the prescription of authenticity, the axiology or ethics hidden in the concept of authenticity, which is a theme only in *Sein und Zeit*, this axiology or this ethics no longer at all have the meaning they might have in any tradition whatsoever. And this implicit ethics, this ethics in quotation marks, once it is no longer determined by a classical theology or a theology of value or a philosophy of courage, of coming to consciousness, of the heroic projection of knowing one's truth, and so forth, this implicit ethics occurs at the level of the implicit ethics that governs

thinking like that of Marx, Nietzsche, Freud: that is, an ethics the source of whose prescription either is not defined, or else, when it is defined, ought to be so in a language radically foreign to the whole of classical metaphysics,
294 whether or not it is so in fact.

This notion of *Sichüberlieferung* does indeed, then, refer us to the root of historicity: namely, finite temporality, as was said in the passage that I read out at the beginning, and that we have basically done nothing but comment on. Up until now, at bottom, as I suggested, all the conceptual material we made use of was borrowed from earlier analyses. No original concept marked our access to the problematic of historicity, which is thus not yet original. It is true that there are the terms *Geschehen* and *Geschick*, but they are just names for the historical. The concept of *Sichüberlieferung* could function rigorously, as we have seen, in an analysis of temporality. The only concept that appears to me properly to belong to a problematic of history and that emerges as dependent on that of *Sichüberlieferung*, is the concept of *repetition (Wiederholung)*. *Sichüberlieferung* is the general structure of temporality as auto-affection: it cannot fail to happen, whether it does so explicitly or not. Repetition will be the movement of *Entschlossenheit* when it *resolutely* and *explicitly*, *expressly*, takes up transmission, the return of the past, going back to the origin, and so on; repetition will be the phenomenon of the freedom of auto-transmission. Freedom is repetition. Repetition is explicitly tradition, says Heidegger. "It is not necessary," Heidegger points out,

> that resoluteness *explicitly* know the provenance of the possibilities upon which it projects itself. However, in the temporality of Dasein, and only in it, lies the possibility of explicitly fetching (*holen*) from the traditional understanding of Dasein the existentiell potentiality-of-being upon which it projects itself. Resoluteness that returns to itself and hands itself down then becomes the *repetition* of a possibility of existence that has been handed down. *Repetition is explicitly tradition*, that is, going back to the possibilities of the Dasein that has been there [for example, choosing one's heroes. But this return to the past, if it is to be authentic] is grounded existentially in anticipatory [pre-cursive] resoluteness; for in resoluteness the choice is first chosen that makes one free for the struggle over what is to follow and fidelity to what can be repeated. (*Being and Time*, 366–67)

295 The concept of repetition, if one remembers what has already been said, implies that repetition is something quite other than a becoming-present-again, than a restoration of the past of what has been left behind. We are dealing with the very opposite of a traditionalism or a philosophy of repetition as immobile recommencement or the return to the origin like a falling

back into childhood. This is why repetition has its origin in the *future*; and as repetition is the possibility of an authentic history, history has its possibility in the future and in death as the possibility of the impossible.

"History," says Heidegger,

> as a mode of being of Dasein, has its roots so essentially in the future that death, as the possibility of Dasein we characterized, throws anticipatory existence back upon its factical thrownness and thus first gives to having-been [to *Gewesenheit*] its unique priority in what is historical. Authentic being-toward-death, that is, the finitude of temporality, is the concealed ground of the historicity of Dasein. Dasein does not first become historical in repetition, but rather because as temporal it is historical, it can take itself over in its history, retrieving itself. For this, *Historie* is still not needed. (*Being and Time*, 367)

Comment.

The general and formal, structural concept of repetition that obliges us to stop opposing the past to the future can lead us to think that we are dealing with a highly abstract, empty and basically rather serene, undramatic description of repetition, when one compares it to Nietzschean or Freudian concepts. One can get the impression that, for Heidegger, repetition is in fact always possible, that it is merely a passage from the implicit to the explicit that a movement of our freedom would make possible and continuous, and so on.

Do we need to make clear that this is not at all the case, and that to lend this naïveté to Heidegger, one must have naïveté to spare, and even a surplus of it to sell? Once we have clearly understood Heidegger's destruction
of the classical concepts of freedom, consciousness, and so on, and all their 296
connotations, it goes without saying that repetition could not be this kind of serene awakening, of confident reanimation of the origin—that is, of death—operating in the diaphanous ether of coming to consciousness.

Simply, once again, Heidegger is defining the general and ontological structure of repetition, within which, and as a modification of it, one could think the repetitions at issue in this or that determinate, non-ontological discourse (this repetition, for example, or else that one); determinate repetitions would not be possible if the fundamental structure of *Dasein* did not provide an opening for them. What Heidegger brings to light is the ontology hidden in the so-called human sciences that work with, for example, the concept of repetition.

What I have tried to formulate today, by designating, at least from afar, this extreme point of Heidegger's intention that can be enveloped by no past gesture of metaphysics or science, does not contradict what I said last time under the heading of *running out of breath* at the end of *Sein und Zeit*. Both things are true at the same time and the running out of breath comes from the fact that, as Heidegger himself points out, at the end of an uncommon itinerary one realizes—I quoted this passage last time—that one has still been using metaphysical conceptuality and that one cannot go on in this way . . . .[18]

This is why the end of §74, in particular, does not present itself in any way as an answer or a solution, but as a deepening of the enigma. What in particular is meant by a historicity and a privileging of the past as rooted in the future? The enigma is again that of temporalization and of that condition of the present as the past of a future.

This is the enigma that remains to be thought; this is the question that remains to be questioned. The question has perhaps not received an answer because it has not been sufficiently questioned, sufficiently problematized in its formulation and in its very origin. Before seeking to respond precipi-
297 tously to this question, we must ask about the origin and the meaning of the question itself and about the ontological horizon of the question.

We now know—and I won't go back over what I said about this last time—that the ontological trace of the question, the trace of its origin, cannot be found in the path of *Sein und Zeit*, but will call for a turning (*Kehre*), as Heidegger says. It will be necessary to retrace one's steps without this gesture being the sign of an impasse, a stepping back or a renunciation: rather a deepening of the re-petition.

I shall conclude this introduction next time.

18. See above, session 7, pp. 159–60.

SESSION NINE

29 March 1965

Last <time>, we continued to reflect on what I called the running out of breath at the end of *Sein und Zeit*, on the signs of it, on its architectonic manifestation, on its *motifs*, which prevented one from thinking of the unfinished character of *Sein und Zeit* simply as an impasse or simply as a turn or simply as a pause. I will not go back over that again, any more than over everything we were saying about *Entschlossenheit*, and about Heidegger's destruction of the Present and of a metaphysics of temporality dominated by the privilege—in itself and philosophically irrecusable—of the present. Philosophy or onto-theology being basically nothing but the dominance of the present and the presence of the present.

Searching—with difficulty—for some new and original concept in *Sein und Zeit* allowing us to distinguish historicity from the temporality in which historicity is rooted, we found *almost* none. The notion of *Sichüberlieferung* which at least in name presented itself as original, referred us to the theme of time as the other, pure affection, which made us take a long detour via *Kant and the Problem of Metaphysics*, whose strange relationship with the end of *Sein und Zeit* we pointed out.

Then we got into §74, the only section in which Heidegger plans to set out from the authentic historicity of *Dasein*, whereas, as I had tried to announce the time before, it seemed, paradoxically, that it was not a matter of historicity *properly speaking*—that is, authentic historicity—in *Sein und Zeit*, and 300
perhaps not even that of *Dasein*.

Because the authentic historicity of *Dasein* depends, as does the authentic temporality in which it is rooted, on *Entschlossenheit*, we paused over this concept. In spite of the suspicions I tried to justify with respect to it, we did our best to recognize its originality and to avoid all the possible misunderstandings that threatened to arise if one understood it within the horizon of morality, of psychology or of metaphysics in general. In the same way, we interrogated the related concepts of *Schuldigsein*, of *Geworfenheit*, of *Entschluss*,

and navigated safely around the Sartrian shoals. This necessarily led us to the theme of the finitude of temporality. This alone allowed historicity to be made into an existential and not merely existentiell (factical) structure and the present to be made no longer the originary and absolute form of experience but the past of the future, a product constituted on the basis of the to-come [*l'à-venir*] and a future [*avenir*] made finite—in an original sense of the word *finite* that is difficult to think—by death. This led us to the difficult concept of being-toward-death and, after a long digression on the function of metaphor in philosophical discourse and in Heidegger's thought, we returned to the primary condition of authentic historicity: namely, first of all not merely *Entschlossenheit* but the auto-traditionality of *Entschlossenheit* that alone can open up a *Schicksal* (destiny: a notion still to be rethought) and a *Schicksal* which originally, and to be a *Schicksal*, can only be a *Geschick*—that is, a co-destiny. No *Geschehen* without *Geschick*. And once again we had to have Heidegger dialogue with Hegel. That detained us for the entire second part of the session. We chose as arbiter—as a bad and provisional arbiter—of this dialogue Kojève, and a particular remark in his book comparing Hegel, Marx and Heidegger on the themes of being-toward-death, struggle and labor. I do not have the time to summarize what we said about this in order to mark, beyond some noteworthy affinities, the radical and decisive differences. Hegel and Aristotelian time (the Present). And *I concluded*: (1) with the
301 proposition according to which the hidden ethics ("ethics" in scare-quotes) that was putting Heidegger's discourse into motion here was none other than the one that put into motion discourses which, like those of the Marxist, Nietzschean and Freudian type, could not refer to a motivation whose concept was borrowed from the philosophy they were destroying. Simply, Heidegger makes a theme of this motivation which is elsewhere a driving force. (2) With the concept of repetition (*Wiederholung*), which is doubtless the only concept that is truly original and proper to a thematic of historicity in *Sein und Zeit*. It still had to be understood appropriately and without misunderstanding. It still had to be understood as authentic transmission—that is, as we saw, deepening the enigma of temporality and historicity, and of the privilege of a past that is not a past present.

Let's continue. Having thus announced to us in its very enigma the site of the authentic historicity of *Dasein*, Heidegger will schematically operate a sort of ontological deduction—a descriptive deduction, a derivation rather than a deduction—(1) of what he calls *Welt-Geschichte* (world history); and (2) of historical science.

What is important is the sense, the direction of the derivation. The historiality of the world is not before the historiality of *Dasein*. It is not a prior site or milieu in which a more determinate historicity, that of *Dasein*, would happen. *Welt-Geschichte* can only be thought on the basis of the historicity of *Dasein* as being-in-the-world, in the specific sense we have granted this expression. Furthermore, history, historical science, as we already saw, is not what allows history to be thought; it presupposes history and is rooted in it in a very determinate way.

I'll move rapidly over the origin of *Welt-Geschichte* in the historicity of *Dasein*. If one has followed Heidegger when he showed that the world is not a milieu in itself in which *Da-sein* would be immersed (which presupposes being outside the world), but that the world worlds in the transcendence of *Dasein*, which is in an original sense *In-der-Welt-sein*, one will understand that the world, both in the sense of nature, or else in the form of culture, in the form of *Vorhandenheit* or *Zuhandenheit*, that equipment, works, books, *302*
buildings, goods for production or consumption, institutions, and so on, have a history only on the basis of the ek-sistence of *Dasein* that must be conceived of neither as simple activity nor as simple passivity. This refers to earlier analyses that I cannot and do not wish to revisit here. I shall take from §75 only the following point, which once again connects all these themes with the destruction of the so-called vulgar concept of time, especially in its Aristotelian-Hegelian form.

History is not and cannot be historical linkage, *Zusammenhang*, cannot link modifications of objects or sequences, *Folgen*, of subjective experiences. History has its place in the linking, *Verkettung*, of subject and object. But as this linking can be originary only if it does not link in a secondary manner an object and an already-constituted and therefore ahistorical subject, this linking is the very origin of the two terms it links. "The thesis of the historicity of Dasein," says Heidegger,

> does not say that the worldless (*weltlose*) subject is historical, but that what is historical is the being that exists as being-in-the-world. *The occurrence of history* [historizing of history: *Geschehen* of *Geschichte*] *is the occurrence* [historizing] *of being-in-the-world*. The historicity of Dasein is essentially the historicity of the world which, on the basis of its ecstatic and horizontal temporality, belongs to the temporalizing of that temporality. In so far as Dasein factically exists, it already encounters that which has been discovered within the world. *With the existence of historical being-in-the-world, the Zuhandenes* [available beings] *and the Vorhandenes* [substantively present beings] *have always already been drawn into the history of the world*. Equipment and works, for example books, have their "fates"; buildings and institutions have their history. And even nature is historical. (*Being and Time*, 369)

What does this mean, that nature is historical? This does not mean taking the opposite position to the Hegelian or Husserlian assertion according to which *303* nature has no history, according to which natural history is a contradictory concept, according to which nature is at bottom the non-historical itself, subject to a model of iterative repetition that excludes that other model of repetition, the historical model. No, Heidegger is not here taking the opposite position to the classical thesis, and also denies that he is doing natural history. But nature, insofar as its meaning as nature is constituted on the basis of the ek-sistence of *Dasein*, its nature-meaning as landscape, as field of cultivation, place of worship, field of battle or conquest, raw material, and so on.[1] To this extent nature is historical (no *life*). So the totality of the world is historical, whether one designate by "world" the world of nature or the world of culture; the world is historical; that means that the world *is* not, but *worlds* in the ek-static transcendence of *Dasein*, in the historialization of *Dasein*. A fundamental historialization on the basis of which alone one will be able to define different types of production of historical meaning, different lines of historical productivity.

And each determinate historicity, each determinate historial line, has its irreducible originality, its own movement and temporal rhythm: the historicity of equipment, of technology, the historicity of institutions, the historicity of works of art, and within the historicity of art, the historicity of different types of art, and so on. All these historicities have their meaning, and their own type of concatenation, their own rhythm, their fundamental inequality of development [one added illegible word], an inequality without reference to a common *Telos* (I tried to show, in response to a question from Tort[2] a few weeks ago, why and how there is no teleology in Heidegger, such that here one should not even say *inequality* but *anequality*, inequality presupposing a defect or a shortcoming with respect to a measure or a *telos,* to a common entelechy, to a measure of all things. The concept of anequality is the only one
304 able to respect this originality, and the radicality of the difference of which Heidegger was always primarily concerned to remind us, an originary difference: that is, one not thinkable within the horizon of a simple and initial or final unity.) So, an irreducible multiplicity of historicities. But this irreducible multiplicity does not signify that historicity in general has no meaning. To speak of historicity in general is not to affirm that there is a general history; it is to affirm that there is a meaning to historicity, not a meaning of history, but a meaning of historicity without which I could not even speak of determinate historicities. Without at least implicit reference to this meaning of historicity in general, I could not even affirm that there are histor*ies*.

1. [Translator's note:] This sentence is incomplete in the manuscript and the French edition.

2. Michel Tort. See above, session 4, p. 89, n. 12.

Because a young interlocutor of Socrates could not, as Socrates points out to him, say that there are sciences (. . .)[3] without reference to the scientificity of science.[4] To speak of a meaning of historicity in general is no more to affirm that there is a general history than to speak of the meaning or the question of the meaning of being in general signifies for the beingness of Being in general. Being in general is nothing, but the multiplicity of beings and of types of beings could not be thought as such, beings could not be thought *as such* without pre-comprehension at least of the meaning of being in general.

So, just as there is meaning of being, just as the meaning of being comes about only because *Da-sein* ek-sists, so the historicity of history and therefore of histor*ies* only comes about because *Dasein* produces it and is produced (both things have to be said at once) in the historicity of its *In-der-Welt-sein*. Precomprehended meaning of historicity and not of history in general.

As historicity in general does not signify general history, there is no common history (any more than there is, to pick up the scholastic expression, any common *ens*); each line, each type, each mode of historical productivity has its style of movedness and its own time. And consequently it would be pointless to think historical movedness on the basis of a common type of *mobility*. And this is what I wanted to get to. Heidegger says this: the things that are 305
in the world, not in the sense of ek-sistence but <in the> banal <sense> of *in-sistence* (for example, bodies, equipment, etc.), have not only their own general innerwordly history (equivocal *Welt-Geschichte*)—and historicism (I showed at length a little while ago how Heidegger criticized it) consists not only in that, but also in interpreting the historicity of *Dasein* and of being *on the basis of* this determinate model of inner-worldy histories—but have each their own type of ontological movement, of *movedness*: *Bewegtheit.* And this *Bewegtheit* does not answer to what is believed to be the general concept of *Bewegung*, of movement. For example, the movement of production and circulation of equipment and work as such, says Heidegger expressly on [German] p. 389,[5] has a proper, original character of *Bewegtheit* (*einen eigenen Charakter von Bewegtheit*), which has for a long time remained in total obscurity (*der bislang völlig im Dunkel liegt*). This movement is not a simple change of place. For example, a ring, says Heidegger (and I suppose he chooses this example because of its simplicity and its complexity, the ring being both a bodily thing, a made object, an object of precious metal, a symbol of fidelity and union and a circular object that is made, given and worn), is affected

3. Thus in the manuscript.

4. [Translator's note:] Probably a reference to the *Theaetetus*, 146e–147c.

5. [Translator's note:] This whole paragraph is a very close paraphrase of *Being and Time*, 370.

by a movement, is even constituted in its very being by a movement, by a circulation that is not merely a change of place. And it is historical only to that extent. Which signifies that the historical movedness or sequence (the movedness of *historizing*, of historical production: *die Bewegtheit des Geschehens*) in which something happens, historializes itself (*geschieht*), cannot be thought, grasped, on the basis of movement (*Bewegung*) as change of place. And the enigma of the *Geschehen* toward which Heidegger calls us back is this *Bewegtheit* unthinkable on the basis of *Bewegung*. For what we have just said about the ring can be said of the totality of what are called historical events or advents.

Without resolving this enigma, one can thus already define its place and
306 exclude some models of reading. For example, if one still does not forget that temporalization is the root of historialization, well, it is already obvious that the time of this *Bewegtheit* that cannot be thought on the basis of *Bewegung*, the time of this movedness which is not yet movement or mobility—that this time cannot be an Aristotelian-type time, a time thought of as the number of movement that is, in any case on the basis of movement as change of place (in the world). Now onto-theological metaphysics never called into question this Aristotelian determination of time. No break with Aristotle on that score. And not even when for the first time history was taken seriously in this metaphysics: that is, with Hegel. Hegelian historical time, says Heidegger, is wholly inherited from Aristotle's *Physics*. In its relations with space, in the dominance of the now, in the idea of punctuality, and so on. I cannot here go into the final pages of *Sein und Zeit* and especially §82 entirely devoted to the Hegelian concept of time as a derived and vulgar concept. I refer you to it. These pages are perhaps the least spectacular but philosophically the most decisive in the book. Recapitulating the comparison between Aristotle and Hegel, a comparison the systematization of which he hopes to pursue elsewhere, Heidegger summarizes things thus in a table of concepts on [German] p. 432:

> Aristotle sees the essence of time in the *nun*; Hegel in the *Jetzt*. Aristotle conceives the *nun* as *horos*; Hegel interprets the now as "*Grenze*." Aristotle understands the *nun* as *stigmē*; Hegel interprets the now as *Punkt*. Aristotle characterizes the *nun* as *tode ti*; Hegel calls the *Jetzt das "absolute Dieses*." Aristotle connects *khronos* with *sphaira*, in accordance with the tradition; Hegel emphasizes the "*Kreislauf*" of time. (*Being and Time*, 410n)

And so forth.

And this more or less dogmatic and inherited determination of time
307 governs in Heidegger's eyes the whole of Hegel's thought since it governs,

as Heidegger goes on to show, the concept of negativity and the relations between time and spirit, negativity and spirit.

Same for Bergson. (Would have to be looked at. Take up not taken up [*reprendre pas repris:* uncertain words] after *Sein und Zeit*.)[6]

You see by this indication the architectonic necessity in which Heidegger found himself at the end of *Sein und Zeit*, to return very rapidly, after a foray in the direction of inauthentic historicity, to the temporal root—that is, to inauthentic temporality—the *they*—the present and history. Past on the basis of the present ⇒ *Telos* ≠ Entelechy. Aristotle. History ≠ telos.

This was the point I wanted to emphasize apropos *Welt-Geschichte*. I believe that the problem of *Bewegtheit* as non-*Bewegung* was the most important problem in the eyes of Heidegger himself. Naturally, his gesture is here merely *destructive*. Heidegger tells us only that historical movedness is not movement, that the concept of history must be liberated from that of movement. But he does not tell us here what the *Bewegtheit* proper to *Geschehen* is. He situates the enigma and, once more, for the second time in this chapter, he calls us back to the enigma. But it is still in the general enigma of the question of being that this enigma of history happens. The appeal to the vulgar temporality of movement was not an accidental and local misstep on the part of traditional ontology. It governed or was of a piece with the whole traditional determination of the being of beings. So one has no chance of seriously re-discovering the meaning of historial *Bewegtheit* without systematically destroying classical ontology and without thinking historicity in the open horizon of the question of being. It is to that question that we are called back by the end of this §75, which I will now translate. It will at the same time bring us to the question of the ontological origin of historical science. [German] p. 392:

> The existential interpretation of the historicity of Dasein constantly gets caught up unexpectedly in shadows. The obscurities are all the more diffi- *308*
> cult to dispel when the possible dimensions of appropriate questioning are not disentangled and when everything is haunted, *sein Wesen treibt* [<pro>-verbial expression: is up to its tricks, is at work, is on the job] by the *enigma* of *being* (*das Rätsel des Seins*) and, as has now become clear, of *movement*. (*Being and Time*, 372)

And Heidegger goes on, bringing us to another question:

> Nevertheless, we may venture an outline of the ontological genesis of historiography (*Historie*) as a science in terms of the historicity of Dasein. (*Being and Time*, 372)

6. Thus in the manuscript.

And this is what he undertakes in §76 of *Sein und Zeit*, entitled: "The Existential Origin of Historiography from the Historicity of Dasein." Let's note first of all that Heidegger intended this project to be generalized and extended to all the sciences. The question of the origin of all the sciences and of each science must be posed on the basis of the ontological analytic of *Dasein*. Heidegger says so expressly at the beginning of the section. But naturally, historical science has in this regard a privilege to the extent that it gives itself out to be the element through which, for example, all questions as to the origin and the history of the other sciences must pass. The history of science presupposes the possibility of the science of history, and historical science must be appropriately thought, and primarily in its origin, in order to be able to give rise to a history of science. If the history of science *already* presupposes that Dasein is historical and that *historical opening* is possible for it, this is *a fortiori* presupposed by the science of history. [Comment]

The origin of the sciences, says Heidegger, is still not very transparent (*durchsichtig*). And if, he says further on, "the being of Dasein is fundamen-
309 tally historical, then every factical science evidently remains bound to this historicity." But it is in a particular and privileged way that historical science presupposes the historicity of *Dasein*.

In this project of an ontological genesis of historical science, I shall merely pick out a few reference points.

(1) Historical science is historical: it has a history. It is not; it historizes itself and its object is historical. And it can have an object only if *Geschichte* precedes it, as it were. As Hegel said, the twin possibilities of history and *Geschichte* are of a piece, but, says Heidegger, history is in its essence belated with respect to *Geschichte*. It is constituted as this belatedness itself.

(2) The guiding thread for this ontological genesis of historical science cannot be borrowed from existing history, such as it is practiced in fact by historians. And this for *de jure* reasons. First because nothing tells us that the practice of historians corresponds to what an authentic historical science should be. And in truth to judge what the *de facto* practice of historical science is worth I have to refer to the Idea (in the sense of the Idea of [illegible word] authentic history.

(3) The problems that are called problems of historical objects and objectivity, however important and decisive, are secondary. Secondary with regard to what? Here things are more difficult.

As we have said, for historical science to be born, the path toward the past must already be open. And this is possible only insofar as a relation to the past in general is possible for *Dasein* in the ek-static movement of temporalization. Now, as we also saw, the *Gewesenheit* that lets itself be discovered is not a past present, a past now, it is, as present, the past of a future, the past object, it is something possible determined in return on the basis of a future bounded by death. What I grasp as past present is a movement of *Dasein*—that is, a present secondarily constituted as the past of a future. 310

Consequently, because history is rooted in time, what will be grasped under the name historical past is something that will never have been first *present*, but possible and past of a future, what is called past present being merely the dissimulation of this past of the future, which is what is originary. What by a metaphor and a dangerous false concept one calls the field and object of historical science is thus a certain *possible*. But as the movement of historical science is itself a *projection* and a certain resolute deployment of the *possible*, the relation of the historian to what is called the historical past will be the relation of a certain possible to a certain possible, of a certain projection to a past projection of *Dasein* (project ≠ consciousness). It is on this condition alone that there could later emerge and be derived a problematic of the positive historical fact, of historical objectivity, of the available historical material. Things, monuments, documents, and so forth, can become historical material only on this condition and because they are comprehended within a historical world. It is not the work of the historian (gathering testimony, critique and elaboration of these testimonies, etc.), that opens the historical field, but the opposite.

It follows that the value of a historical science, if such is its origin, depends primarily on the authenticity of the historical repetition that—before seeking or finding "positive facts" (*Tatsachen*), "a positive presence" (*Being and Time*, 375) resuscitated—will place itself in relation with the silent force of the possible without which there would be no *Dasein* and no *Gewesenheit*. This possible, if one understands it correctly and not as indeterminacy, freedom, individual potential, and so on (metaphysical determinations), is the true theme of history. It is in this direction that one must seek the "positive," the authentic *Tatsächliches*. It is on the basis of the future that the historian must repeat, and he must repeat toward a past that was also an opening toward the future, which never was a present and positive fact.

Only the opening of this *repetition*, the very possibility of repetition, creates a primordial element of generality or universality. Historical repetition can open only in language and it is therefore from the outset general in a certain 311
sense. And with respect to this fundamental generality that appears as soon as a repetition is possible, and even when historical repetition is dealing, as always, with something of the origin—with respect to this primordial generality the classical problems of generality and singularity, of law and singular event, of the model or the structure and concatenation of singular facts, and

so forth—all these problems, however important and inevitable, are derivative and at bottom superficial. And when one takes them to be the problems of the historicity of history, they are simply false, factitious and illusory.

Consequences of this are: *first point*, a certain engagement of the historian, a certain decision, a certain choice that is always already pronounced, always already necessary for historical science to open, and this engagement, far from affecting the research with what is called the subjectivity of the historian, is the sole condition of any historical "objectivity" (in scare-quotes). It is the audacious and resolute authenticity of the repetition, more than the so-called rules of historical objectivity, that will guarantee the opening of the past. It could easily be shown that the now classical theo-ontological historical science that claims to be so concerned with objectivity, with neutrality, and so forth, is itself guided in advance by an implicit and determinate choice. (Hegel already said similar things in the *Lectures*.) And this reminds us that history is historical, that the science of history has its tradition, its auto-transmission, that it ceaselessly explicates itself in its work, that it has its epochs, and that it hides or dissimulates itself from itself: for example, without speaking of the histori*cism* that was criticized elsewhere by Heidegger, histor*ism* (i.e., the imperialism of the historical preoccupation), is an epoch of historical science and is not necessarily the most authentic from the historical point of view. It is not in moments of historizing fever that there is the most authentic history. Just as there can be aestheticism and romanticism in the claim to get to the bottom of the *Weltanschauung* of an epoch, there can be an authentic historical projection in the work of the historian who is content simply to publish sources. Just as the historicity of a time pre-
312 occupied with extending its historical science as far as possible in time or in space, with citing so-called primitive cultures, can manifest an inauthentic historicity, so can epochs ignorant of historical science be historical, understand, mark and form history more profoundly.

If with respect to this place of origin thus designated the internal problematic of historical objectivity is highly derivative, then all the questions about the use, the good or bad use of historical science, will be still more derivative. Must one be a historian or not? This is a question the meaning of which can be understood only if it is referred to the place of origin thus designated.

Here Heidegger performs, on the basis of the movement of the *Geschehen* of *Dasein*, a sort of deduction of the three possible types of science and historical interest. He begins by referring to an earlier triplicity or ternary distinction. Not Hegel's. You know that, at the beginning of the introduction to the *Lectures on the Philosophy of History*, in a passage that André is going to explicate during a seminar on *Hegel and History*,[7] Hegel distinguishes between three sorts of history: original history, reflective (pragmatic and critical) history, philosophical history. I will not dwell on this since we shall have to speak about it again and since Heidegger is not referring to it. Heidegger is referring to Nietzsche, and to the second of his *Unzeitgemässe Betrachtungen*, entitled "On the Uses and Disadvantages of History for Life."[8] You are aware of Nietzsche's hostility towards the historicizing fever of his epoch and the sign of degeneracy, the threat to life, that he saw in it. And without advocating animal forgetfulness of the past, he is trying to determine the moment and the stage at which history threatens life and becomes destructive.

"There is," he says, "a degree of sleeplessness, of *Wiederkäuen*, of repetition, of rumination, of the historical sense, which is harmful and ultimately fatal to the living thing, whether this living thing be a man or a people or a culture." (*Untimely Meditations*, 62) 313

The point, then, as always with Nietzsche, is to define in terms of intensity, degree of force, the degree and the limit (*Grad und Grenze*) at which

> [. . .] the past has to be forgotten if it is not to become the *Totengräber des Gegenwärtigen*, the gravedigger of the present, one would have to know exactly how great the *plastische Kraft* [plastic power] of a man, a people, a culture is: I mean by plastic power the capacity to develop out of oneself in one's own way, to transform, to transfigure (*umzubilden*) and incorporate into oneself (*einzuverleiben*) what is past and foreign, to heal wounds, to replace what has been lost, to recreate broken moulds. (*Untimely Meditations*, 62)

We are indeed dealing with the limit of a force and of an intensity, of a power to tolerate and assimilate history, to such an extent that one must not simply abandon oneself to destructive history nor refuse it. Nietzsche's principle is therefore the following: *das Unhistorische und das Historische ist gleichermassen für die Gesundheit eines einzelnen, eines Volkes und einer Kultur nötig*: "the unhistorical and the historical are necessary in equal measure for the health of an individual, of a people and of a culture" (*Untimely Meditations*, 63).

Life for Nietzsche must always protect itself within a kind of haze of

7. We could neither identify the person meant by this name nor situate the aforementioned "seminar," which perhaps was no more than a session devoted to student presentations. [Translator's note: see also the note on p. 109.]

8. Nietzsche, "On the Uses and Disadvantages of History for Life," trans. R. J. Hollingdale, in *Untimely Meditations*, ed. Daniel Breazeale (Cambridge: Cambridge University Press, 1997).

absence of historical sense. When this haze, this atmosphere, dissipates, life is destroyed. But as the ignorance of history can also threaten life, life must make use of history, subjugate history to itself. History must belong to the living. "History pertains to the living man in three respects," says Nietzsche:

> It pertains to him (1) as a being who acts and strives [*Strebenden*: is ambitious], (2) as a being who [is] *Bewahrenden* und *Verehrenden,* preserves (*wahren*) and reveres, (3) as a being who suffers and seeks deliverance. This threefold relationship corresponds to three species of history—insofar as it is permissible to distinguish between a *monumental*, an *antiquarian* (*antiquarische*: archeo-
> 314 logical) and a *critical* species of history. (*Untimely Meditations*, 67)

Monumental history is a history from which one draws teachings, examples, and models, an authority to create great things today. Antiquarian history is a history of veneration of the past *qua* past, and is always a pious history, as it were. (If time, read [French] p. 239.)

> *History thus belongs in the second place to him who preserves and reveres—to him who looks back to whence he has come, to where he came into being, with love and loyalty; with this piety he as it were gives thanks for his existence. By tending with care that which has existed from of old, he wants to preserve for those who shall come into existence after him the conditions under which he himself came into existence—and thus he serves life. The possession of ancestral goods changes its meaning in such a soul: they rather possess it. The trivial, circumscribed, decaying and obsolete acquire their own dignity and inviolability through the fact that the preserving and revering soul of the antiquarian man has emigrated into them and there made its home. The history of his city becomes for him the history of himself; he reads its walls, its towered gate, its rules and regulations, its holidays, like an illuminated diary of his youth and in all this he finds again himself, his force, his industry, his joy, his judgment, his folly and vices. Here we lived, he says to himself, for here we are living; and here we shall live, for we are tough and not to be ruined overnight. Thus with the aid of this "we" he looks beyond his own individual transitory existence and feels himself to be the spirit of his house, his race, his city. Sometimes he even greets the soul of his nation across the long dark centuries of confusion as his own soul; an ability to feel his way back and sense how things were, to detect traces almost extinguished, to read the past quickly and correctly no matter how intricate its palimpsest may be—these are his talents and virtues. (*Untimely Meditations*, 72–73)*

Critical history is the history of the one who judges and condemns in order
315 to be able to live. Critical history summons the past to appear before its tribunal, interrogates it without mercy and readily condemns it. Always con-

demns it. The tribunal *of* history, here (objective genitive) is the tribunal that judges history and always condemns it, for, Nietzsche says, every past deserves to be condemned. To be condemned not by a theoretical or practical verdict, by knowledge or by morality, but by life, by its obscure, driving, power (*Macht*), insatiably avid for itself. The judgment of life on the past is always dangerous both for life and for the epochs and the people who pronounce this judgment. "[. . .] history can be borne only by strong personalities [. . .]" (*Untimely Meditations*, 86).

So one must understand *critique* here in a sense that has nothing to do with historical critique as guarantee of objectivity. We are dealing here with a critique that demolishes, with an active and destructive critique that is not the respectful gesture of the historian. And it is even primarily the critique of historical objectivity. Historical objectivity is the disease, the degeneration of life, its disinterest, and so forth. Just as—*analogically*— for Heidegger, historical objectivity is a derivative preoccupation with respect to the original repetition of history, so—*analogically*—for Nietzsche, *objectivity* is a derivation of life, or rather a failure, a setting adrift of life. In the very narrow sense of this word = something like a castration. The objective attitude is castrating; it castrates both the one who assumes it and what it is aiming at. What's more, we must not say that the objective attitude is castrating: it is castration itself; castration is access to objectivity. To say that castration is objectivity is to say that it is neither masculine nor feminine, but that it is the privation of sex . . . And it would be difficult to say whether, in Nietzsche's eyes, critical history (in the sense he intends it [non-objective]) is masculine or feminine. One might be tempted to think that it is masculine, since it considers objective historians to be eunuchs, but one might think just as well that *critical* history is *feminine* since history (*Geschichte* = reality) is masculine for Nietzsche and can therefore be exhausted and critically destroyed only by 316
a woman. This means that the masculine and the feminine are one and the same thing which, in objectivity, is affected by castration.

What I am saying is not over-embroidering. It is Nietzsche who says this, or very nearly so, in the pages I am going to read, [French] 277–81:

*[. . .] *history can be borne only by strong personalities, weak ones are utterly extinguished by it.* The reason is that history confuses the feelings and sensibility when these are not strong enough to assess the past by themselves. He who no longer dares to trust himself but involuntarily asks of history "How ought I to feel about this?" finds that his timidity gradually turns him into an actor and that he is playing a role, usually indeed many roles and therefore playing them badly and superficially. Gradually all congruity between the man and his historical domain is lost; we behold pert little

> fellows associating with the Romans as though they were their equals: and they root and burrow in the remains of the Greek poets as though these too were corpora for their dissection and were as *vilia* as their own literary *corpora* may be. Suppose one of them is engaged with Democritus, I always feel like asking: why not Heraclitus? Or Philo? Or Bacon? Or Descartes? —or anyone else. And then: why does it have to be a philosopher? Why not a poet or an orator? And: why a Greek at all, why not an Englishman or a Turk? Is the past not big enough for you to be able to find nothing except things in comparison with which you cut so ludicrous a figure? But, as I have said, this is a race of eunuchs, and to a eunuch one woman is like another, simply a woman, woman in herself, the eternally unapproachable and it is thus a matter of indifference what they do so long as history itself is kept nice and "objective," bearing in mind that those who want to keep it so are forever incapable of making history themselves. And since the eternally womanly will never draw you upward, you draw it down to you and, being neuters, take history too for a neuter. But so that it shall not be thought that I am seriously comparing history with the eternally womanly, I should like to make it
> 317 clear that, on the contrary, I regard it rather as the eternally manly: though, to be sure, for those who are "historically educated" through and through it must be a matter of some indifference whether it is the one or the other: for they themselves are neither man nor woman, nor even hermaphrodite, but always and only neuters or, to speak more cultivatedly, the eternally objective. If the personality is emptied in the manner described and has become eternally subjectless or, as it is usually put, objective, nothing can affect it any longer; good and right things may be done, as deeds, poetry, music: the hollowed-out cultivated man at once looks beyond the work and asks about the history of its author.* (*Untimely Meditations*, 86–87)

Naturally, our great *castrator*, as Nietzsche recognized, is God the father or his philosophical pseudonym, Hegel. Hegel is ultimately, for Nietzsche, the name or the origin of historicism and objectivism, of the historical devotion of the eunuch who bows down before the positive, objective fact, acknowledges it from a distance as untouchable. So much so that the hour of absolute historical objectivity would be the final hour of history. Objective history, respected like a virgin by a eunuch, would be sterile, sterilized and paralyzed. Now this devotion before the objective fact [*fait*] is also a devotion before the *fait accompli,* a history that is not *critical* in the Nietzschean sense because it is trying to be too *critical* in the philosophical sense or in the sense of historical methodology. This philosophical or methodological *hypercritique* becomes *dogmatic* because it is content to affirm and to believe without destroying, and it becomes *empiricist* because it is content to record the fact, what it takes to be the virgin fact. As though one could know virginity without violating it.

Nietzsche sees in this historical degeneration which signals or signifies itself as Hegelianism, as end of philosophy or German ideology, a degeneracy of life and a phenomenon of *vulgarity*. For Nietzsche, Hegel is philosophy as vulgarity. To which Hegel would no doubt retort that that is a vulgar reading of his philosophy, as he often did preemptively, pointing out the schemas that ought not to be followed in order to read him, and that are often the very ones that his detractors, Feuerbach for a start, followed with 318
an infallible and instructive assuredness. One can imagine for example what Hegel would say about the vulgarity of Nietzsche's interpretation of *absolute knowledge*. And since we were talking about this last Friday[9] and were wondering how such a flat reading of the end of the *Phenomenology* had managed to become dominant, I shall read you this passage from Nietzsche that shows it in a glaring light. Read [French] p. 331–37:

> *[. . .] Even if we Germans were in fact nothing but successors—we could not be anything greater or prouder than successors if we had appropriated such a culture and were the heirs and successors of that.
>
> What I mean by this and it is all I mean is that the thought of being epigones, which can often be a painful thought, is also capable of evoking great effects and grand hopes for the future in both an individual and in a nation, provided we regard ourselves as the heirs and successors of the astonishing powers of antiquity and see in this our honour and our spur. What I do not mean, therefore, is that we should live as pale and stunted late descendants of strong races coldly prolonging their life as antiquarians and gravediggers. Late descendants of that sort do indeed live an ironic existence: annihilation follows at the heels of the limping gait of their life; they shudder at it when they rejoice in the past, for they are embodied memory yet their remembrance is meaningless if they have no heirs. Thus they are seized by the troubled presentiment that their life is an injustice, since there will be no future life to justify it.
>
> But suppose we imagine these antiquarian latecomers suddenly exchanging this painfully ironic modesty for a state of shamelessness; suppose we imagine them announcing in shrill tones: the race is now at its zenith, for only now does it possess knowledge of itself, only now has it revealed itself to itself—we should then behold a spectacle through which, as in a parable, the enigmatic significance for German culture of a certain very celebrated philosophy would be unriddled. I believe there has been no dangerous vac- 319
> illation or crisis of German culture this century that has not been rendered

9. Every session of this course was held on a Monday, with the exception of the third, which fell on a Thursday. Derrida might be here once more referring to a session—which we were unable to locate—devoted to student presentations.

more dangerous by the enormous and still continuing influence of this philosophy, the Hegelian. The belief that one is a latecomer of the ages is, in any case, paralysing and depressing: but it must appear dreadful and devastating when such a belief one day by a bold inversion raises this latecomer to godhood as the true meaning and goal of all previous events, when his miserable condition is equated with a completion of world-history. Such a point of view has accustomed the Germans to talk of a "world-process" and to justify their own age as the necessary result of this world-process; such a point of view has set history, insofar as history is "the concept that realizes itself," "the dialectics of the spirit of the peoples" and the "world-tribunal", in place of the other spiritual powers, art and religion, as the sole sovereign power.

History understood in this Hegelian fashion has been mockingly called God's sojourn on earth, though the god referred to has been created only by history. This god, however, became transparent and comprehensible to himself within the Hegelian craniums and has already ascended all the dialectically possible steps of his evolution up to this self-revelation: so that for Hegel the climax and terminus of the world-process coincided with his own existence in Berlin. Indeed, he ought to have said that everything that came after him was properly to be considered merely as a musical coda to the world-historical rondo or, even more properly, as superfluous. He did not say it: instead he implanted into the generation thoroughly leavened by him that admiration for the "power of history" which in practice transforms every moment into a naked admiration for success and leads to an idolatry of the factual: which idolatry is now generally described by the very mythological yet quite idiomatic expression "to accommodate oneself to the facts." But he who has once learned to bend his back and bow his head before the "power of history" at last nods "Yes" like a Chinese mechanical doll to every power, whether it be a government or public opinion or a numerical majority, and moves his limbs to the precise rhythm at which any "power" whatever pulls the strings. If every success is a rational necessity, if every event is a victory
320 of the logical or the "idea"— then down on your knees quickly and do reverence to the whole stepladder of "success"! What, are there no longer any living mythologies? What, the religions are dying out? Just behold the religion of the power of history, regard the priests of the mythology of the idea and their battered knees! Is it too much to say that all the virtues now attend on this new faith? Or is it not selflessness when the historical man lets himself be emptied until he is no more than an objective sheet of plate glass? Is it not magnanimity when, by worshipping in every force the force itself, one renounces all force of one's own in Heaven and upon earth? Is it not justice always to hold the scales of the powers in one's hands and to watch carefully to see which tends to be the stronger and heavier? And what a school of decorum is such a way of contemplating history! To take everything objectively, to grow angry at nothing, to love nothing, to under-

> stand everything, how soft and pliable that makes one; and even if someone raised in this school should for once get publicly angry, that is still cause for rejoicing, for one realizes it is intended only for artistic effect, it is *ira* and *studium* and yet altogether *sine ira et studio*.* (*Untimely Meditations*, 103–5)

You see what is signified by the accusation of vulgarity that Hegel and Nietzsche are flinging, or would fling, at each other. Now you know that if, as we saw, what governs the whole of Hegelianism in Heidegger's view is a *vulgar* (his word) concept of time as intra-temporality, worldly temporality thought in the mode of the movement of *Vorhandenheit*, Heidegger says elsewhere, in passages I read at the beginning of the year, that Nietzsche is merely a reversal of Hegel: that is, he still belongs to the sphere of metaphysics in which this reversal takes place. He too, then, would be a victim of Hegelian *vulgarity*.

Let's leave this general schema and approach more closely this Nietzschean theme of the three histories. Heidegger proposes a repetition of it, seeking to get back to the common root of these three histories and explaining how, starting from this common root, the triplicity Nietzsche talks about comes about. According to Heidegger, Nietzsche thematized only the triplicity but he thought more than he was saying, and it is this unspoken thought
that Heidegger wants to repeat. He thinks more than he says and this unspo- *321*
ken thought will be the thought spoken by Heidegger who writes, for example, at the beginning of this repetition, that the triplicity (*Dreifachheit*) of history (*Historie*) is prescribed, pre-scribed (*vorgezeichnet*), in the historicity (*Geschichtlichkeit*) of Dasein. And, he says, "Nietzsche's division is not accidental. The beginning of his Betrachtung makes us suspect that he understood more than he made known" (*Being and Time*, 376).

The unspoken thought is the rootedness of historical science in historicity and of this latter in temporality. It is in the unity of the three temporal extases that the three histories are rooted, in the unity of the three *Entrückungen*, the three ways of taking a distance, of getting outside oneself:

> Dasein exists as futural authentically in the resolute disclosure of a chosen possibility. Resolutely coming back to itself, it is open, in repetition, for the "monumental" possibilities of human existence. The historiography (*Historie*) arising from this historicity (*Geschichtlichkeit*) is "monumental." As having-been (*gewesendes*), Dasein is delivered over to its thrownness. In appropriating the possible in repetition, there is pre-scribed at the same time the possibility of reverently preserving (*Bewahrung*) the existence that has-been-there, in which the possibility taken up became manifest. As monumental, authentic historiography (*Histoire*) is thus "antiquarian" (*antiquarisch*). Dasein temporalizes itself in the unity of future and the having-been

> as the present. The present, as the Moment, discloses the today authentically. But insofar as the today is interpreted on the basis of the futurally repetitive understanding (*zukünftig-wiederholenden Verstehen*) of a possibility taken up from existence, authentic historiography (*Historie*) is de-presentification of the today (*Entgegenwärtigung des Heute*); that is, it becomes the painful way of detaching itself (*Sichlösen*) from the entangled publicness of the today [a precise concept for Heidegger]. As authentic, monumental-antiquarian histo-
> 322 riography is necessarily a critique of the "present." (*Being and Time*, 376–77)

(You see how the anti-Hegelian theme of the destruction of the present as parousia and the critique of the present as engaged critique of the today and decision in the situation, as refusal of the *fait accompli* and empiricist passivity and so forth, are united here.) This is nothing short of saying that this powerful anti-empiricist movement that Hegelianism is, no doubt the most powerful in the whole history of philosophy, is an empiricist movement. And Heidegger concludes the paragraph that I am translating thus:

> Authentic historicity is the foundation (*Fundament*) of the possible unity of the three kinds of historiography. But the ground on which authentic historiography is founded (*der Grund des Fundaments*) is temporality as the existential meaning of being of care. (*Being and Time*, 377)

What Heidegger has just sketched out in this way on the basis of the origin of historical science must be re-commenced according to him for the origin of all the human sciences, for everything that since Dilthey was called the sciences of spirit as opposed to the sciences of nature, just as understanding was opposed to explanation. But because the origin of each science of spirit refers back to the history and the historicity of *Dasein*, well, the theory of the sciences of spirit always presupposes a thematic existential interpretation of the historicity of *Dasein*. This common root not only does not reduce the originality of each science and its proper history; on the contrary, it makes it possible.

As I must break this course off here, this course which will, then, have been no more than a long introduction to the introduction it promised to be, I will attempt, cutting a considerable number of decisive corners, to sketch out the conclusions toward which it is heading, toward which it would have traveled if, beyond *Sein und Zeit,* we had indeed patiently followed the path
323 along which we have nonetheless constantly proposed rapid reference points.

During the session before last, in a series of architectonic considerations, I tried to indicate what the move from *Sein und Zeit* to the other writings signified: notably the move from the *Geschichtlichkeit* of *Dasein* to the *Ges-*

chichtlichkeit of *Sein*. We also recognized along the way what was signified by the epochal essence of being and, by the same token, the simultaneously unveiling and dissimulating essence of language. This essence opened us to the meaning of metaphoricity as such, before any linguistic determination of language, or any scientific or onto-theological determination of beings.

It was implied in all these considerations that Heidegger's path of thought presented itself as epochal and historical: that is, as metaphorical. But here what is announced in the metaphor is the essence of metaphor, metaphoricity *as such*, metaphoricity as historicity and historicity *as such*. But it belongs to this *as such* that it hides what it announces (i.e., that it not reach proper meaning as such). There is history only of being and being is only history, but by its essence this proposition is still metaphorical.

Heidegger knows this and says so. No doubt the thinking of being announces the horizon of non-metaphor on the basis of which metaphoricity is thought. But it does not announce itself prophetically like a new day (prophets only ever announce other metaphors), as something that will be; it announces itself as the impossible on the basis of which the possible is thought as such (announce ≠ event here). One can call it death, the possibility of death essentially inscribed in the history of *Dasein* who knows better than ever today how the death of man, of the human, for example, is announced. So the thinking of being announces the horizon of non-metaphor. But the gesture whereby it announces this horizon, even though it denounces the entirety of *past* metaphor (onto-theology), happens in a metaphor about which it does
not yet know—because it is irreducibly to-come—what that metaphor is 324
hiding. The thinking of being is even the only respect for the future as such, far from being a sentimental and nostalgic traditionalism. It is that on the basis of which all thoughts that claim to be *progressive* can arise as what they are. What is said in the Heideggerian metaphor does not belong to Heidegger but to the epoch and to the total pro-position of the epoch, to the total statement of the epoch, to its total saying. Heidegger says in the "Letter on 'Humanism'" ([French] p. 149), "Historically, only one saying [*Sage*] belongs to the matter of thinking, the one that is in each case appropriate to its matter" (*Pathmarks*, 272). Literally: "There belongs to the thing of thinking (thing in general: *Sache des Denkens*) only one saying (*eine Sage*) that is up to its *Sachheit*." This is why, in particular, there is no Heideggerianism and no Heideggerian.

The metaphorical dissimulation of this statement happens, one might say, in that difference between meaning and signification that we recognized at the outset and whose particular character we recognized in the case of the meaning and signification of *Being*. To speak of a question of being is, by the

simple elocution of the word *being*, to determine it, to determine metaphorically the cipher of non-metaphor. Determine it in what way? Well, for example, still by the linguistic determination to which one cannot fail to make appeal. And this linguistic determination still remains a determination by the present, by the presence of the present, at the very moment when, in the name of the question of being, one is destroying the domination of presence. Heidegger knows this and says it, very early—for example, in that passage from the *Einführung* ... (1935) of which I spoke,[10] where he lets it be understood that the infinitive form of the word *be* is thought on the basis of the third person *present indicative*. This irreducibly grammatical dimension of meaning, this writing, this necessary trace of meaning is the metaphorical process itself, historicity itself. And Heidegger's remark showing that the
325 word *be* still belongs to a thinking of presence, finds confirmation in the well-known text to which I also alluded (*Zur Seinsfrage*, 1955), where I was explaining why Heidegger judged it necessary to cross out the word Being.[11] This crossing out, this negative writing, this trace erasing the trace of the present in language is the unity of metaphoricity and non-metaphoricity as unity of language.[12]

Given this, if the signification *be* is still a metaphor and if the signification *history* is thinkable only as history of being, well, the signification *history* is also, like that of Being, a metaphor to be destroyed. This destruction will not be a philosophical gesture, of course, since it is in the destruction of philosophy that the question of being as history has been brought about. This destruction will not be a gesture decided and accomplished once and for all, by someone in a book, a course, in words or deeds. It is accomplished slowly, patiently, it patiently takes hold of the whole of language, of science, of the human, of the world. And this patience is not even ours, it is not an ethical virtue. It is the auto-affection of what one can no longer even call being. Being and history would thus still be metaphorical expressions. (Destroy the word *metaphor* = linguistics. Heidegger does not use it.)

If being and history are metaphorical expressions that are in the process

10. See above, session 3, p. 119.

11. Martin Heidegger, "Zur Seinsfrage," in *Wegmarken*, 239. See above, session 2, p. 21 [Martin Heidegger, "On the Question of Being," in *Pathmarks*, trans. William Mc Neill, p. 310.]

12. We have chosen not to reproduce crossed-out sentences when they occasionally appear in Derrida's manuscript. Exactly at this point, however, he draws a big cross—a big *kreuzweise Durchstreichung*—over the following sentence in between large parentheses (see plate 15): "It is in this sense that one can speak of an end of philosophy, an end of history and an end of being that are nothing less than the future itself."

of destroying themselves as such, well, one can speak of an end of history and a death of being that are, no less, what by *another* metaphor we call the future itself. What is hidden under this other metaphor is the opening of *the* 326
question itself: that is, of difference.

The title of this course was, I recall: "Heidegger: The Question of Being and History." You remember that I tried at the outset to justify each of the words of this title. Each of them, even the name Heidegger, has turned out to be metaphorical. There is one word, perhaps you remember, that I did not try to justify, and that was *question.*

INDEX OF NAMES

The index covers only those names mentioned by Derrida in the text of the seminar.